D0604847

BARNSTORMING OHIO

ALSO BY DAVID GIFFELS

Furnishing Eternity: A Father, a Son, a Coffin, and a Measure of Life

The Hard Way on Purpose: Essays and Dispatches from the Rust Belt

All the Way Home: Building a Family in a Falling-Down House

Are We Not Men? We Are Devo!
(cowritten with Jade Dellinger)

Wheels of Fortune: The Story of Rubber in Akron
(cowritten with Steve Love)

BARNSTORMING
OHIO

TO UNDERSTAND AMERICA

DAVID GIFFELS

hachette
BOOKS

NEW YORK

Hachette Books
Hachette Book Group
1290 Avenue of the Americas
New York, NY 10104
HachetteBooks.com
Twitter.com/HachetteBooks
Instagram.com/HachetteBooks

First Edition: August 2020

Published by Hachette Books, an imprint of Perseus Books, LLC, a subsidiary of Hachette Book Group, Inc. The Hachette Books name and logo is a trademark of the Hachette Book Group.

The Hachette Speakers Bureau provides a wide range of authors for speaking events.

To find out more, go to www.hachettespeakersbureau.com or call (866) 376-6591.

The publisher is not responsible for websites (or their content) that are not owned by the publisher.

Print book interior design by Sean Ford.

Library of Congress Cataloging-in-Publication Data

Names: Giffels, David, author.
Title: Barnstorming Ohio: to understand America / David Giffels.
Description: First edition. | New York: Hachette Books, 2020. | Includes bibliographical references.
Identifiers: LCCN 2020011097 | ISBN 9780306846397 (hardcover) | ISBN 9780306846380 (ebook)
Subjects: LCSH: Political culture—Ohio. | Public opinion—Ohio. | Ohio—Social conditions—21st century. | Ohio—Economic conditions 21st century. | Ohio—Politics and government—21st century. | Giffels, David—Travel—Ohio. | Presidents—United States—Election.
Classification: LCC F496.2 .G55 2020 | DDC 977.1—dc23
LC record available at https://lccn.loc.gov/2020011097

ISBNs: 978-0-306-84639-7 (hardcover), 978-0-306-84638-0 (ebook)

Printed in the United States of America

LSC-C

10 9 8 7 6 5 4 3 2 1

For Evan and Lia

With any luck,
You'll find a rainbow purged of sullen promises.
—Elton Glaser, "Drowning in Ohio"

"Build It Like We Own It!"
—Plant motto, GM Lordstown Assembly

CONTENTS

BARNSTORMING OHIO

1

A FUNHOUSE MIRROR

The predawn moon poured its cold white shine through the kitchen window and across a countertop spread with two dozen freshly frosted Ohio-shaped cookies. The lights were still off, but I could see the cutouts, lined up from the night before, pale blue with navy piping, in rows on waxed paper. The coffee dripped one last time, then the *beepbeepbeep* of the machine. Ready.

First Monday in March, 2019. By day's end, those cookies would be decimated by a wide-eyed pack of fourth graders, my twenty-three-year-old son would walk through the back door wearing an Akron Police uniform for the first time, the GM Lordstown auto plant just up I-76 would be tooled for its demise, and Luke Perry would be dead.

A farmer down in Delaware County was loading corn to market, preparing for a trip later that day to Virginia, where he would talk to legislators at an agriculture conference, all the while worrying about the prospect of another wet spring. After months of speculation, one Ohio politician was preparing to announce that he would not run for the Democratic presidential nomination, while another was preparing to announce that he would. My local paper that morning carried the death notice for a "beloved son, brother, father, uncle, best friend," a man just thirty-two years old, who "struggled for many years against his disease of addiction until God carried him to Heaven," a jarring obituary verse that had suddenly become standard in a county where death by opioids was an epidemic.

Three miles away, a recently discharged twenty-two-year-old army vet was waking up in the same low-income housing project LeBron James used to call home, preparing for his daily hour-long walk to a downtown Akron community college, working to correct his life's course. A baby would be born that day at Mercy Medical Center and a miniature orange Massillon Tigers football would be placed in his bassinet, a longstanding tradition in the town where American high school football began. Nine random people in Dayton were starting another morning with no reason to think the unthinkable: a nightclub horror of gunfire that awaited them five months hence.

People got up. They dressed for work. They argued with their spouses, they urged their dogs to do their business, they fretted over bills on the desktop, they phoned in prescription refills, they asked what's for dinner tonight.

Mrs. Gina Giffels, a teacher at St. Vincent de Paul Elementary, Akron, Ohio, entered the kitchen in her bathrobe, turned on the light, poured herself a coffee, and began her workday, arranging those cookies side by side in plastic containers. I helped.

Not everybody in Ohio celebrates Statehood Day, but Mrs. Giffels's students sure do. In commemoration of the Buckeye State's 216th birthday, she would spirit those cookies into her classroom, breaking them out for the afternoon lesson. She would show her students how the dark blue icing along the edges designated the water borders—Lake Erie to the north (assuming one uses compass directions to navigate baked goods) and the Ohio River curving down the eastern and southern edges. She would tell them how important these waters have been to every part of life in Ohio, and she would point out the red dot of icing she'd put near the upper right, indicating their shared hometown. State history is a fourth-grade educational standard across the country. Students learn the story of their home place, the territory that designates them part of America but that also gives them the beginning of a notion of their own unique version of Americanism.

Ohio isn't any more American than any other place, but it is *completely* so, a unique cross section that maps the persona of the nation in a way that has prompted others to turn here again and again to plumb our collective identity. In my lifetime here, it has been easy to believe, as novelist Dawn Powell once observed, that "all Americans come from Ohio originally, if only briefly." It is an ur-place, sublimely average in both the dispositional and mathematical senses, an intersection of lifestyles and economies, of geographical characteristics and political tendencies, of climates, of conscience, of concerns, a place with answers to the most important question: *Who are we?*

I was born in Akron and am a lifelong, doggedly committed citizen of a state that's often easier to leave than to love. I have spent much of my adult life thinking and writing about this place in widely ranging forms. For eighteen years, I covered Northeast Ohio as a newspaper journalist. The books I've written all have Ohio themes and settings. I talk about it—a lot—sometimes in bars, sometimes in classrooms, sometimes to outsiders looking to understand this place. I teach a course at the University of Akron on Ohio literature. My go-to beer is brewed in a district called Ohio City. I used to play in a band named after Cleveland's flag-ship department store, the May Company. Most important, my son and daughter, born and raised here, were just then coming into their own as adults, as citizens, as young people preparing to commit, each in their own way, to Ohio as their home and to a set of ideals that I still want to believe in.

Gina left for school as the sun was coming up and I completed my morning like I always do, reading the newspaper at the little table under the window, finishing what was left of the coffee, wishing there was a half cup more.

I can't say that I was worried that morning in the way I might identify now. Like most people, I was occupied by the immediate concerns of the day, my classes to teach, an eye doctor's appointment, my expiring license plates. But I was worried, the way most people are, for my children, the son who was beginning police academy, the daughter leaving for class at the downtown university, still fretting over her path, asking me and Gina for an answer that we wished we had. *What is my life going to be?* I was worried, the way most people are, about the slim, black smartphone at my side, the way it distracts and narrows my focus, the drag of social media and the ways we no longer listen and the ways we no longer speak. I was worried, the way most people were in 2019, about the chaos, division, and acrimony surrounding the presidency of Donald Trump. I was feeling, that morning, like most people, the troubling misalignment of my country. And I was wondering about Ohio, a topic I wonder about perhaps more than any other.

What I knew that morning and was beginning to consider in a newly urgent way is that I live in a very particular America, the America of Ohio, which has forever served uniquely as a reflection of the nation, a conscience of sorts. Even in a time when that reflection felt more like one from a funhouse mirror, I believed that in the far reaches of my territory, on farms and in little towns, in factories and in kitchens, there would be an answer to what that misalignment meant. So that's what I set off to find.

* * *

The Ohio I was about to explore is such a remarkably reliable gauge of Americana that "bellwether" is our default political cliché and test marketers beat a perennial path to our food courts. Pulitzer Prize–winning native son Louis Bromfield observed nearly a century ago (in verbiage few other self-respecting midwesterners would use): "Ohio is the apotheosis of Americanism."

Geographically and culturally, the state is an all-American buffet, an uncannily complete everyplace. Cleveland is the end of the North, Cincinnati is the beginning of the South, Youngstown is the end of the East, and Hicksville (yes, Hicksville) is the beginning of the Midwest. Across eighty-eight counties, Ohio mashes up broad regions of farmland, major industrial centers, small towns, the third-largest university in the country, the second-largest Amish population, and a bedraggled vein of Appalachia. It is coastal, it is rural, it is urban and suburban. Mainly because of the industrial age migration of Europeans, white Appalachians, and black southerners to the cities for factory jobs, Ohio developed a rich cultural and political melting pot. The state's four distinct seasons, each intense unto itself, unfold like Currier and Ives without the soft edges. It is the birthplace of professional football, rock 'n' roll, the airplane, and chewing gum. As my friend Seth Borgen, author of a book called *If I Die in Ohio,* said over beers one night, "Ohio has a little of everything, and an abundance of nothing."

Our uncanny knack for choosing the American president, therefore, should come as no surprise. Since 1896, Ohio's voters have sided with the winner in twenty-nine of thirty-one presidential elections. No state has a higher percentage of accuracy. No Republican has ever won the presidency without winning Ohio. We are the only state to have a perfect record choosing the victor since 1964.

In a 2015 interview with Cincinnati public radio station WVXU, Eric Ostermeier, a research associate at the University of

Minnesota's Humphrey School of Public Affairs Center for the Study of Politics and Governance, remarked on Ohio's electoral clairvoyance: "The electorate in Ohio is willing to flip back and forth," he said. "They have done that plenty of times. But the vote in Ohio *always* mimics the national vote. It's extraordinary."

The building on the University of Akron campus that houses my office is of vaguely brutalist design—but only in the way that what we call "style" gets diluted by the time it reaches Ohio—a hulking, midseventies poured-concrete structure the color of a dirty labradoodle, its windows set slightly inward like a criminal's hooded eyes. The campus library next door was built at the same time, in a similar design, so much concrete that no one has ever been able to figure out how to plumb a sprinkler system through its walls. The books might burn, but that ungainly building won't.

When I arrived that morning and entered through the set of glass doors, I passed the department directory hanging in the hallway, a sign I've always appreciated for its unintended poetic juxtaposition:

BLISS INSTITUTE

followed by

CONFLICT MANAGEMENT.

The Ray C. Bliss Institute of Applied Politics is a nationally prominent think tank whose political scientists are active in polling and research, regularly called upon to comment on national topics, and pretty much ubiquitous during presidential election seasons, when journalists and other seekers come parachuting into Ohio from around the world to take measure of us. In part to address the questions they know will be asked, four of the institute's faculty—Daniel J. Coffey, John C. Green, David B. Cohen, and Stephen C. Brooks—coauthored a book in 2011 titled *Buckeye Battleground*. The title is a reference to Ohio's other *B* cliché, which often accompanies *bellwether*: battleground.

I started that day by digging into the institute's archives. The Bliss researchers have outlined in great detail the key feature of Ohio that allows it to serve so reliably as a microcosm of the nation: its distinct regional diversity, which journalists and political observers refer to as "the five Ohios," broken down thus: (1) the densely populated, urban, industrial/postindustrial Northeast; (2) the rural, agricultural, more culturally "midwestern" Northwest; (3) the central region whose epicenter is state capital Columbus, a growing, modern city defined (and in some ways divided) by government and the huge Ohio State University campus as well as prosperous exurbs; (4) the more sparsely populated, more Appalachian Southeast; and (5) the conservative, southern-influenced Southwest, anchored by Cincinnati, which abuts the Ohio River and which I often refer to as the largest city in Kentucky.

In a section of its website describing these five Ohios, the Bliss Institute asserts:

> Ohio's regional diversity is unlike any other state in the country. Many states, it is true, are a mixture of urban and rural areas. Geological features such as coasts, plains, and mountainous areas often divide states as well. Yet, Ohio is perhaps unique in that, while some of these factors are present, the existence of such regional diversity belies a simple explanation for Ohio's complex political character. . . . Each region represents a unique collection of big cities, suburbs and rural areas, one or more media markets, and at least one

major newspaper. Each region has a distinct political ethos and votes in a different fashion.

As a newspaper columnist in 2004, I had found this to be a highly useful road map for the two months preceding the presidential election, which I spent touring the state in my cranky old Volkswagen, traveling to far-flung corners to listen to people. I wasn't out to ask folks who they were voting for. I was simply looking for a true voice. When that season ended, the understanding I'd gained of what I guess I'd call "my people" far outweighed whatever I'd come to understand about an election. I came away with the deep sense of an authentic America. So now, with the five Ohios back in mind, I drew a crude outline of the state on a sketch pad and began plotting places I wanted to visit.

On the basis of historical evidence, *Buckeye Battleground* concludes that Ohio has a long and unmatched track record of not only electoral precision but also of significantly increased value as immigration diversified the state over the course of the twentieth century. "Ohio," the authors write, "has become a more accurate presidential bellwether over the course of its history."

In addition to this diversity, Ohio's character of Americanism derives from its legacy as the cradle of presidents: seven natives have occupied the White House—second only to Virginia's eight—never mind that the last was born in the nineteenth century. Ohio was also the home state of the first female to run for president—not Hillary Clinton, but a woman named Victoria Woodhull, who declared her candidacy in 1872.

All these factors come to a head every four years, when the national and international media, as well as the key candidates, descend upon Ohio, with its coveted eighteen electoral votes, trying to understand its people and their stories. It is a quadrennial battleground. Outside of the political seasons, however, our place is more often ignored or misunderstood. Regardless, whether we're being prodded like a county fair heifer or dismissed as flyover country, we have always retained our American quintessence. Many of us who live here know it as a point of pride, a key part of our identity, even if that "identity" is defined by hyper-averageness. Ohio likes to think of itself as the "heartland," a fundamentally American domain, the sort of place Bruce Springsteen would write about. The sort of place Bruce Springsteen *did* write about. For a long time, the state slogan was "The Heart of It All." Our very borders suggest the shape of a valentine. Look at those frosted cookies. The western boundary is straight, surveyed by Manifest Destiny and the linearity of farmland, until the river curves it inward toward the bottom. The northern edge dips downward, then back up, tracing the Lake Erie coastline. The eastern border curves easily into the soft *V* of its underbelly, following the Ohio River, the largest tributary of America's main vein, the Mississippi.

I took a long walk across campus that afternoon, down a concrete mall where students wearing jackets, some bearing the names and logos of nearby high schools they'd recently attended, rushed through the cold, ducking quickly into doorways. It was twenty degrees and sunless, deep into the ass end of the midwestern winter, which puts the "season" in seasonal affective disorder. Ohio's cities perennially rank near the top of those listings of American municipalities with the fewest sunny days—for some reason, Akron always seems to be jockeying for higher position with Buffalo, a competition that seems unhealthy for several reasons—and nothing feels more familiar here than our monochrome sky.

The University of Akron is a commuter school. Most of its students come from nearby, many from middle- and working-class families. They attend a college that in 2019 was struggling to pay down debt and reverse declining enrollment, to maintain its relevancy amid four state universities within an hour's drive. It's located in one of only seven Ohio counties that Democrat Hillary Clinton carried in the 2016 election, all of them urban and densely populated except one, the anomalous Athens County, where most of the population is concentrated in a liberal college town that exists as a distinct blue contrast to the vast red Appalachian region surrounding it.

Eighty-one of the state's eighty-eight counties swung to Trump in 2016. Most of those are Ohio's smaller or more sparsely populated territories, the farmlands, forests, and hills, but Trump managed to squeeze out more votes from them than previous candidates could. Down Ohio's side roads, out in its river valleys, along its margins, he found something here that hadn't been found before. I live in a city with a blue-collar legacy, and it would have been almost unthinkable not so long ago for a factory worker, employed or not, to support a Republican for president. But in working-class Lorain County, up near Cleveland, as reliably blue as it gets, Clinton squeaked past Trump by only 131 votes, a far cry from Barack Obama's margins of 18 percent in 2008 and 15 percent in 2012. Little Monroe County, which clings to the Ohio River down in the Appalachian Southeast, swung hard for Trump, giving him 72 percent of the vote after supporting Obama by 10 percentage points in 2008 and barely leaning in the direction of Republican Mitt Romney in 2012, when he took 52 percent of the vote.

The nineteen thousand students on my campus come from families that tell a story, and those families ripple outward across our highways and meadows and downtowns, deep into the question of where we are now and where we are headed. In 2016, in Ohio as in other Industrial Belt states, unexpected numbers of blue-collar workers turned away from their traditional Democratic roots, and rural Appalachians became more visible at the polling booths, pulled by a candidate who said things out loud they'd been thinking among themselves, stoking fears and frustrations, and who promised to revive the state's lost manufacturing and fossil fuel jobs, a long-held (and probably long-lost) hope. The wealthy suburbs and the deep southern part of the state—the upper buckle of the Bible Belt—remained reliably Republican. Ohio's white women voters, meanwhile, did not support Hillary Clinton; a CNN exit poll found only 39 percent had voted for her. Many were openly averse to a female candidate.

As one of the most gerrymandered states in the nation, Ohio's Republican-drawn district maps portray a sometimes-tortured misrepresentation of reality, cramming blue votes into tiny corners of a state Republican lawmakers have painted overwhelmingly red.

"I'll tell you a joke," Bliss Institute director emeritus John Green said to me one morning as we talked in his campus office. "This is a *real* joke."

He'd invited Ohio Republican Party chairman Bob Bennett and Democratic Party chairman Chris Redfern to speak to one of his classes.

"Chris said, 'You know, Bob, you guys drew the most *awful* set of districts. Just terrible. I mean, there's this district—we call it 'the snake by the lake'—that joins eastern Toledo with western Cleveland, right along the Lake Erie shore. And, you know, at one point, it's only one lane wide.'

"And Bob said, 'Chris—you're exaggerating. It's at least *four* lanes wide.'"

It's a battleground within a battleground. In 2019, a federal court ruled the state's congressional map unconstitutional, with a three-judge panel declaring that "the 2012 map dilutes the votes of Democratic voters by packing and cracking them into districts that are so skewed toward one party that the electoral outcome is predetermined." The November 2018 election results offer compelling evidence: all the major statewide races were won by Republicans except one, incumbent senator Sherrod Brown's victory in one of the few blue districts. The governor, attorney general, treasurer, auditor, secretary of state—all are now Republicans. Ohio has always been shaded slightly red but maintained the diversity that has kept it a bellwether. New districts are to be drawn following the 2020 census, but for now, questions persist: Is this a temporary shift? A Trumpian anomaly? Or is Ohio telling us something new about America?

As I was returning to the lot where my car was parked, I came across one of my students, a kid who goes by the nickname Skunk for a reason you do not need to know other than that he picked it up as a teenager in a scrappy old river town in the middle of the state. I call him a kid, but he's in his midtwenties, divorced, and has done enough cage fighting and hard drinking to qualify as a character in a Tom Waits song. We talked for a short while. He asked what I'd been up to and I told him about this undertaking I was beginning, to travel around in an attempt to understand just what the hell was happening to our country.

"Listen, I can give you some Trump-lovin' old boys from Gnadenhutten who'll give you all the stories you want," he said.

I knew him well enough to know what he meant, that he was offering me a cartoon. Ohio knows this code. Thanks in part to the notoriety of J. D. Vance's *Hillbilly Elegy* and in part to the overgeneralizations that plague the locales of flyover country, we have a perpetual instinct to define ourselves to the world, a hedge against stereotype and misconception. I didn't know exactly what I was looking for yet, but I knew I was pursuing an important question of identity at one of the most critical junctures in modern American history, and the only way I could find an answer would be to let people speak for themselves. In Ohio, especially, this happens less often than you might think.

* * *

"You look good in your police costume," I said to my son, Evan, that afternoon when he returned home after finishing his first day at the academy. He had boomeranged back here after moving out during college. My greeting was only half in jest. Though he was twenty-three, it was difficult not to still see the ten-year-old that remains imprinted in my impression of him. When he was sworn in two months later, he would become the youngest officer on the force.

That same week in March, three toddlers were shot in Akron. Separate incidents: a two-year-old, a three-year-old, and a four-year-old. I don't know if the statistics that accompanied the news reports made me feel better or worse: Akron's gun violence was not measurably increasing, and Ohio's violent crime rate remained slightly below the national average. There are plenty of reasons for a parent to be scared shitless when their kid becomes a cop. Before that week, I believed I had thought of all of them.

I was proud of him, proud of his commitment to serve others as well as his commitment to his hometown. I was proud, too, of my daughter, Lia, who was preparing to apply to in-state graduate programs in physical therapy, also aiming her career toward helping others and also charting a path that would keep her in Ohio. This state, like others in the old industrial regions, has struggled to maintain population through an era of "brain drain," the loss of young, promising people to places with more apparent opportunities. With 11.7 million citizens, Ohio remains the seventh-largest state in the nation. But its growth rate is nearly flat, just over 1 percent in the past decade, and the population is slowly growing older and less diverse. To stay or to leave was a decision of great consequence.

In many regards, Ohio, like the rest of the country, felt like it was teetering, like things could go one way or another, fast.

*   *   *

I was back in the kitchen that evening, chopping onions with the radio playing in the background, when I heard the news that Luke Perry had died. To most American entertainment consumers, the dreamily handsome actor was associated with one highly specific place: Beverly Hills, 90210. But when I heard the report of his passing, I automatically connected him to another highly specific place, the city of Mansfield, right smack in the heart of Ohio, where he was born and grew up. I know this because we Ohioans always know if someone is from here, no matter how tenuous the connection. It is a habit of humble places. If you mention Wolf Blitzer to someone in western New York, you will immediately be told "You know, he's from Buffalo." Everyone in Little Rock knows Pharoah Sanders played his first gigs there.

This is not a cultural quirk so much as an earnest statement of identity by places that struggle against anonymity, that struggle to be heard. It's a way of understanding one another with careful nuance. It is something near to empathy. And it is a way to calibrate relevance, to say: we are here, we exist, and we have something to tell you. The small voices are important. In times like ours they are more important than ever.

2

ONE MAN, ONE VOTE

"I took that libertarian test and I came out more libertarian than the libertarian!"

This is one of the first things Jim Renner told me on a sunny Saturday morning as we sat in the kitchen of the rustic hillside home he had gutted and rebuilt with his own hands, the same hands that now rested on the plastic tablecloth, sometimes sliding it askew as he worked the arcs and punctuations of his storytelling. His pale blue eyes drew tight at the corners as he cackled in response to his proclamation. He's not a libertarian, or maybe he is, but that's not how he defines himself. He liked the Tea Party just fine till the Republicans took it over. He's not a Republican—hell no; he makes a sour face every time he says the word—but he voted for Donald Trump in 2016 and thinks his presidency is the best thing that's happened to America in a long time. Renner is a lifelong Democrat, a former steelworker and union steward, the son of a truck driver, and he thinks all drugs should be legalized. He's also been a CEO, supports tax cuts for corporations, favors a border wall, and owns a Cadillac. When he spoke before a Tea Party gathering in 2010, he was introduced by the emcee as "the most conservative Democrat I've ever met," but as we talked on that spring morning, he pointed his thick index finger across the table at me and opined, "If you throw all that stuff aside"—meaning fiscal issues—"I'm probably more liberal than you are."

Jim Renner is not an easy answer, and that's why I came here to his home in North Benton, Ohio, to begin with the important truth that there won't be many easy answers. The Trump candidacy flushed a lot of ambiguity, a lot of conflicting loyalties and curious deviations. It illuminated contradictions, force-feeding light through an anomalous prism. It galvanized a divide, but one that can't be characterized simply. A few years before he cast his vote for the man, Renner thought Trump was "just some rich crazy guy." Trump didn't really change in the intervening years, and neither did Renner. So, what did change?

Although Ohio represents an American "typicalness," it's unreasonable—and I'm sure scientifically unsound—to assume a demographic cross section could animate a "typical" Ohioan, much less that this hypothetical Buckeye could somehow explain what happened on November 8, 2016, or what will happen in elections yet to come. But what the hell. Let's give it a ride.

Based primarily on averages from 2018 US Census data, our archetypical Ohioan is a white, native-born female, 38.9 years old, who owns a house worth $135,000 and lives there with 1.44 other people. According to Social Security Administration data on the most popular names for girls born in Ohio in 1980, she is called Jennifer. She graduated high school, but not college, earns $29,011 a year, and has health insurance. She lives in a metropolitan area. She roots for Ohio State Buckeyes football and believes that the Cleveland Indians should spend more on their payroll. (This is anecdotal.) There is a computer in her home. It has internet access. If she voted in 2016, Jennifer cast her ballot for Trump.

By this accounting, she's two years older than the average American, earns $2,000 less per year, paid nearly $60,000 less for her home, and is just as likely to have voted for Trump as if she lived somewhere else.

Many of us in Ohio found ourselves making personal calculations after the 2016 election, measuring our voting selves against an imagined "other," someone like Jennifer, or maybe someone real—a friend or family member who'd voted for someone we couldn't imagine any sane person voting for—Clinton or Trump—driven by the existential question that arises when there's a national identity shift: Who am I in relation to who we are?

That was the question vexing Ohio artist Michael Loderstedt, a question rising in pitch after the 2018 midterm elections, when Ohio turned almost completely red while something of a blue wave washed over other places. The recently retired Kent State University art professor found himself "analyzing what I felt was a difference between myself and 'most Ohioans,' now having lived here so long." Based on research about the state he has called home since 1982, he created a graphic, a word sculpture oriented sideways to mimic Ohio's north-coast shoreline (think of the black field as Lake Erie and the word field as Cleveland's northern edge), and posted it on his social media pages.

Following the 2018 gubernatorial election, when Ohio voters selected Mike DeWine, whom Loderstedt described as "a milquetoast, anti-abortion Republican," over Democrat Richard Cordray, "a nationally-recognized leader in consumer rights protection," the artist found himself considering moving away from a state he still loves.

Most Ohioans believe they are not racist, but seldom associate with people of color.
Most Ohioans believe their dead loved ones are waiting for them in heaven.
Most Ohioans believe there should be laws to protect the environment.
Most Ohioans don't like politics, or government and often do not vote.
Most Ohioans are ok with Trump, as long as the economy is good.
Most Ohioans spend less than 1% of their money on art.
Most Ohioans have never been in a boat on Lake Erie.
Most Ohioans eat meat with every meal. Every. One.
Most Ohioans spend more on their pet than on art.
Most Ohioans believe in absolute right and wrong.
Most Ohioans do not have a college education.
Most Ohioans have never left North America.
Most Ohioans wish there were no abortions.
Most Ohioans have never swam in Lake Erie.
Most Ohioans make less than $37K per year.
Most Ohioans call themselves conservative.
Most Ohioans believe in heaven and hell.
Most Ohioans eat fast food once a week.
Most Ohioans do not belong to a union.
Most Ohioans like to listen to talk radio.
Most Ohioans believe Hillary is a bitch.
Most Ohioans identify as Christians.
Most Ohioans were born in Ohio.
Most Ohioans live in the suburbs.
Most Ohioans do not own a gun.
Most Ohioans believe in ghosts.
Most Ohioans are over age 39.
Most Ohioans are overweight.
Most Ohioans pray every day.
Most Ohioans believe in God.
Most Ohioans are women.
Most Ohioans have a dog.

In an email exchange, Loderstedt told me:

I've described Ohio as an abused housewife who always settles with what she's got, always afraid to go in another direction. I'm afraid that describes our situation politically. When I taught at Kent, I'd often quiz students about who cast a ballot the day after an election, and the results were always shocking. Of a class of fifteen to twenty, often less than five would vote, and half of those were probably not telling the truth. When I'd ask why, they'd cite reasons from not wanting to stand in line, the risk of missing a class (I always made election day voting an excused absence), going to the wrong polling place because they forgot they were registered in their hometown. But mostly they thought it didn't matter to them, that they didn't connect with any candidates or issues (unless it was legalization). I'd try and explain how arts funding, student loan access, and grants are often tied to political decisions; it didn't matter.

The more he thought about it, the more this apathy and resignation to powerlessness bothered him. If just the student populations of three of Ohio's state universities had voted for Al Gore in 2000, he said, Gore's hundred-thousand-vote margin of defeat here to George W. Bush would have been erased, and Ohio would have swung the electoral college in Gore's favor.

"That alone would have changed the course of history for this country," he said. "Who knows, by now we would be facing an investment in green technology, pursuing alternative energy sources, rebuilding infrastructure and a host of other issues our society needs and government should take initiative towards. Instead, we're mired in turning back the clock to the 1950s, in other words, settling for something presumably safer and more self-serving."

So, by 2019, Loderstedt was feeling alienated and marginalized, as though he no longer fit in Ohio, or Ohio didn't fit him anymore.

It's not just that the country is divided, it's how loud each side rings within its own ears and how little each listens to the other. This isn't a groundbreaking observation, but I've been struck since the election of Donald Trump by how many times I've heard the national dynamic described within families.

I did not vote for Donald Trump in 2016, but I know plenty of people who did—among my birth family and my in-laws, I was definitely outnumbered—and one thing I know for sure is that his presidency has introduced the most uncomfortable political conversations of my lifetime. And I'm talking about a lifetime that includes returning home from my first-ever trip to the voting booth and telling my very traditional, white Republican father that I'd just voted for Jesse Jackson.

Before he died in 2018, my dad had Sunday dinner at our house every week. Now that he's gone, I regard those evenings among my fondest times with him, especially in the way this generally reticent man grew more candid and open-minded in the final years before his death at eighty-five. We always began with cocktail hour, gin and tonics in the summer, Manhattans when it grew colder. In the early fall of 2016, as the election babel loudened up, we found that the first drink would usually be enough lubrication to get us talking about the week's news, a topic that sometimes could extend into the second round. But with him being a Fox News guy and me more of an NPR man, we always knew when the debates had gone far enough and it was time to change the subject. There was a reasonable civility to the exchange. (I took the libertarian test, too, after Jim Renner and I talked. I came out about where I expected—solidly moderate. Many years ago, I picked up a nickname: "the playful diplomat." It fit then and has served me well since.)

I'm pretty well certain my dad had voted for a Republican in every presidential election of his lifetime, but I also know he voted mostly for Democrats in local races, because in urban northern cities like Akron, Republicans just don't have enough base to build a comparable roster of talent. He was also a devout Catholic. In that light, the most noteworthy of those Sunday evenings followed the week in which the soon-to-be president of the United States had been broadcast over and over boasting about his ability to grab women by their pussies without retribution, a word neither of us was comfortable using in front of my children, and these were children who were both legal adults. This still seems impossible, all of it. As we neared our threshold of tolerance for the topic, he lowered his head, shook it, and said, "I just can't vote for that guy."

But then he did.

And I can't say I don't understand, because I understood *him*. I understood that he was not an easy answer either. At the very least, I can't allow myself to judge his actions without scrutinizing my own.

A few weeks later, the evening after Election Day, I had to decide whether to keep preexisting plans to attend a University of Akron football game with my dad, my brother Louis, and our friend Joe, all of whom I knew had voted for Trump.

"We are not allowed to talk about politics," I emailed Louis that afternoon. "Unless I get drunk."

Jim Renner learned early how to start at the bottom. When he was a kid, his truck-driving father followed his union out on a strike. The lost paychecks led to a complete collapse—loss of the family home and just about everything in it. The family moved into a trailer, Jim bumped around a couple of schools, graduated high school a semester early just to get the hell out, married at nineteen, took a low-paying job as an extruder in a plastics factory, had a son, then divorced and found himself living as a young single dad. He married again, to a woman who also had a son, and found a place he could afford to buy, a trashed Hells Angels house in a rural township, and he got to work fixing it up for his growing family to call home. He landed a job making good money in a steel mill, American Spring Wire, and settled into a life that looked something like the promise he understood, in which hard work, ambition, and loyalty were rewarded in kind. This was the early 1980s, when that transaction still remained a basic principle of Americanism, especially in the industrial Midwest, where a high school diploma was enough to claim a factory job, which in turn was enough to claim middle-class comfort, which in turn was enough to set up a secure retirement and finally an obituary whose narrative reinforced that standard agreement. I see them all the time in my hometown newspaper: Someone in their eighties who retired twenty years ago after forty-odd years at Goodyear Tire and Rubber, or at Firestone Tire, or any of the other industrial patriarchs. Someone who made it all the way through to the very end in the way that had been promised.

In a dozen years as a steelworker, Renner and his coworkers were represented by three different unions—the United Steel Workers, the United Auto Workers (because the company produced automobile springs), and, "another one, that I don't even know why they were in a steel mill—textile workers or something."

He had some ambivalence about organized labor, especially the old-school, hardline, us-versus-them battles that still permeated the culture of what was then becoming the Rust Belt. He never understood scrapping for the last nickel in contract negotiations, which often occurred. He favored something more like trickle-down economics.

"My attitude was you should be as eager for those guys [the company] to do good as for you to do good," he said.

He became frustrated with some of the union dynamics, especially the quick-trigger tendency to call a strike, only to have half the members cross the line before the first Styrofoam cup of coffee had gone cold. So, he became a union steward and put his ideals and his penchant for a rousing debate to work.

"I was so good," he said, "they demoted the HR guy and brought in a corporate lawyer to argue with me. And he was *good!*"

His whole face—framed by a thick, dark bowl cut and a clavicle-length gray biker beard—lit up when he entered this part of his story. He knew he was as smart as any college-educated corporate suit, and he loved nothing more than a game of wits. When computers first arrived on the shop floor, he became fascinated with them, exploring their functions and contents. Soon he realized he was probably accessing information he wasn't supposed to be seeing. He asked his foreman if anything in there was off-limits. "You're not smart enough to find anything that can hurt anyone," he was told, and soon enough he and a few others were buzzing around inside the company databases like rats in a food pantry. When another worker veered closer to sabotage, messing with materials prices, someone caught on.

Whenever one of his stories reached its moment of confrontation—and most of them were aimed directly toward that—they generally climaxed in a dynamic like this one did: Jim, the little guy in his workingman's clothes, ushered into a conference room full of powerful people, suited up and seated strategically in a way to maximize their advantage. The big boss always at the head of the long, shiny table. Each side lined shoulder to shoulder with lieutenants. Jim placed at the farthest end, as though centered as the target for a cannon shot whose propulsion would be maximized by its passage through the opposing forces. And finally, Jim trying to decode the battle dynamics in the midst of it all. In this case, he recalled a courtroom-style examination:

Did you access classified information in the shop-floor computer?
Yes.
Did you know you were somewhere you weren't supposed to be?
No.
Why not?
Because I was told there was nothing off limits in the computer.
Who told you that?
He pointed across the table to where the foreman was sitting among the company brass.

"He did."

Renner laughed when he said that, finishing with the denoue-ment that completed pretty much all the stories he told me that day, the moral in which the powerless turns the tables on the powerful. They're like Aesop's fables, which, it's worth noting, are attributed to a slave, a storyteller who is overlooked, under-estimated, yet wise. Sometimes the mouse wins, sometimes the lion, but the teller always understands what has transpired. In this case, Renner walked out grinning and exonerated, with a scolding not to do it again, feeling a little bad for the foreman who was left with the blame, but only a little.

Ohio is divided in a lot of ways. Here is one.

From the early twentieth century until around 1970, an Ohioan like Jim Renner with a high school diploma could enter the middle class reasonably certain of steady work, good money, and solid benefits. In factory towns, unionized workers often had more job security and better perks than college-degreed white-collar workers. But as that string started to play out in the last quarter of the twentieth century, those multigenerational factory families urged their children to go to college and forge a new path to what they hoped would be the same quality of life. Those college students often paid their tuition working summer and part-time jobs in the mills, standing temporarily on the shoulders of giants, gazing for new vistas. I know a guy who likes to tell the story of paying his way through the University of Akron in the 1970s by working as a "fan cleaner" at the Firestone Tire and Rubber headquarters, where the executive offices were in such close prox-imity to the factory soot that such a job—wiping smokestack residue from desk fan blades—had its own category. Years later, after establishing a successful company of his own as Firestone spiraled through its decline, the entrepreneur bought one of the industrial icon's decommissioned factory buildings to house his operation.

"Firestone Parkway," he told me one time. "I thought that was a classy address."

The portal into the middle class, however, has increasingly narrowed. First, it was a good union job. Then, as that security faded, it was college. But as tuition costs took a radical upturn beginning in the 1990s, the burden of student debt has raised a harsh and legitimate cost–benefit question. In present-day Ohio, employers are eager for candidates with trade school training—machinists, electricians, HVAC technicians. According to the Ohio Department of Job and Family Services, the state's most in-demand occupation in 2020 was "Laborers/Freight/Stock/ Material Movers." Meanwhile, many college degrees go unused or underrewarded. One of my wife's young elementary school teaching colleagues heads straight out of work every day to her second job at Target, just to make ends meet. Amid all this is the difficult question of what "middle class" even means anymore, and just how endangered it is.

Jim Renner didn't go to college, but he was no dummy. He seems, all his adult life, to have known what he wanted and how to get it. His supervisor told him he wasn't smart enough to figure out those new computers, so Jim popped open a screen and found his way deep into the works, as deep as he could go, mostly just to prove the guy wrong. He didn't have the diploma, but he spent most of his downtime on the shop floor reading newspapers and magazines, trying to understand the world. When the twenty-four-hour cable news cycle first appeared on his TV out there in the sticks, he was immediately fascinated. At first, he was tickled by what might now be called an unintended version of reality TV—on-air personalities unaccustomed to filling so much time, bumbling through the hours.

"I used to watch these guys, cuz they didn't know what to say," he recalled, mimicking the awkward live-in-studio banter. "It was funny as hell."

But then he continued watching as they figured something out. They could fill that time by bringing politicians into the studio, and between the talking heads and the polished speechmakers, the programming found its stride.

"It was good for them but bad for us," Renner said of the politicians and their new mass audience. "Because it takes them away from us and gives them more perceived power."

What he saw were politicians who now only had to listen to whoever was across the studio desk—and to themselves. Their ears and instincts retuned themselves to the new vibe.

At the same time his interest in politics was growing, the dynamics of power, both in his immediate world and that world beyond the television screen, were changing.

And Ohio is united in a lot of ways.

Many of us—I'd guess most—have either been here all our lives or were born here, left, and found a reason to return. The former is the case with Renner, who has never lived more than a few miles from where he was born. With its 11.7 million residents, Ohio, the seventh-largest state in the union, ranks among the top ten in population density. But it's also among the slowest-growing states, with a population increase of only about a half million people in the past twenty-five years. Most of the big cities have lost significant numbers of residents over the past two generations. Generally, this means that the people who are here tend to have been here for a while. A bumper sticker appeared a few years back: STUCK IN OHIO. As a lifer who has watched plenty of people leave, I find myself annoyed. If you've got a bumper, you've got a car, and if you've got a car, you are literally not stuck in Ohio. With one of the largest Interstate systems in the nation, there are abundant routes of departure.

Most of us who've stuck here on purpose have a reason to stay, and we share a rich, finely tuned cultural familiarity. Cincinnatians have an inside joke—the way you can tell someone is from there is if, by way of introduction, they ask what high school you went to. Once, as I was running a 5K in Akron, a densely packed group of us passed under an old bridge. In the enclosed stone corridor, I recognized a high-quality sonic resonance and shouted, "O-H!" and was met with an immediate, unanimous, booming "I-O!" When Renner casually mentioned his first job was delivering newspapers, I spontaneously and instinctively asked if it was the *Record-Courier,* and his big face lit up in sublime recognition. Of course it was. I understood where he was from, down to its circulation zone, in a way that only a fellow lifer could, an understanding as spiritual as it was tediously literal, which in some way validated our mutual relevance. In Ohio, this is important.

Where he is from is a place next to one of the prettiest lakes in Ohio, its surface sliced on this spring morning by the hulls of fiberglass boats and ringed with the ripples of fishing bobbers. The highway exit that leads to his house is flanked by a Midwest Fireworks billboard and a place selling prefab sheds, giving way to a Dairy Queen and a campground entrance, the state route softening into thick, green roadside foliage cut with vistas revealing old red barns and tidy houses set far back from the road. Boats in the carports, four-wheelers by the porches, the occasional truck bed out front for sale. It's the kind of place people sometimes call nowhere, which is why I wanted to come here.

The latest edition of the local *Farm and Dairy* newspaper sat at the edge of the kitchen table the morning Renner and I talked. He was dressed in Wrangler jeans and a well-worn Carhartt pocket tee. The room smelled faintly of maple syrup, the hint of a recently cleared breakfast. A big dog eventually romped through, tired of being cooped up because of company. A breeze lilted through the screen door. Outside was the kind of country quiet that reminds someone like me, someone who's always lived in the city, how different life can be even for two people who think of themselves as from the same place.

This country place is how one might rightly imagine Ohio. But so is the soot-stained red brick of the factories of my hometown, with their grimy, green-tinted windows and tall, round smoke-stacks with defunct company names lettered down their sides. So, too, are the weathered clapboards of a dog-chained shack in the Appalachian foothills not far south from here and the mansion built by a wealthy Buckeyes booster in the golden ring around Columbus and the doggedly evolving skyline of Cleveland. All very different, and all very Ohio.

Renner's home in little North Benton, unincorporated, nestled between those lakes and woodlands, is just as much the epicenter of what was once steel country as it is of rural recreation. It doesn't fit easily into any of the five Ohios, but it is as "Ohio"—and as American—as a place could be. Renner, too, could be viewed as a quintessential representation of his place, but can't be cast into a single role. Maybe his most Ohio quality is his adaptability to change, which, paradoxical as it may seem, is among the state's most consistent traits.

In 1991, Renner quit his factory job to start a contracting business with his brother, a carpenter who had a little bit of seed money. Jim's only construction experience came from rehabbing that Hells Angels house, but he had plenty of Rust Belt gumption, do-it-yourself instincts, and belief that hard work is a better route to prosperity than luck or expertise or the government. They bought some property, built a house, and put it on the market. A cash buyer showed up out of the blue, and the sale of that first house got them on their feet. They built and sold a couple more, then connected with a guy who'd won the lottery and wanted to invest, and their homespun enterprise grew, eventually doing nearly $3 million in annual business and employing eleven people. Jim's brother handled sales and Jim built the houses. Eventually, they disbanded the company. Jim attended some home builders' seminars, learned more about the business side, and has worked for himself ever since.

Along the way, his interest in politics and his independent spirit led him to run for office. In 2010, he filed a petition to challenge incumbent Charlie Wilson in the Democratic primary for Ohio's 6th congressional district, a wide stripe of mostly rural Appalachian territory trailing the Ohio River along the state's eastern border. Described in press accounts variously as "a virtual unknown" and "a political newcomer," Renner spent no money on his campaign. On an election questionnaire, he listed jobs and spending cuts as his top priorities. In their book *The Roads to Congress 2010,* authors Sean D. Foreman and Robert Dewhirst write, "The outcome of the Democratic primary was known before the race started. . . . Wilson was treated as the incumbent who was not in a competitive race." One local Chamber of Commerce after another invited Wilson to speak. None invited Renner.

A YouTube video of an April 2010 Tea Party event in Lisbon, Ohio, shows Renner taking the microphone at the town square gazebo, dressed in jeans and a white T-shirt emblazoned with an American flag and the slogan KEEP FLYING! UNITED WE STAND. He starts with a crack on Nancy Pelosi—"She's from California, she had to be smoking somethin'!"—and then criticizes Congress for its inside factions, pork-barreling, and association with lobbyists.

"It's not just voting in the right people," he says, "it's making them do the right thing once they get in there."

Renner lost the following month, but all things considered, he made a decent showing, receiving 31 percent of the votes, 15,674 to the incumbent's 34,772. (Wilson, who'd spent nearly $30,000 on his primary campaign, went on to lose that November to Republican Bill Johnson.) Renner considered running for Congress again in 2020, this time as an Independent, but got busy building a house for his daughter and instead registered the domain name "greatamericanmiddle.com," with the notion to start either a political action committee or a new political party.

Until then, he had been a Democrat "by necessity," with little remaining faith in the traditional two-party system. He considered Trump a right-leaning moderate Democrat who used the Republican Party as a means to an end. In the ensuing months, the impeachment trial and the growing federal dysfunction only deepened Renner's disgust.

"The Democrats are completely out of their minds, and the Republicans are just, I dunno, crazy," he told me in early 2020.

As for himself, his politics are more influenced by his daily dealings with practical-minded people in the construction industry than what he calls "the liberal slant—the wish list."

"I'm down there every day with the construction workers," he said. "The people I'm with all the time, they're like, 'This is what I can do today. So this is what we'll do today.'"

Just like them, Jim Renner, an "unknown" in a place you might call nowhere, gets up every day and goes to work, smart enough not to expect too much but still hoping for better.

3

LORDSTOWN

The closer I got to Lordstown, the more self-conscious I was of my Subaru. I knew I was driving into a raw nerve. Even as a fellow Ohioan, a self-perceived ally, I was a stranger with questions entering a jilted place where people had good reason to be wary. I knew I was driving my Japanese car into an elaborately American territory, where the first thing folks notice is what you're driving. I know this, because I had departed that very morning from a not-so-different place, the "Rubber City," where nearly four decades after the last passenger tire was manufactured, people still take note of the brand on your sidewalls. Places that make things are primally attuned to where things were made and who made them.

Lordstown, more than most places, had always been about what was made there. Cars. Specifically, General Motors cars. By the time it was incorporated as a village in 1975, its namesake Lordstown Assembly plant (motto: "Build It Like We Own It!") had already been producing GM automobiles for a decade. There's really nothing about this place that isn't about the auto plant. My GPS destination was called Hallock Young Road on the map, but

31

was marked Honorary Chevrolet/UAW Parkway on its sign-post. In Ohio, *Lordstown* doesn't refer to a municipality; it refers to a livelihood.

Three weeks before, in early March 2019, a white Chevrolet Cruze LS had made its way down the assembly line at Lordstown, a sort of death march, heavy with ceremony. An American flag was draped across its windshield. Its route down the dual tracks of the long, tunnel-like, fluorescent-lit workspace was flanked by reporters, photo-snapping shift workers, and worried union officials. When it reached the line's end that Wednesday midafternoon, it became the last car built there before the plant entered "unallocated" status. The shutdown of the machinery that day represented the first time the plant had been taken completely out of operation since the inaugural Impala was completed back on April 28, 1966. It also represented the first time since the dawn of the automobile age that GM would not be manufacturing vehicles in Ohio. More immediately, and more to the dark heart of the matter, it represented a wholesale loss of employment and identity for a whole lot of people. GM was laying off some 15,000 employees at five facilities nationwide, including all 1,700 hourly workers at the Lordstown plant. The factory's force of dedicated, experienced autoworkers had already endured a slow, steady reduction, with two shifts eliminated since 2017, representing a loss of nearly 3,000 good-paying jobs. At its peak in 1976, the plant had employed 12,000. Through the late twentieth century, following the collapse of steel manufacturing, GM Lordstown was the region's largest employer.

Nearing the complex, I passed a sign directing where to turn for the United Auto Workers Local 1112 union hall, where a steady drumbeat of concerned members had been dropping in for information and advice and support, the news still fresh and hard to believe, the ambiguity of "unallocated" leaving open the hope—a dangerous word in such a time and place—that something could change, that they could be "allocated" again soon. And then, a couple of miles farther down the trucking route, the sprawling utilitarian factory complex unfolded, dominating the view. The first thing visible from the road was a bigger-than-billboard banner covering the side of a building, featuring a shiny blue sedan, logos for the UAW and GM (in that order), and finally:

LORDSTOWN
HOME
OF THE
CRUZE

It's hard to overstate the pride and emotional investment carried by those five words. Lordstown, a village of some thirty-four hundred people, covers just thirty-two square miles. But its resonance, both pragmatic and symbolic, carries far beyond this immediate place and time. Its employees arrived at their shifts each day from all over the region, some with commutes of more than two hours, from Cleveland and Pittsburgh and central Ohio, aware of how precious these jobs were, especially in 2019. Experienced workers made more than thirty dollars an hour, a far higher wage than for most blue-collar jobs in the region.

Everywhere I went in Northeast Ohio that spring, people were talking about the layoffs the way people talk about disasters that strike to the heart of all our shared fears and vulnerabilities, with new emphasis on the "home" part of something hitting close to home. In Akron, for instance, many of us related the shutdown directly to the demise of Ohio's tire manufacturing a generation before. In Cleveland and the small towns near the Pennsylvania and West Virginia borders, it echoed the steel layoffs. Here in the region known as the Mahoning Valley, which has lived and died with the swells of manufacturing, it was both a cruel déjà vu and a terrifying direct hit. Forty-two years earlier, Youngstown Sheet and Tube had closed a steel plant that was nothing short of the Valley's life force, an event that people still talk about like it was last week and whose psychological and economic tremors pulsed straight into Lordstown. The GM plant was the region's long-nurtured ember of hope. In surviving every lurch of the industrial economy, it validated the pride and goodwill people had invested there. The facility withstood labor unrest and strikes in the 1970s so bitter that the media introduced "Lordstown syndrome" as a generic term to describe worker discontent.

GM had planned to close the plant in 2002; the community rallied and it persevered. A succeeding series of union concessions helped keep Lordstown in the fight; in the wake of GM's 2009 Chapter 11 reorganization, the company invested $350 million to retool the plant for production of the Chevrolet Cruze compact, one of its most popular models, a resounding victory that inspired pride across Northeast Ohio, where so many other battles had been lost. Up until that last chassis rolled through, the plant operated at peak efficiency.

And now it was closed. That's what people said. If they used GM's term—"unallocated"—they did so with bitterness and confusion, a word received as a disingenuous mock of corporate jargon that only added uncertainty to the already unsettled deal. You can't achieve closure when something isn't closed, even when it is so obviously closed.

The main road into the factory complex is (and not by accident) situated directly off a ramp of the Ohio Turnpike, a major trucking route linking the East to the Midwest and just one of many characteristics, presented by both nature and design, that made Ohio such an attractive locale for major manufacturing. On this cool spring morning, though, the roads were notably, eerily, deserted.

Under a broad, glaucomic sky drifting with directionless clouds, the landscape felt lethargic, a distant whoosh of highway traffic dissolving lazily through my open window, the slow glide of grackles and other common birds tracing the horizon. Occasionally, a semi whizzed by, not slowing at the entrance. The grass median dividing the ceremonially named Chevrolet/UAW Parkway was lined with wire-legged plastic signs featuring a blue silhouette of Ohio and the directive DRIVE IT HOME / SUPPORT GM LORDSTOWN. These signs, promoting a campaign of awareness and resistance, were ubiquitous that spring in Lordstown and the surrounding communities, where every aspect of the economy and civic well-being was linked to the fate of the plant and the spending power of its employees.

Most entrances to the parking lot of the 6.2-million-square-foot facility were blocked by concrete barriers and orange barrels. Beyond, not a single human in sight. A few dozen cars were parked close to the building in a lot made for hundreds, its faded asphalt crystalled with gravel and glass. The 905-acre campus was surrounded by chain-link fence topped with razor wire.

Driving away, I passed one more sign at an intersection that marked the final corner of the Lordstown complex, a truer representation of the anguish and protest that had arisen in the wake of General Motors's pronouncement. It was a sheet of graying plywood screwed to a couple of two-by-fours, crudely lettered in black spray paint: SAVE THE GM PLANT.

The plea was raw, and when I talked to people around there, their anger and concern distilled into two distinct but inseparable messages: save our jobs, and keep your promises. Many hearkened back to a much-publicized 2017 Trump rally in downtown Youngstown, where the president said Ohio's departed manufacturing jobs are "all coming back." They quoted his sound bite again and again: "Don't move; don't sell your house."

Over and over that spring in the Valley, the warning was repeated: if it can happen here, it can happen anywhere.

Monty Woolley was standing on the line the day the last Cruze came down. A union electrician, he had worked a quarter century at the plant, nearly half his life, following in the footsteps of his father, who'd made his career there, straight to retirement. In his navy-blue coveralls and dirty white shop-floor sneakers, Woolley had stepped out of the plant's paint shop and crowded in with his coworkers, surrounding the half-completed body, all of them wanting to be near their final product. Some of these were close friends he'd known for decades, others passing figures at the time clock, folks dressed in hoodies and ball caps, coveralls and yellow safety vests, along with the wrist and elbow sleeves and the knee braces necessitated by the toll the work had taken on their bodies. He knew that some of these people had new mortgages and babies on the way, aged parents in their care, and dreams that would have to be set aside.

"You could look in people's eyes. Even up to that point everyone had hope. Everyone thought, something's gonna happen good. Something's gonna change," he recalled. "And you just look in their eyes and you just see the sadness, the lack of hope."

Amid the crowd of coworkers, he could feel the lump rising in his throat, an emotion he did not want to show. He turned and walked away.

Two months later, I sat with him in the dim shadows of his living room in the middle of a cloudy weekday morning when everyone else in this quiet Youngstown neighborhood was off at work. Woolley, with a shaved head and full white goatee, dressed in denim shorts and a teal T-shirt, rested his stockinged feet on the footrest of a brown recliner, a spot where he'd been spending more time lately than he'd prefer. He and a handful of other

UAW workers had been kept on for about six weeks following the shutdown, tasked with bringing perpetual motion to a stop. This process represents one of the harshest of the narratives that have echoed across American industrial cities for the past three decades: the longtime shop-floor worker whose final assignment is shutting down his workplace, sometimes having to dismantle his own machine, sometimes even preparing it for shipping to a plant in another city or another country, where someone else will do the same work for less money.

Woolley, that morning, was waiting anxiously for the mail carrier. He'd been expecting his letter, thought it might have arrived yesterday, but it hadn't. That letter, like so many others arriving in homes around the Valley and beyond, would reveal his fate.

Employees who'd been laid off from Lordstown were receiving mailed offers of positions at other GM plants, a prospect that for many was just as fraught with upheaval as unemployment. Lives would have to be uprooted, children pulled from school, families separated, homes dumped for a loss, all to keep a paycheck that couldn't be duplicated nearby or to maintain a track toward retirement that required sticking with GM.

The week of the shutdown, my local newspaper and a few other news outlets carried an op-ed column by a soon-to-be-jobless twenty-year Lordstown veteran named Nanette Senters, who called the relocation offer "a false choice."

"I can't just pick up and leave," she wrote. "My entire family lives in the Lordstown area—my 84-year-old mother is too frail to move, and she relies on me for her care. I'm also expecting my first grandchild here in June. But if I don't relocate, I may not be able to find another job that pays a living wage."

Echoing a resentment I heard repeatedly throughout that season, she called out politicians whose promises had manipulated people's hopes and their votes, only to come up empty. In a region where union Democrats had made a tidal electoral shift toward Donald Trump, his rallying words reverberated: "Don't move. Don't sell your house."

I contacted Senters to ask if we could talk, and for several weeks we tried to schedule a meeting. But throughout that time, she was overwhelmed by the turbulence of losing a job she'd valued specifically for its stability. Few people work in factories primarily for the love of it. They do it for the good pay and benefits, the steadiness that allows them the possibility of a comfortable, meaningful existence beyond work. There's dignity in that transaction, a basic American contract of trust: hard work traded for its reward. In our final text exchange, Senters reflected the turmoil that occurs when that contract fails, giving way to forces beyond one's control:

> Hi David. I've been trying to organize all the things necessary for me to move on a moment's notice. Put my 85 year old mother in Assisted Living last month and am selling her house. Had my first grandchild yesterday. A beautiful baby girl. I have elderly pets and am waiting till the last minute because when the call comes they will have to be euthanized. The change would kill them anyway. The whole thing is devastating. I have 5–6 years of service before I can retire. I'm considering refusing the offer and retraining but I'm terrified that I may not be able to get a new job at my age. So anyway, I would be happy to speak with you. Send me a message before you call and I will answer.

I tried, but never heard from her again.

Meanwhile, Monty Woolley waited for his own letter and the choice he'd have to make. Just a few months before everything was ripped from each individual's control, his birthday had brought him to the union contract's magic number for retirement, in which his age, fifty-nine, and years of service, twenty-six, added up to eighty-five. But he had planned to work longer, with his retirement target in 2023.

"This threw a monkey wrench into everything," he said.

If he retired now, during his layoff, he would risk losing the opportunity to take a buyout once a new contract was ratified, something he estimated would happen in the coming fall. He'd put in twenty-six years and didn't want to lose out on a final reward. But to remain employed till the contract was settled, he'd need to relocate to another GM facility. That's what the letter would reveal. He could be offered a position in Bowling Green, Kentucky, or Arlington, Texas, or Wentzville, Missouri, or maybe he'd be lucky enough to be offered a job in Ohio, at parts plants in Toledo or Lorain. When the letter arrived, he would begin the difficult decision of whether to walk away from GM or uproot and relocate temporarily. For now, all he could do was wait.

He was so close. He'd given his loyalty and his well-being to a job whose physical demands had led to two back surgeries. "You trade your youth for the money," he told me. He'd given his patience, too. He was originally hired at Lordstown in 1979, then got laid off after less than a year. He went back to school, got his degree in electrical engineering, and took a job in Grand Rapids, Michigan.

"But it wasn't where my heart was," he said. "I wanted to work with the tools. I wanted to get my hands dirty."

So, when GM contacted him after a fourteen-year layoff and offered him a job in the Lordstown complex as a union electrician, he decided to take it. He did not, however, do so blindly. His father had seen enough of the power plays and downturns to encourage Woolley to stick with engineering. And Woolley himself, having already been laid off once, quietly kept up his guard.

"I never really trusted GM, to be honest with you," he said. "I always, in the back of my mind, was expecting something like this."

Two years before, guided by that caution, he and his wife, Susan, had downsized from the home where they'd raised two sons, taking up residence in this modest, pale blue bungalow, deliberately cutting expenses. Just in case. Always with his eye on the long game, Woolley thought he was going to make it out clean. Now he sat in limbo, fifty-nine years old, stuck on that recliner, waiting for a letter that, no matter what it said, would unsettle his life.

Woolley wanted to make sure I understood that he considered himself among the fortunate. His sons were grown and out on their own. Susan had a good job working as a computer programmer at Joy Cone, the ice cream cone company, not far across the Ohio border in Hermitage, Pennsylvania. He'd been careful with his savings. Moving temporarily would represent a significant financial hit, in addition to a separation, probably for the better part of a year, from Susan, who would need to stay here for her job. But he would still be able to finish his GM career on something close to his own terms.

Describing himself as "one of the lucky ones," however, was not an expression of relief. More than once in our conversation, he followed such statements with references to what he knew was happening in other households across the Mahoning Valley. Many of those people he'd stood with on that final production day were at the mercy of GM, midcareer, living lives that relied on the income that had built them. Some had recently taken on large mortgages. Some were married couples who'd suddenly lost two incomes. Most would not have any option other than to move to wherever GM would have them.

"I don't know how it is where you live," he said, "but this area, there's very strong family ties here. People don't like to move away from family."

He shook his head.

"What do you say to someone like that?"

In a region where job stress is part of the fabric, he knew what layoffs did to people. He'd been laid off himself; through twenty-six years inside Lordstown Assembly, he could never feel at ease. For the past two generations, anxiety had been creeping into the psyche of the people who'd built America, who'd created its middle class and validated the notion of its "dream." As the twentieth century ticked down and the twenty-first began, there was a vague unshakeable sense that something was slipping away.

So Woolley knew there would be domestic strife, fistfights, arrests, drinking and drug habits spiraling toward crisis. A week after the GM announcement, a friend from Youngstown told me of a dark story buzzing through his neighborhood, that a laid-off worker there had committed suicide.

"In a few cases, but too many," Woolley said, "we're hearing of people getting divorces already. Families are really paying for this, and unfortunately, kids are paying for it. In a layoff, you're gonna wreck families. You're gonna wreck people, basically. It hurts because it didn't need to happen. It was a mean-spirited thing for the company to do. We did everything they wanted us to do and they still turned around and stabbed us in the back."

Near the close of the twentieth century, when Bruce Springsteen was of a mind to write about a lost and forgotten America, to reckon the accounts of people who'd been left out of a changing calculation, people who'd once been something like royalty under "a beautiful sky of soot and clay" and who now were foundering, he turned to Youngstown. Springsteen's album *The Ghost of Tom Joad* is widely recognized for its grittily authentic chronicle of the poor and disenfranchised. In his autobiography *Born to Run,* Springsteen cast the album as a confrontation with a moral question that had dogged him amid his dizzying commercial ascendancy: "Where does a rich man belong?"

The album's fourth song was inspired by a book, *Journey to Nowhere: The Saga of the New Underclass,* written by Ohio native Dale Maharidge and photographed by Michael Williamson, a duo that has collaborated on four books, each variously exploring the plain and overlooked people of America: an aged hobo, the citizens of a small Iowa town, and the southern poor, whose tale they documented in *And Their Children After Them,* which was awarded the Pulitzer Prize for nonfiction. *Journey to Nowhere,* published in 1985, chronicled the human and social burdens of the industrial downturn in Northeast Ohio, a region just then becoming known as the Rust Belt. "The history of steel in the Mahoning Valley is the history of America," writes Maharidge, who'd begun his journalism career at the *Cleveland Plain Dealer,* dead center in the debris field of industrial implosion. You didn't have to go looking for authenticity in Northeast Ohio then; it crunched underfoot. Springsteen had acquired the book upon its release, but never got around to reading it. As *Rolling Stone* reporter Brian Hiatt tells it in *Bruce Springsteen: The Stories Behind the Songs,* the songwriter, in the midst of the *Tom Joad* sessions—recorded in the library of his California home's guesthouse ("the library of his California home's guesthouse" may be a partial answer to the question of where a rich man belongs)—picked up *Journey to Nowhere* in the middle of a sleepless night, fell into its thrall, and finished it by morning. Almost immediately, he wrote "Youngstown."

With *Tom Joad,* Springsteen seemed almost desperate for humility, and wary of it, too. For such a master of artifice and persona, "humility" could have meant adapting a new Steinbeckian cloak, a costume change from his "Racing in the Street" leather. Instead, he seemed determined to use his privilege to illuminate the character of people whose dignity was at great risk, and to do so before it was too late—for him. The line between fetishization and sincere illumination was dangerously thin. And the bullshit detector in places like Youngstown was exquisitely tuned, as happens in places that have been force-fed a diet of the stuff. If Springsteen wanted to offer his voice to the voiceless, he needed to do right by his subjects. "They traveled light," Springsteen wrote in his memoir of these people he invoked; "they were lean, direct in their expression, yet with most of what they had to say left in the silence between words."

Despite the album's old-timey echoes, the Ohio he tapped there in the waning twentieth century was as raw as a gunshot wound. "Youngstown" begins with the early-nineteenth-century discovery of iron ore in a creek valley near the titular city and the subsequent establishment of the Hopewell Furnace, the region's first iron mill. (Worth noting: Hopewell Furnace is also the name of a death metal band in neighboring Pennsylvania.) The song tells of the families that endured the heat and filth of the mills as their penance for a life in the middle class and evokes the role of steelworkers in winning America's wars and creating its millionaires. "Once I made you rich enough," Springsteen sings, "rich enough to forget my name." In the final lines, the narrator prays for an afterlife in hell, the only appropriate counterpart to the blast furnaces of Ohio. Most important, however, is the chorus, addressed to a "darlin'" named "Jenny," the most bittersweet word in all the rich, shopworn lexicon of the Mahoning Valley.

"Jenny" was the local nickname for the Jeanette Blast Furnace, which smelted ore into pig iron, dominating the operation inside the Campbell Works of Youngstown Sheet and Tube, a steel mill that employed nearly thirty thousand people at its peak, and whose towering, belching, unglamorous profile defined the region's silhouette.

The steelworks was an outsized, elementary fact of life for all who lived within reach of its stinking shadow. In "Sticks and Bones," an essay of his Youngstown youth, Gordon Murray recalls, "The mill was so long that it seemed only to have a middle." The adjective *paternal* is usually applied to large corporate industrial employers, but in the Valley, Youngstown Sheet and Tube—YS&T for short—seemed much more maternal, a nurturing presence, an essence, a warm, pulsing thing watching over everyone: Jenny.

Murray's essay was published in an anthology of writing and photographs about Youngstown, *Car Bombs to Cookie Tables,* in which YS&T appears again and again, beginning with the cover photograph of the mill's interior. The steelmaker, established in 1900, is a touchstone first for nostalgia, then collapse.

On September 19, 1977, still referred to in the Valley as "Black Monday," YS&T announced the closing of the Campbell Works, putting five thousand people out of work, destroying countless lives, and eliminating a region's very identity and purpose. Here's how Springsteen described the corporate axe: "Them big boys did what Hitler couldn't do." Jenny was the last blast furnace still operating in a community whose entire ecosystem had relied on the steel industry. The Valley was decimated. Whatever hope remained was housed at Lordstown Assembly.

It's hard to overstate the effect Springsteen's song had in this part of Ohio. When it came out just before Thanksgiving 1995, the Jeanette Blast Furnace still held its profile alongside the Mahoning River, rusty and dormant, an ugly symbol of an unhealed wound. Most people in the region agreed that the song got it right, both in its somber, bitter lyrics and its haunting, unadorned delivery. Even more welcome was that someone had taken note. Youngstown, Cleveland, Toledo—most of Ohio's cities as well as Ohio itself—were long accustomed to a different sort of invocation, our place-names used as punch lines or as cultural code for a backward, unsophisticated place. A Mark Twain quip whose veracity has been disputed, but whose message is achingly familiar, is well known to Ohioans: "When the end of the world comes, I want to be in Cincinnati because it's always 20 years behind the times."

Springsteen's song was on local radio a lot that year. He came to Youngstown in the middle of a January snowstorm to play a sold-out solo acoustic concert at the city's Stambaugh Auditorium, the twenty-six hundred seats filled with people whose story was in those lyrics. *Los Angeles Times* music critic Robert Hilburn was in the audience and described a room that fell silent as Springsteen introduced the song: "This is about the men and women who lived in this town and who built this country. It's about [the people] who gave their sons and daughters to the wars that were fought...and who were later declared expendable."

The crowd remained silent, other than an unavoidable, spontaneous yawp upon hearing their city's name emerge from the lips of the fabled singer, hanging on every word until the song's final chord, then erupted into a standing ovation. Springsteen received the key to the city and, buoyed by the warm reception, stayed an extra day to see some of its sites.

I remember not long after the song came out settling into the passenger seat of a car driven by a sportswriter friend who lived in Warren, another scruffy pin in the Mahoning Valley map, arranging my feet so as not to disturb the paperback he'd tossed onto the floor mat as he cleared the seat for me: *The Grapes of Wrath*. More memorable than the Springsteen-inspired reading material was the miniature set of vice grips jury-rigged to replace the broken stem of the dashboard radio's volume control. When I asked him about it, he deadpanned, "Everyone in the Valley owns a car like this."

"Youngstown" remains a staple in Springsteen's live repertoire, the hushed acoustic ballad translated by the E Street Band into a six-minute-long burner whose final phrase— "the fiery furnaces of hell"—gives way to Nils Lofgren's extended, searing guitar solo, mournful and defiant. In concert footage, he plays himself into a frenzy, whirling midstage, refusing to be ignored.

Meanwhile, *Journey to Nowhere*, the account that inspired the song, is out of print.

It wasn't getting any more comfortable, driving these roads in my Subaru, trying to formulate a rationale that I could articulate if confronted, and finding no words that satisfied. I was reminded of a long-ago exchange with a brother-in-law who, laying eyes on my newly purchased (albeit very used) Volkswagen, accused, "You bought a *Jap* car?" My dryly self-righteous response was, "No, actually it's German." It didn't occur to me till later that his motorcycle was a Suzuki.

Most modern consumers don't think at all about where their products were made, a condition that's only increasing, and increasingly dangerous. In an age of online commerce, when there's no difference between purchasing something from the next county or from a continent across the globe, it seems that products come from both everywhere and nowhere. Japanese automaker Honda operates one of the industry's most highly regarded auto manufacturing facilities right in the middle of Ohio; your neighbor's Chevy Blazer may have been built in Mexico, where GM is that nation's leading carmaker.

Any such nuance was stopped in its tracks, however, as I slowed to turn into the driveway of the UAW Local 1112 union hall, three miles up the road from the Lordstown plant. A warning was boldly announced in the yellow lettering of a large sign directing ALL NON-GM, FORD, [AND] CHRYSLER VEHICLES to park behind the building. If a Subaru Outback can slink, that's what mine did, as I made my way to the farthest reaches of the asphalt, wishing to indicate respect.

Inside, I waited to talk to David Green, the local president, who, only recently elected to the position, had found himself a very busy man, speaking very publicly for his members and working to try to convince GM to reactivate the plant once the new contract was negotiated later in the year. Three days before my visit, he had appeared on Fox News, where he referred to a Twitter post by President Trump that called for GM to reopen the plant, saying a tweet was not enough to prompt the help his people needed. Trump responded with a tweet aimed at Green:

> Democrat UAW Local 1112 President David Green ought to get his act together and produce....Stop complaining and get the job done!

Green arrived at the glass front doors of the union hall, dressed in jeans and a black hoodie featuring the Local 1112 logo, a backpack slung over his shoulder. He breezed through the lobby, barely waiting for me to rise from my seat to follow him. He paused to answer impromptu questions from staffers as we passed through the large, cafeteria-like common room, where laid-off workers consulted with union officials across folding tables, weighing their options and fates. When we reached his office, the forty-nine-year-old, thirty-year GM veteran dropped his backpack and leaned wearily into his chair behind a cluttered desk, pulled out a bottom drawer, kicked off his sneakers, and propped up his feet. I asked him what it feels like to be in a tweet-storm with Donald Trump. He smirked.

"It's a little overwhelming," he said. "I didn't tweet back. You can't win that war. I didn't take it personally, because he clearly doesn't know me. I don't think he has a lot of high regard for me even though he doesn't know me. Which is kind of disappointing, that this is the leader of the free world, and he's passing judgment on what he knows nothing of. I'm busy as hell trying to do something to entice General Motors to get a product here."

Green, who previously had written two letters to the president asking for his help—both unanswered—wasn't Trump's only target. In that same tweet, the president wrote, "G.M. let our Country down, but other much better car companies are coming into the U.S. in droves. I want action on Lordstown fast."

On that point, there was agreement. Every day that the massive facility sat idle, the fear increased that it would stay that way. Green likened the unallocated status to "having a loved one in a coma on a life support system and wondering, is it better to pull the plug or is it better to wait it out?"

He was joined by laid-off workers, community members, business and political leaders, and other unions in waging the "Drive It Home" campaign, lobbying in Ohio, as well as in Detroit and Washington, for either General Motors or another company to get Lordstown back to work, to restart a production line that had been clicking right along. The Cruze, a compact sedan, had sold briskly amid the Great Recession and high gas prices. But now General Motors was placing greater emphasis on the rebounding SUV market, with vehicles produced in other places. Lordstown had a wealth of experience, dedicated autoworkers eager to get back to work, assets Green tirelessly promoted.

"Even after GM made that announcement, up until the very last day, we outperformed quality and productivity standards," he told me. "We were done a couple days early just because our people were that good. They just kept working. I think people from this area, there's just a lot of work ethic. People want to get up and go to work. They believe in that."

Long, agonizing weeks would pass before any real discussion of a possible new use for the facility emerged, and when it did, it was not what laid-off union workers wanted to hear or how they wanted to hear it. In May, Trump tweeted:

> GREAT NEWS FOR OHIO! Just spoke to Mary Barra, CEO of General Motors, who informed me that, subject to a UAW agreement etc., GM will be selling their beautiful Lordstown Plant to Workhorse, where they plan to build Electric Trucks.

No one up here had ever heard of Workhorse, which was based in Cincinnati. GM would quickly clarify that there was no deal, only negotiations. Ohio's governor, Mike DeWine, recognizing that this was far from a done deal, warned, "This is probably not the day to celebrate," and, "If things are not in place for this to happen, this would be very cruel to the workers and the people in Lordstown and the Mahoning Valley."

It would soon be revealed that Workhorse was putting all its chips on a potential $3.6 billion contract with the US Postal Service. In the company's twelve years of existence, it had lost $150 million; in 2018, its revenues totaled a mere $763,000. Everyone seemed to be responding to the president's tweet, to the viability of the deal, to the viability of Workhorse. Few seemed to be recognizing the other, potentially game-changing question: Would Workhorse employ union labor?

Even after the significant concessions of recent years, the UAW Lordstown employees were earning a living that, though far from extravagant, couldn't be replicated in Northeast Ohio. Some were uprooting, at great expense, to continue making union wages. Others were downsizing their expectations of their lives. A distinct possibility was dawning: regardless of the outcome, whatever Lordstown had represented for half a century was likely gone forever.

As weeks, then months dragged on, the unallocated Lordstown

facility was beginning to look more and more like a familiar and unwelcome icon of the Midwest: an empty manufacturing plant, left hollow. I returned there in May. The big plywood Save the GM Plant sign was still standing. The UAW's plastic Drive It Home campaign signs were gone. Another handmade sign, propped on the ground against a fence at the facility's entrance, began:

Keep Hope…

Unmown grass had grown over the rest of the words.

The worst part is the promises.

In the aftermath of "Black Monday," schemers and speculators had descended into the Valley promising new industries that would create hundreds or thousands of jobs, building hopes without either the intention or the means to follow through. A blimp factory, an airplane works, a brewery. Nothing. Four decades later, few had forgotten the sound of those voices. The closing of Lordstown Assembly was described around town as another broken promise, in forsaken tones. Proposals like Workhorse were met with well-earned skepticism.

Trumbull County, where the Lordstown plant is located, went 51 percent for Trump in 2016 to Hillary Clinton's 45 percent, the first time since Richard Nixon that the county had voted in favor of a Republican presidential candidate. Four years before, Barack Obama had taken Trumbull by 23 points. Every person in the region who told me they'd voted for Trump said their previous vote had been for Obama, whose picture—snapped during his presidency when he made a visit to the Lordstown shop floor—still hung in the local union hall.

"I'm not a strong Democrat; I'm not a strong Republican. I've voted both ways," Monty Woolley said. "To be honest with you, I voted for Trump because I felt like he made a little bit more sense. People were tired of politics as usual. But for him to make the promises he did, and to backpedal on his promises—he just turned his back on the UAW.

"The things he said he was going to do, in my opinion, were all good things and that made me vote for him. But like my dad used to say, 'He's got an alligator mouth and a Tweety Bird ass.'"

I asked him what all this meant for 2020. He grinned and answered without hesitation: "A new broom sweeps clean."

David Green, the union president, said plenty of his Lordstown brothers and sisters had voted not so much for Trump as against Clinton. Others supported Trump because he'd told them he would restore a lifestyle they believed in, one they and their ancestors had helped create.

"You come into an area like Trumbull County, Mahoning County, where unemployment is higher than the national average...when you come to an area like this and you start talking about jobs, people listen," he said. "They want to hear that. But over the last couple years, we've seen nothing but jobs leave here."

As for 2020?

"I don't think Donald Trump is gonna get as many votes in this valley as he did then, for sure."

Five days after our visit, I received a text from Monty Woolley:

Told you I'd let you know I just got my invite to go to Arlington Texas plant. Good luck with your book

Thanks for the update. How are you feeling about that?

It is what it is. I'll stay there until the contract. Then retire

This is what it felt like to be one of the lucky ones in Ohio in 2019.

*   *   *

The summer passed with no answers and more distress. In July, still laid off and after months of fighting to save the Lordstown plant, David Green reluctantly accepted GM's offer of a position at a plant in Bedford, Indiana. In moving, he'd be leaving behind his parents and a daughter who'd recently graduated from the local Youngstown State University, as well as his position as union president.

"I was on the fence about going," he told the local *Tribune Chronicle* newspaper. "If I wait much longer, I end up getting forced some place. I would rather decide my fate. I don't have a lot of confidence in General Motors to decide my fate or do anything in my best interest."

Two months later, the contract between GM and the UAW expired and forty-nine thousand autoworkers nationwide walked off the job, embarking on a forty-day strike, the longest such walkout in half a century. Through September and October, negotiations dragged on as picketers stood outside the empty Lordstown plant holding signs and chanting slogans, hoping the new contract might bring it back to life. When the agreement was ratified, though, it was revealed that GM had used Lordstown and two other plants as negotiating chips. In return for a concession to close all three permanently, GM sweetened the financial pot for UAW employees at its remaining facilities.

In November, General Motors sold the massive Lordstown facility to a newly formed company, Lordstown Motors Corp., which planned to build electric trucks there. The revived plant, where twelve thousand had once worked, would employ four hundred people.

A month later, GM announced plans to build a new facility near Lordstown to manufacture batteries for electric vehicles, with eleven hundred new jobs expected. A Trump campaign spokesman called it a "huge win" for the Mahoning Valley. Those who remained, though, knew the faces behind all those numbers. They knew what had been lost.

Daily life in the Mahoning Valley has always been about power, in all its permutations. The company might hold your fate in the ultimate sense, and the clashes between corporation and government might seem like battles of the gods playing up above, but there were countless ways, many of them seemingly small, to maintain a sense of control, of independence, of dignity. As monumental forces played out in the tiny village of Lordstown, David Green told me something at the union hall that stayed with me. I had asked him what lesson Lordstown might hold for the rest of the nation.

"I think the biggest thing is knowing where your products come from. Specifically, automobiles," he said. "A car purchase, a truck purchase, is the second-largest purchase people make. Where that vehicle is finally assembled puts people to work, a *lot* of people to work. . . . I would argue that every American should care that that vehicle was made here in the States. I would rather people bought a Honda that was made in Ohio than a Buick made in China."

Then he told me how. The first three characters in a vehicle identification number—that little plate at the edge of the driver's side dashboard—represent the World Manufacturer Identifier. They tell you where your vehicle was made. If the first digit in your VIN is a 1, 4, or 5, your car was assembled in the United States.

When I got home that day, I leaned over the hood, peered beneath the windshield wiper, and scrawled the long series of letters and numbers into my notebook. I went into the house and keyed them into my web browser.

My Outback was built by American workers in Lafayette, Indiana.

4

MAIN STREET

Late in the lunch hour on a random Wednesday, bumblebees drowsing in the warm afternoon, the circular brass twinkle of arcade music lazed across the intersection of Fourth and Main and drifted down into the stretch of restaurants and shops, the "Carrousel District" of Mansfield, Ohio, which, if you narrowed your focus, would allow you one version of America, and if you widened it, would allow you another. In the neatly landscaped park at the end of a brief concrete promenade flanked by a pair of bronze horses and beds of crimson begonias and yellow sedum, the carrousel—they use the extra *r*—made its breezy circuit. Empty wooden horses and their brightly shellacked companions—a bear, a giraffe, an ostrich, a cat—rose and dipped and rose and dipped, passing in a merry blur. Along the perimeter, tall wooden rocking chairs for nonriders sat empty. A single horseman, a white guy in a mullet and T-shirt, grasped the shiny brass pole, seeming either too old or not old enough to be doing such a thing in the middle of the day in the middle of a small town in the middle of Ohio.

Main Street slopes gently downward from the little park, past the town's oldest restaurant, Coney Island Diner, opened in 1936, and the original Art Deco sign for City News, now a smoke shop that also sells magazines (a potentially flammable business model, but who am I to say?), past an art gallery and an independent bookstore, and a shop selling vinyl records and vintage clothing, and Relax, It's Just Coffee, and Martini's on Main, and just like that the district ends, the sidewalk immediately devolving into broken concrete and humped, cracked asphalt, the townscape ahead anchored by an old brick building with no sign of activity, its side patchwork-painted beneath an anachronistic white-on-black frieze: BISSMAN & CO. WHOLESALE GROCERS.

That building, like much in this part of America, asks an all-important question: Is this something to be saved, or something beyond salvation? Is it an end or a beginning?

The impression of Oz ends at one block and begins again on another, the broken-pattern fits and starts of hard reclamation. Turn the corner and you enter an empty shadow, trailing an abandoned set of train rails embedded in asphalt, then hang a right up the next block and there's the sunlight and the old downtown funeral home, its name carved into a stone above the big arched upstairs window: Schroer's Mortuary. It's a modestly handsome brick building in a city full of modestly handsome buildings, some that call for a better fate, others that confirm the good that can come when someone gives them one. The mortuary is one such example, scrupulously repurposed as the Phoenix Brewing Company, where the tawny smell of malt carried into the air on the morning I stopped in. Duncan Macfarlane, the head brewer, a former chemist dressed in gym shorts and a T-shirt, was bouncing between tasks, silver vat to silver vat, as his wife and business partner, Carmone Macfarlane, showed me around the place they had sunk their life savings into in 2014, exactly a century after this building began its life. Like many of Mansfield's downtown commercial structures, it had sat vacant for a long time before someone saw it as an opportunity, or at least a risk worth taking. The building was owned by a man named John Fernyak, who for decades had quietly played a savior role, buying downtown properties that had been left behind, finding new uses for them. The carrousel was his idea.

Carmone showed me around the Phoenix taproom, formerly the funeral home's chapel, a bar area with exposed brick walls and the mortuary's original windows, heavy sashes operated via chunky, chain-pull latches, steampunk deluxe, painstakingly reconditioned as though to prove their worth against the modern argument that it's easier to tear down and start anew. The taproom tables featured thick wooden tops cut from the scavenged lanes of a nearby bowling alley. Most of the materials used in the renovation came from the region—the back bar was transported from the nearby town of Ashland, its chalkboard was salvaged from a school building in Madison, its antique light fixtures plucked from a local office building undergoing renovation, the outdoor patio's old street bricks scavenged from Cleveland.

Like many start-up small businesses, the entire operation felt distinctly personal, which it was. Duncan and Carmone met as students at Bowling Green State University. After marrying, they moved to Mansfield, Duncan's hometown, in 1999. By then, the city had been hit hard by Rust Belt forces, with many of its large industrial employers either closing, downsizing, or relocating in the seventies and eighties. The year the Macfarlanes settled in Mansfield, AK Steel, the last significant manufacturing entity in town, began an epic, savage battle between labor and management, a three-year grind of lockouts and strikes that left the whole town feeling beaten. Its center had been all but gutted by the exodus of retail and restaurants to the suburbs. The loss of jobs was evident in empty buildings and shallow bank accounts. In 2020, the city's per capita income was $19,125, far below the national average of $31,177. As had been the case for years, unemployment was significantly higher than the national average and projected job growth was significantly lower.

Still, Carmone and Duncan were able to make a life there. She taught art for twenty years in local schools while he worked as a chemist. He started home brewing in the 1990s, with a "Mr. Beer" kit. The hobby grew increasingly serious, as Duncan studied up on grains and began harvesting his own yeast. The beer got better, too. Duncan taught his friend Scot Cardwell how to brew, and as their skills and interest expanded, Scot began prodding for the two of them to open a microbrewery. Duncan was hesitant, but Scot persisted, convincing his friend to take an evening business class with him. Soon, the pair, along with their wives and another friend, formed a partnership and opened Phoenix Brewing. Its 2014 launch was followed by steady, encouraging growth; by 2019, the business employed fifteen people, five of them full-time.

Carmone said she worried at first whether the community would accept a craft brewery, and whether people would accept the sincerity of their purpose to make their town better. It's not just easy in a place like Mansfield to be skeptical of someone's motives or potential for success; it's prudent. The balance is delicate and real harm can be done by the wrong action or message. For Carmone, true success arrived when Phoenix brewed a specialty beer for a local charity event, bonding the business and its owners with the community in a way that, as we talked, brought a glint of tears to her eyes.

"Deciding to commit to Mansfield," she said, "that was the easy part."

She envisions Phoenix as a "community hub," a role played by many of the thousands of local craft breweries that have opened across the country in the past decade. Phoenix is a regular fixture at a downtown outdoor concert series and had recently participated in a local celebration of the twenty-fifth anniversary of *The Shawshank Redemption,* much of which was filmed at Mansfield's historic Ohio State Reformatory. (A life-size cardboard cutout of Morgan Freeman's character, Red, peered out that day from an upstairs window.)

The brewery's owners buy Ohio products whenever possible, from local grains to a walk-in refrigerator purchased at a school auction. The beers themselves dip deeply into the local waters for their iconography and nomenclature. Their Schroer Pilsner takes its name from the old mortuary, while Orange Eyes Pumpkin Ale, Mary Jane Chai Baltic Porter, and Ceely Rose Belgian White IPA all derive from local folk legends—a monster, a witch, and a murderer, respectively. (There is an undeniably macabre vibe to the whole operation. Phoenix's wooden flight paddles and tap pulls are coffin-shaped in homage to the old funeral home. And, yes, the building has a ghost. "He's friendly," Macfarlane said. "We call him Charles. He doesn't like beer. But he does like people.") A brown ale, Danger City, takes its moniker from a nickname Mansfield got saddled with after its downtown businesses failed or moved out to the malls, leaving the streets to crime and debauchery. Ironically, the parallelly named "Safety Town" school program for kids to learn about traffic rules, 911 calls, stranger danger, and the like was also founded in Mansfield. Danger City or Safety Town? The identity remains a matter of perspective.

Mansfield's story is a familiar one in these parts, told in the broken windows and rusting rooftop water towers of dead factories, and in a population that peaked at fifty-five thousand in 1970 and has been in decline ever since, and in the stubborn contrarian hope of a craft brewery and a carrousel and an independent bookshop. These latter things don't seem to stand a chance against the monumental loss of manufacturing and the lure of an easier life somewhere else. "Hudson was made for leaving," essayist Ian Frazier once wrote of his Ohio hometown, noting how easy it was to jump a fence and hitchhike the adjacent I-80 straight to New York City, which is precisely what he did in his youth, hence the essay's pointedly unidirectional title, "Out of Ohio." (It worked out well for him: he's written for the *New Yorker* ever since.) It's hard not to trace a narrative of unintended consequence in the state's highly evolved transportation system, its network of interstates developed in the mid-twentieth century to aid the rampant distribution of manufactured goods, a network that for the past four decades has instead provided myriad escape routes for anyone interested in an easier way of life. Because life is not easy in Mansfield, Ohio, and there's just no way around that. That's not its meaning here.

I sat talking about this with Llalan Fowler in the upstairs loft of Main Street Books, where she makes the two-minute walk to work every day from her downtown apartment. The loft, overlooking the bright, neatly arranged bookshop, is a cross between a parlor and a performance space, with a sofa and a couple of armchairs, work by local artists hanging on the walls, a fireplace, and a piano. How, I wondered, does one get a piano up a narrow staircase into a bookstore loft?

"My artist friend and two of his strongest art students hauled it up there with ramps and pulleys. It was quite the thing," Fowler told me.

The bookstore hosts a thriving series of author readings and other events in this space, bringing in writers and performers from around the region. So, it's a rewarding life, but hardly a lucrative one for Fowler, who has managed the store since moving back to her hometown in 2011. In her bio on the Main Street Books website, she writes that she came back home at the end of her twenties "to live, work, make friends, find love, start writing again, and drink good beer."

Yes, she's one of the ones who left. That, too, is the familiar story, the "brain drain," the exodus of young, talented people from cities and states that had lost their economic power and the identity it carried. Fowler lived in Washington, DC, Boston, and New York City, the sorts of places that do make Ohio seem made for leaving. A blue-black tattoo on her wrist underscores her departure and return. It's the outline of Ohio with a human heart situated where Mansfield would be, a network of lines extending from it this way and that, invoking the highways that take our young people to their new fates. Less often told is the story of return, which happens more regularly than the prevailing perception suggests, yet raises the question of why. To put it bluntly, if a bibliophile is going to accept the poverty vow of running a funky little book-shop, why starve in Ohio when you can do it more glamorously in Brooklyn?

"In none of those places did I feel the kind of community I find here—the way community is supposed to be," Fowler answered. "Some days it feels like Sesame Street when I walk through downtown," she said, pivoting her head as though following the greetings from storefront to storefront. "It's like, 'Hey! Hey!'"

Even so, she said, when she first returned it felt like a mistake. People told her Mansfield "wasn't ready" for what she envisioned—a bookshop/performance space that would be con-nected to a local hub of DIY music, art, and culture, all fostered by the younger generations, all hived in the little downtown anchored by a carrousel audacious enough to sport that extra *r*.

Many midwestern cities whose downtowns were abandoned in the seventies and eighties began their grind toward renewal in the nineties with a cornerstone project intended to attract people, business, and energy back to the central city. In my hometown of Akron, it was a minor league ballpark, built with city funds and opened in 1997, sparking new investment and activity in restaurants and bars and, gradually, a return of residential life to downtown. In 1995, on a larger scale, Cleveland opened the Rock and Roll Hall of Fame and museum as a new anchor on its downtown lakefront, prompting a narrative of "renaissance." In Mansfield, it was the $1.25 million carrousel, built with private funding and opened in 1991. Its cheery nostalgia, bright, shiny colors, and downright Norman Rockwell–ness seemed like a brazen and possibly misguided stab at renewal, as though Don Quixote himself might be seen mounted on one of those wooden steeds. To an outsider, it could easily come across like that episode of *The Simpsons* when a *Music Man*–styled con artist talks the residents of Springfield into buying a monorail as a town attraction, an episode that aired just a short time after Richland Carrousel Park opened. A merry-go-round? In the middle of a blighted Rust Belt town? What suckers fell for that one?

Just beyond the façade, however, is a reminder of the city's former promise and imagination, with a relevance that might be lost on the outsider but that reinforces the community-building synergy between past and future. The carrousel was not a random caprice, and the town didn't have to go far to find one. Mansfield is home to the Carrousel Works, the largest manufacturer of merry-go-rounds in the world. The company built this one on a site designed by a local architect, outfitted with a band organ crafted not far away, by a company in Bellefontaine, Ohio. It is a counterstrike of optimism against blight, a highly public and deeply nuanced answer to the question that vexes these cities and towns: Who are we?

And you may be asking yourself what people have been asking me—an impenitent optimist—for as long as I have maintained the value of such benchmarks: What does any of it matter without jobs?

In the depth of hard times, Akron cleared out a block of long-empty buildings in the center of downtown and dropped thirty-two million precious dollars on construction of its ball-park, money that will likely never be recouped dollar for dollar, prompting that very question.

Two decades later, candidate Trump came to the Rust Belt offering the easy answer, that he would bring back manufacturing operations that used to employ hundreds inside places like that hulking empty shell I passed on the way into Mansfield, an answer that in many Ohio communities played warmly and dangerously into the native ear, a very different echo of *The Music Man*. There are places in Ohio and across the manufacturing states—plenty of them, many small and isolated and vulnerable—where a community-funded carrousel offers more realistic promise than the notion of a long-departed economic model.

That's not easy to understand if you're not from here. Just like it's not easy to understand why a young woman living in New York City would return to Ohio to run a bookstore that gets by on charm and the simple belief of its investor that, as Fowler shared, "a downtown needs a bookstore."

Shops like hers, and like the vinyl record store next door and the vintage clothing boutiques and the comics shops and the quirky museums and microbreweries you find in small towns and the downtown districts of medium-sized midwestern cities, have found a resurgence in recent years. They employ handfuls of people, not the hundreds who worked in those soot-stained mills that define the skylines. But that's not their point, not their main value. They provide a civic service, Fowler said. They bring people downtown, and "they offer things our community deserves." They recognize quality of life as part of an economic model.

Authenticity—that overplayed and elusive concept—is one resource that the postindustrial Midwest has in spades. Dan

Auerbach, the Akron-born singer and guitarist of the Black Keys, once told me that he will always love his hometown for the fact that Hollywood directors spend fortunes trying to re-create settings that look exactly like our everyday surroundings.

Why does the nation turn to Ohio every four years to understand itself? Because all our struggles and all our scars and all our little bandstands and diners and neat little lawns have withstood fortunes and failures and promises and lies, quietly proving Robert Frost's three-word definition of life: it goes on.

Fowler, dressed in jeans and a T-shirt decorated with the Main Street Books logo—a vintage typewriter overlaying Ohio's silhouette—leaned forward earnestly when I asked her what the nation, what our leaders, need to understand about us, about Mansfield, and Akron, and all the other dots along the highway, and she paused a long moment because she wanted to get it right. Because we don't often get to tell this on our own terms.

"I feel like we are poked and prodded because we look like what America looks like," she said. "This downtown is what I think people *want* America to be. But we can't do that if America is Walmart. I go to the doctor downtown, I buy my jeans downtown, I go to dinner downtown. I'm putting money in the pockets of my neighbors, not Walmart or Amazon, where the money goes into the pockets of a CEO who keeps it. I want people to be more mindful of their shopping, and of their relationships to each other."

The carrousel, she's certain, did make a difference, bringing activity back to a downtown nicknamed Danger City, but not in a nostalgic return to a past that itself is a myth. (Never forget that the heyday of midwestern mass manufacturing was also a heyday of industrial pollution, institutionalized racism and sexism, nepotism, greed, violence, and rancor.)

"I don't think we're coming back," Fowler said. "I think we're making something totally new."

There are countless towns and small cities like Mansfield in Ohio and Michigan, Pennsylvania and Wisconsin, the so-called battleground states of a region also known, not coincidentally, as flyover country. The latter designation describes places that the rest of the nation, and especially those with the most power, don't pay much attention to. Superficially, these communities once sustained by manufacturing jobs now look broken and unworthy. But who accounts for the forty-six thousand people who still live in Mansfield, or the thirty-seven thousand people in Lima, or the sixty-four thousand people in Lorain? Who listens to why they stay put and what they do to try to make their place better? Who recognizes their value? Who asks them what they need?

At the beginning of 2012, Ohio was home to 47 craft breweries. By 2020, that number had surpassed 300 and continued to grow. Ohio's not alone; the craft brewing industry has been thriving nationally for the past decade. In 2010, according to the Independent Craft Brewers Association, 100 new microbreweries opened in the United States. In 2018, that number rose to 724—not 724 total, but 724 *new* microbreweries that debuted in that year alone. Keeping track is a dizzying concern. Rick Armon, considered Ohio's preeminent beer writer, has tried to do just that. For more than a decade spanning the rapid rise of the craft brewing industry, he wrote a weekly beer column for the *Akron Beacon Journal*, where he worked as a reporter, and a popular blog for its online edition. He's written two books on Ohio's beer industry; his (then) comprehensive *Ohio Breweries*, published in 2011, profiled the state's (then) forty-nine beer producers, but his introduction warned that in 2010 alone, eight new Ohio breweries opened while five closed. A new version of that book would update the tale with a radically expanded set of characters and a breathless advance of plot.

As is often the case with national trends, Ohio was slightly behind the curve. But, for a variety of reasons, by 2019 the Buckeye State had emerged as one of the top five craft beer producers in the country, representing a $3.12 million economic impact, and ranked eleventh in consumption, 4.9 gallons annually per drinking-age adult. By comparison, beer-guzzling Vermont leads the nation, at 21.3 gallons per adult, far outpacing the pack, with Delaware's 12.5 gallons a distant second. (For the record, West Virginia is last, at 0.4 gallons per adult.) As of 2018, the craft brewing industry accounted for some 8,300 jobs in Ohio.

In just about every Ohio small town and just about every urban neighborhood, an independent brewery has opened in the past decade or so, often accompanying a renewal in communities making the slow grind back from Rust Belt decay. I met Armon for a beer one afternoon at the Akron tasting room of Hoppin' Frog Brewery, set inside the nondescript, low-roofed World Headquarters complex (so says the sign on the brown cinderblock wall across the driveway), which, if you didn't know that's where you were going, you'd mistake for a storage facility. In this regard, Hoppin' Frog belies the hipster gentrification model most of us associate with the craft beer culture. Its neighbors off an industrial-heavy state route consist of a semitruck dealer, a Marathon station, the former Goodyear Zeppelin airdock, and Majestic Trailer & Hitch. Despite the lack of a funeral-home backstory or a brick-and-exposed-ductwork reclaimed factory space, Hoppin' Frog is one of the more successful breweries in the country, with a slew of prestigious awards and the distinction of being the only internationally distributed Ohio craft beer brand.

In a cultural sense, it isn't hard to decipher why Ohio would be a prominent producer and consumer of beer. The beverage's blue-collar association fits right in with the regional personality, as does the association of beer drinking with sporting events, perhaps the highest-profile cultural activity in the Buckeye State, which, not coincidentally, shares its nickname with the massive Ohio State sports machine. (An old joke: Ohio only has one professional football team. They play in Columbus.)

As we sampled the Hoppin' Frog Lemon Lime Turbo Shandy, Armon explained the main reason Ohio has risen toward the statistical top, both in production and consumption. It has more to do with politics than one might think. The state government, in recent years, has taken significant steps to encourage development, empowering small operators. In 2013, then governor John Kasich signed a bill reducing the license fee for small brewers by nearly 75 percent, from $3,906 to $1,000. That difference was enough for many hobbyists to turn professional.

In 2016, Ohio lawmakers lifted the maximum cap on the alcohol content of beer—12 percent—allowing craft breweries freer rein in their creativity and the distinction of their product. Hoppin' Frog, renowned for its bold, boundary-pushing brews, thrived with the new freedom. (Later in the afternoon, owner-brewer Fred Karm, who'd stopped by to chat, quipped about his reputation for high-alcohol-content beers: "Life begins at 6.0." [Budweiser is 5.0.])

In addition, Governor Kasich passed a law allowing breweries to operate on-site tasting rooms without purchasing costly liquor licenses.

"It's an economic driver in the state, and that's why state lawmakers have been friendly," Armon said. "These breweries can turn around a neighborhood."

Even before the recent trend began, he recognized this, back in the late 1980s, when he was a student at an inner-city Catholic high school, waiting every afternoon for his ride home in a run-down Cleveland neighborhood.

"I can say firsthand that Ohio City was a shithole in the 1980s, because I went to St. Ignatius. And then Great Lakes went in in 1988 and began the gentrification. You're seeing that around the state now—craft brewers are going in and you're seeing people showing up."

When Great Lakes Brewing Company opened, it sat at the end of an alley in a neglected historic neighborhood, with a scrappy rock club across the way and not much else, save for plenty of empty parking spaces. It was a pioneer, Ohio's first craft brewery, debuting just four years after the Boston Brewing Co. launched the craft trend with its Samuel Adams Boston Lager. It's now the second-oldest operating brewery in Ohio, after an Anheuser-Busch facility in Columbus. The neighborhood it once anchored alone is now rich with small, thriving breweries, boutique restaurants and shops, valet parking stands, sidewalk dining, and a constant flow of foot traffic in a city (like many in the Midwest) still coming to terms with the rules of pedestrian crosswalks. It's part of the same American trend toward localism that explains the existence of Main Street Books and Phoenix Brewing in Mansfield.

A similar story played out downstate, in Cincinnati. There, the notoriously troubled Over-the-Rhine neighborhood has been transformed into an urban village of boutiques, services, restaurants, and cafés. At its foundation was the opening of the Christian Moerlein Brewing Company in 2004, the owners reviving an old Cincinnati brand from the nineteenth century. As often occurs, there's a significant downside to the new version of this old neighborhood, as poor, mostly African American residents who can't afford the new, higher rents have been driven out of the place where they scraped by through generations of blight.

Regardless of the effect, Ohio's beer culture has established a stout national presence. In its 2019 rankings of "Best Cities for Beer Drinkers," the website SmartAsset included five Ohio cities in the top fifty, tied with Colorado for the most on the list. Cincinnati was ranked first in the nation, and Cleveland tenth.

As our second five-ouncer arrived and we continued chatting, Armon regaled me with barroom trivia, listing Ohio's notable firsts in the craft brew culture: Ohio is home to the nation's first strip club/brewery, Pinups & Pints in Dayton. It boasts America's first nonprofit brewery, Carillon Brewing Co. near Dayton, where historic reenactors in period costume brew in the nineteenth-century style. Biker BrewHouse in Austintown is the first brewery in a Harley-Davidson dealership. And Fifth Street Brewpub, also in Dayton, is the country's first co-op brewery.

What we don't have so much of (also reflective of the national profile) are women and minorities. When Flatrock Brewing Company opened in 2012—aided by the state's eased regulations—it was the first African American–owned brewery in Ohio. In 2019, a national beer festival featuring some thirty black brewers had three Ohio participants. A group called Black Brew Culture estimated at the time of the festival that African Americans represented less than 1 percent of brewery owners nationally. When I asked Armon if my perceived stereotype of craft brewing as a white-male domain was accurate, he said no.

"It's really *bearded* white males."

Welcome, then, to Beer Women Rock, a charity fundraiser held one Saturday afternoon in a trendy reclaimed corner of Cleveland's near west side, the "Hingetown" neighborhood near the mouth of the Cuyahoga River, old brick storefronts representing the standard urban-gentrification checklist: cycle shop, juice bar, art gallery, coffeehouse, loft housing, boutique florist. One of the businesses, Cleveland Tea Revival, is in a reclaimed building whose outside wall is covered by an eco-cooling system of plants and grasses, the very woke-ness of green technology. In the near distance, the Cleveland skyline rose through the warm haze, centered by the old Beaux-Arts Terminal Tower, along with the abstract glass and steel of the new Hilton Cleveland Downtown Hotel, one of several major investments that coincided with the city's hosting of the 2016 Republican National Convention. Nobody called this neighborhood Hingetown until it got rebranded in the early twenty-teens. Before that, it was a low-rent gay enclave, the "hinge" between three other resurgent urban neighborhoods, its city blocks characterized by street crime, drugs, and prostitution and described in a 2015 *Vanity Fair* feature variously as "decrepit," "toxic," and "nowhere." Now it is very hip, notably white, seemingly safe, no more or less gay than any other midwestern gentrified neighborhood. In fact, the only thing it seems to be missing is the requisite craft brewery.

But on this day, that void was more than filled by the dozens of beer industry professionals and friends who packed the bar and outdoor patio of Jukebox, a tavern set into the middle of the block. Beer Women Rock is an annual event staged both to celebrate women's role in the region's beer industry and to raise money for charity. The 2019 event benefited a Cleveland-based nonprofit called "Drink Local. Drink Tap," which "inspires individuals to recognize and solve our water issues through creative education, events and providing safe water access to people in need." As always, the menu featured a signature beer brewed especially for the event. This year's was Beauty School Dropout, a pinkish, salted, and grapefruit-infused Belgian-style table beer. And, as always, this beer was brewed by a woman. And, as always, with just one exception, the group had to turn to a home-brewer to get the job done. Because, in 2019 anyway, Cleveland's thriving local breweries employed exactly zero female brewers.

"It's a sausage fest," Leslie Basalla McCafferty, one of the organizers, told me.

Marissa DeSantis, public relations supervisor for the venerable

Great Lakes Brewing Company and the afternoon's DJ, agreed that women are underrepresented in Ohio's beer industry, especially on the production side.

"When people see craft brew, they think 'white guys with beards,'" she said during a break from behind the turntable. "There needs to be a bit of a shift—why not more women?"

This question is especially germane to an industry and culture that gives great lip service to community and social values. Women have worked hard to be seen and heard, with national organizations such as Girls Pint Out and the Pink Boots Society representing females in the brewing industry.

"Part of what's at the core of what we're doing here is equality, making sure everyone is taking care of everyone," DeSantis said.

Cleveland is a beer town. All of the cities in Ohio and across the industrial Midwest carry that vibe, each representing its own distinct version of the factors that contribute to the region's brewskie culture: a blue-collar sensibility, the enduring influence of European immigration, the regional farms that produce grain and hops, the heavy emphasis on sporting events and tailgating, and the general lack of pretension that lends itself to a frosty mug on a Saturday afternoon. One man's T-shirt at Beer Women Rock nailed the vernacular: CLEVELAND—IT'S NOT THAT BAD—HAVE A BEER!

But it can't be ignored that there is a distinct dude-ness to it all, despite the efforts of women in the industry and in the drinking public. My wife, Gina, had accompanied me to the event, and when we stepped inside to order a round—a Beauty School Dropout for me and a Dogfish Head IPA for her—the male bartender pulled the taps, returned, and, without asking, handed the Beauty School Dropout, the "girl beer," to Gina, and the Dogfish Head to me. We switched glasses, clinked in toast to irony, and drank.

5

THE CANDIDATE

The day Tim Ryan launched his presidential campaign, bright April sun and dusty clouds staged a competition above a fenced-in stretch of Youngstown's Federal Street, the city's main drag transformed for that Saturday afternoon into something like a small town square, with American-flag bunting decorating the dais, Tom Petty playing through the PA speakers, and the smell of free hamburgers hanging in the humidity.

One thing about Ohioans is we drive everywhere, and we're accustomed to free parking, generally within a few steps of wherever we're headed. So I wasn't surprised to find plenty of available spaces in the surface lot near the entrance to the Saturday-afternoon rally, but I was as confounded as the three ladies who stood with me after exiting our cars, puzzling over the strange contraption at the edge of the lot: a large white metal box mounted on a rusty post, a 1960s-esque relic, its front surface lined with numbered coin slots and Pay Here lettered above.

"Do you know how to work this?" one said.

"I don't even have any coins," I said.

"Do you think they charge on weekends?" another asked.

I glanced across the street at the line of people snaking toward the sheriff's deputy–staffed security entrance into the rally area. Democracy and justice clicked together in my head: if they ticketed one of us, they'd have to ticket all of us, and that seemed unlikely.

"You know what?" I said. "If I get a ticket, I'll complain to my congressman."

We all agreed it was a safe bet, and off we went. The joke, of course, is that our congressman was the man we'd come to see, Tim Ryan, who had just declared his candidacy for the 2020 Democratic presidential primary. When he made his announcement two days before this kickoff event, he became the seventeenth Democrat to join the race for the nomination, equaling the party's highest total, set in 1976, a number quickly eclipsed as the field would grow to two dozen by late spring.

I approached the line, which resembled a smaller, less drunken version of the procession to get into a Cleveland Browns game, people in ball caps and sneakers, some baring shoulders that were already turning pink on this first warm day of spring. Just as I was about to take my place, I spotted my hometown's mayor, Dan Horrigan, whom I still call "Danny" from when we attended high school together. He waved me over, introduced me to the man he'd arrived with, a local county commissioner, and we settled into the queue. Horrigan was going to be one of the introductory speakers, he told me, then he had to zip back to Akron, where he had another event followed by an evening fundraiser. I reminded him that technically he was about to become my son's boss, with Evan nearing completion of his police academy training. I told him about my ongoing mix of pride and worry. He said he understood and tried to reassure me by reinforcing how extensive the academy training would be. I nodded and thanked him, wanting that to be enough but still wondering when or how I would be able to reconcile this new version of my child in the world. We reached the entrance, the deputies checked us both out, and Horrigan headed off to find the campaign staff.

An hour before the scheduled early-afternoon start, the atmosphere was laid-back, the crowd still arriving. The first hundred or so people were already inside, many of them wearing the free campaign T-shirts handed out by volunteers at a folding table under a tent—TIM RYAN 2020—and holding red, white, and blue placards with the slogan OUR FUTURE IS NOW.

The message rang generic, but this early in the season, that seemed reasonable. It's got to be one of the hardest marketing jobs in America, to distinguish a national candidate who's not already a household name. Ryan, a forty-five-year-old white male who'd been in Congress since 2003, was fighting for attention with the likes of Beto O'Rourke and Pete Buttigieg, John Delaney and Seth Moulton—one clean-shaven Caucasian blending into another, their messages often doing the same.

Ryan's district included the Mahoning Valley, home of Lordstown, and he was entering the race a month after the GM shutdown. It would be wrong to say he "had that going for him," though I suspect a more ruthless political strategist than myself would say that very thing. It's hard to imagine a more urgent moment for a politician to fight for the working people he represented, hard to imagine a more quintessential example of the middle class at risk than hourly autoworkers laid off by a huge corporate employer, hard to envision a better opportunity to coax back the blue-collar Democrats who'd voted for Donald Trump and his promise to revive manufacturing jobs, especially as the president had done nothing to change the plight of Lordstown.

Ohio was already shaping up to be among the most important states in the 2020 election, along with industrial midwestern neighbors Michigan, Pennsylvania, and Wisconsin, all three of which turned from their traditional Democratic leanings to complete Trump's Rust Belt triumph. In May 2019, a *New Republic* headline asked "Is Trump DOA in the Rust Belt?" In his analysis, staff writer Alex Shephard pointed to signs from the 2018 midterm elections that these states would be swinging back in favor of a Democrat for president. He invoked the words of Ohio Democratic senator Sherrod Brown from November 2018: "Let our country—our nation's citizens, our Democratic Party, my fellow elected officials all over the country—let them all cast their eyes toward the heartland, to the industrial Midwest." Although Republicans had dominated statewide races in the midterms and Trump had trounced Hillary Clinton here by 9 percentage points, Ohio, which had long been shaded more red than its neighbors, could still be seen as both a bellwether and a potential battleground for the presidential race, and the narrative of Lordstown could provide one of the most compelling issues to influence working- and middle-class voters.

Ryan was the second Ohio politician that season linked to the Democratic candidacy. The first was Brown, Ohio's senior senator who'd previously served in Congress, representing the same district (though since gerrymandered) as Ryan, covering industrial (or postindustrial, depending on one's perspective) Northeast Ohio. As he considered whether to run for the 2020 nomination, Brown went on a listening tour, with "dignity of work" as his theme. He had a longstanding reputation as a champion of the middle class and had a compelling partner in his wife, Connie Schultz, a Pulitzer Prize–winning former columnist for the *Cleveland Plain Dealer*, now syndicated, with a significant social media presence and her own powerful narrative as a daughter of the working class. The first column she ever published was about the worn-out black lunch pail her father carried every day for thirty-six years as a maintenance worker for the Cleveland power company, "the job he hated every day he was there."

But for now, if the nation was going to elect its first Ohioan to the White House since Warren G. Harding won in 1920, it would be Ryan. A native of Niles, a small town in the heart of the Mahoning Valley, and the son of a steelworker, he, too, would make working people the focus of his message. At the time of his announcement, jobs were a key concern across the industrial Midwest. Among those four key flyover states, the unemployment rate was above the national average in Ohio, Michigan, and Pennsylvania, with only Wisconsin coming in below. Anything could tip the delicate electoral balance, and few topics are more personal to a voter than their livelihood.

The temporary stage was set up at the farthest end of the closed-off area of the street, facing another platform whose tiers were already lined with photographers and television cameras. Between the two structures was a wide-open area of pavement, a sort of political mosh pit, slowly filling with bodies. I spotted David Green, the local UAW president, near the stage, and a few politicians I recognized. I found a place at the edge of the crowd. Next to me was a woman in a black T-shirt with her hometown's name in white block sans serif letters—WARREN OHIO—a style that had become ubiquitous in Rust Belt cities over the past decade or so, hard-knocks places that once had an instinct to apologize for their existence but lately had embraced their narrative via their casual wear, the city names often displayed with defiance: CLEVELAND AGAINST THE WORLD, TOLEDO VS. EVERYBODY, AKRON: WHERE THE WEAK ARE KILLED AND EATEN. The (INSERT CITY) VS. EVERYBODY shirt repeats itself across the region, where it seems that every town—Flint, Erie, Wheeling—is itching to fight back. Slowly, the term *Rust Belt city* is being replaced by the more noble *legacy city,* a nod to the larger history and hard-won experience of such communities.

I asked the woman from Warren, Holly Sandy, what had drawn her to the event, and she nodded toward the two young children gathered against her blue-jeaned legs, her ten-year-old daughter, Tomlyn, and twelve-year-old son, AJ.

"Mrs. Ryan was their teacher," she said, referring to the now potential First Lady of the United States, Tim Ryan's wife, Andrea, who taught first grade in the nearby town of Mineral Ridge.

Warren is a working-class town in the heart of the Mahoning Valley, and we'd barely begun talking before Lordstown came up, as it did inevitably all across the region that spring. Earlier, I'd asked a young campaign volunteer, Shanice Peterson, what was at the front of her mind in relation to the national election, and she phrased her answer by way of where she lived: "I'm from Warren, so my biggest concern is jobs."

Holly told me her dad had worked at Lordstown, and had retired, a condition often expressed with deep relief in times like these, a recognition that he'd made it out before it was too late. But she knew a lot of people whose lives were upended by the layoffs, some directly and others indirectly, and also the greater sense of helplessness, as forces far removed from here were directing people's fates.

"People are sad," she said. "It's just a sad time."

From candidate Ryan, she continued, "I want to hear what he's going to do for this area, for the Valley."

Warren is a tough place, tough enough that one needs a good reason to stick it out there. It's the county seat of Trumbull County, where the unemployment rate that spring was pushing 8 percent, even as President Trump made a regular habit of tweeting the national rate, which that month was 3.6 percent. As someone who has found my own reason to stay in a hometown with a similar struggle, I have sometimes been pressed to justify the choice, as happened in an unexpected quasi-debate during a radio interview a few years earlier. I was sitting in an Ohio production studio, wearing headphones and talking through a microphone to inter-viewer Charles Monroe-Kane in the Madison, Wisconsin, studios of the syndicated public radio show *To the Best of Our Knowledge*. In the midst of the interview, he told me he was from Warren, the son of a steelworker, and that he'd fled a place he defined by job-lessness and foreclosures and methamphetamines and pollution, a place he found depressing and felt he needed to leave, all of this as prelude to one of the most common questions asked of people living in their Rust Belt hometowns: "Why did you stay?"

I explained that I'd spent my college years exploring downtown Akron at its worst, amid the city's industrial collapse, a sort of postapocalyptic landscape that fascinated me. As a young person born after the boom years, I didn't comprehend the social and economic tragedy of abandoned storefronts and factories; instead, I perceived these places as the cast-off treasures of a fallen king-dom. My city was a place full of possibility, a place where anyone of my generation could stake a claim cheaply, could feel needed, a place that LeBron James *chose* to return to, not just validating our often-challenged sense of home but specifically identifying with its hardship, most notably in that remarkable 2014 *Sports Illustrated* epistle, which resonated in this region far differently than it did anywhere else: "In Northeast Ohio, nothing is given. Everything is earned. You work for what you have."

Ultimately, Monroe-Kane and I arrived together at the most vexing question, the one neither of us could answer to the satis-faction of either of our worldviews: If cities like ours are defined primarily by work—and they are—what does it mean when the work goes away?

That was the question looming over downtown Youngstown

that Saturday afternoon, a question of both practical and philosophical urgency, and one that I knew from hard experience
would be twisted and manipulated, sometimes misunderstood and
sometimes ignored, in the coming year. It wouldn't be long before
the reporters and the candidates and the pollsters and the analysts
began arriving at our borders seeking the information that would
suit their needs. I knew that people here would want their stories
told, but not for the gain of someone who didn't really understand
or care. People here trusted Sherrod Brown's "dignity of work"
message because they knew he lived in Cleveland, that he'd begun
his political career in the hard-bitten city of Lorain, and that he
regularly visited these places and listened to their concerns. There's
a reason the black lunch pail from Connie's first column remained
an icon after all these years, because people related to that. Some
of them had one sitting right there on their own kitchen counter,
ready for the next shift. Others wished they still did. In a CNN
town hall session later that spring, Ryan specifically positioned
himself as the candidate most in touch with the working class.

"When these plants close," he said in the broadcast, "I know
who's working in them. They're my family. They're my friends.
When I walk into the Oval Office every morning, no one's going
to have to explain to me why I'm there or who I'm there for."

It's got to be hard to put together the playlist for a political event,
especially when drawing from the American pop canon. Harder
yet is identifying just the right tune to serve as a theme song. It
seems almost inevitable that a Republican candidate plucking a
song from pop radio will get a cease-and-desist appeal from the
artist—American songwriters tending to lean toward the left—as
when Tom Petty's people told George W. Bush's people to stop
using "I Won't Back Down" during the 2000 campaign. (To put
an even finer point on it, Petty went to Democratic challenger Al

Gore's house after Gore conceded defeat and performed the song just for him.) Then there's the problem of the potential fallout of a misinterpreted lyric. Just because something sounds like an anthem doesn't mean it can serve as one. In 1984, Bruce Springsteen's "Born in the USA" seemed like a pitch-perfect patriotic commercial jingle for Ronald Reagan—it was in fact selected upon the recommendation of conservative commentator George Will—until someone pointed out its darkly bitter portrayal of the plight of Vietnam veterans. In a 2019 interview with Yahoo Entertainment, E Street Band guitarist Steven Van Zandt cracked, "Well, in truth, I think that misunderstanding paid a lot of my bills." He broke into a smile and shrugged. "Eh, y'know. It happens."

For his part, Donald Trump ignored the Rolling Stones' pleas to stop using their music, and "You Can't Always Get What You Want" continued playing at his rallies despite the curious fact that it was a song by a British band and that Mick Jagger himself puzzled over Trump's choice of a "sort of doomy ballad about drugs in Chelsea."

So I paid special notice to the songs coming out of the rally's speakers that day. Springsteen's "Glory Days" and Dire Straits' "Walk of Life" were cornerstones of the eighties mainstream throwback vibe that matched the persona of a Gen X candidate—Ryan—who quarterbacked the John F. Kennedy High School football team until his graduation in 1991. James Brown's "Living in America" made sense. But Martha and the Vandellas' "Nowhere to Run" offered an odd implication to the beginning of a presidential campaign, to say nothing of Rick James's "Super Freak."

As the plaza continued filling with people, I spotted a compact, swaggering figure walking my direction. At first I wasn't sure, but then, yes indeed, it was Ray "Boom Boom" Mancini, the former World Boxing Association lightweight world champion and a folk hero in a city that clings to its precious few national icons—actor Ed O'Neill being probably the closest thing to a household name. After Mancini's fighting career ended, he remained in his hometown, so it wasn't necessarily a surprise to see him here, but it's not every day you run into a five-foot-five-inch man who looks like he could drop you with one punch, which, even in a natty outfit of jeans, blazer, and T-shirt and smelling of expensive cologne, Boom Boom looked like he could.

I approached him and introduced myself. He shook my hand with a friendly hello and the handsome visage and TV-ready smile that had helped his post-boxing career as an actor and ringside analyst. For all his accomplishments, Mancini's legend carries the shadow of its darkest moment, a 1982 fight that led to the coma and subsequent death of his opponent, Korean boxer Duk Koo Kim. Towns like this, especially those that have their own dark chapters, tend to support their native children during difficult times, and that was true with Mancini, who stuck close to home. Although not accused of wrongdoing, he endured depression and survival guilt, as well as judgment from afar. Through it all, Youngstown had his back. In return, he has been one of the city's most visible champions, and so it stands to reason that his support for Tim Ryan as a candidate was framed by his relationship to his hometown.

"He's a local guy. You gotta take a shot with a local guy," Mancini told me. "He understands our needs. Youngstown, twenty years ago you could shoot a cannonball down Federal Street. Now, y'know, take the old steel mills, make them into something else. You need new blood, new ideas."

He nodded goodbye and continued forward, stopped every few yards to shake a hand or pose for a selfie, disappearing into a crowd that had grown to about three hundred people.

*   *   *

The rally opened with brief preliminary endorsement speeches by Akron's and Warren's mayors and the leader of a military veterans' group, leading to Ryan's rousing introduction by Youngstown mayor Tito Brown, whose booming preacher's cadence rose to a crescendo: "Why do we have to wait?! Our time is *right now!*"

Ryan came bounding onto the stage, an open-collared light blue dress shirt over his tall, athletic build, sleeves rolled halfway up his forearms, the crowd cheering, Our Future Is Now placards waving and bouncing. Square-jawed and youthful looking despite the gray creeping into his dark hair, he raised the microphone and began in his plainspoken tenor:

"I'm Tim Ryan, and I'm running for president of the United States of America!"

His message ran a gamut of hot topics—the economy, health care, jobs, civility—but throughout, he returned to his identity of place, referring to himself as "a kid from Niles, Ohio," and "a working-class kid who can work his ass off for the working-class community." He invoked "Black Monday," the day in 1977 when the Youngstown Sheet and Tube steel mill closed, throwing thousands out of work, including his own father. He told the story of a cousin who'd had to unbolt the machine that had been his workstation from the factory floor and prepare it for shipping to China. He cast himself as a midwesterner who understands the regions of the country that often feel left out of the national conversation.

"The flyover states are my states. The flyover states are your states. And the flyover states are going to start governing this country!" he boomed, followed by rousing applause.

In addition to his regionalism, Ryan, a practitioner of mindfulness, repeatedly proclaimed his mission to help repair a deeply divided nation.

"I'm running for president first and foremost to try to bring this country back together," he said, bringing more cheers. "Things go up and things go down, but if we're not united, we are not going to be able to fix these structural problems that we have in the United States. And I'm running for president to, first and foremost, try to bring this country back together, because a divided country is a weak country."

Looking into the crowd, he quoted the late basketball coaching legend Jim Valvano: "God must have loved ordinary people because he made so many of us!" Then he turned to the biggest celebrity in the crowd, the man he called "The Champ," the former boxer standing in the makeshift plaza among his fellow supporters.

"We're goin' to DC, Ray," he said. "Bring the gloves!"

His speech concluded after about twenty minutes and "I Won't Back Down" came blaring through the loudspeakers as a campaign volunteer approached with a gym bag. Ryan reached inside, produced a regulation-size football, dropped back into his stance, and lobbed it into the crowd. He pulled out another, sent it off in a different direction, then another and another. As a lifelong Ohioan, it was hard for me to view the spectacle without recalling a similar stunt back in 1980, when Cleveland Cavaliers owner Ted Stepien promoted his new slow-pitch team by lobbing softballs out the fifty-second-story window of downtown's Terminal Tower toward a crowd gathered below, the first ball smashing a car window, the next two injuring bystanders, prompting a chaos of panicked flight in all directions. Nor could I avoid the echoes of *WKRP in Cincinnati* newscaster Les Nessman's horrified response to a similarly misguided Thanksgiving promotional stunt, looking skyward to identify large objects being dropped from a helicopter: "Oh my God, they're turkeys!"

It's Ohio. We were born prepared for the worst.

But Ryan's touch was light and his aim was true. As the music played, he and his family remained on the stage, shaking hands and chatting with supporters. I stood at the edge, watching and listening. People introduced themselves to him, some reminding him of a connection, the small-town "your dad knew my dad" sort of association that binds places together. He posed for selfies and signed autographs. I believe I saw him kiss a baby. Despite the waist-high metal security divider between him and the audience, the casual familiarity even in his impromptu press conference made it feel more like he was running for town council.

As the onlookers slowly trickled away, a shrill, breathy *HOOT* like the sound of a locomotive horn pierced the humid air. It was the old steam whistle from Youngstown Sheet and Tube, salvaged and refurbished by a downtown bar.

In his newspaper column the next day, under the headline "A win for the Valley," Todd Franko, editor of *The Vindicator,* reflected on Ryan's announcement and the hope it gave to a place that hadn't had much go its way of late.

"A person from the Valley could and would run for the most powerful position on the planet," he wrote. The declaration seemed to carry a hint of incredulity, coming as it did from a newspaper that knows well the underdog spirit of its people, that knows what it's like to be anonymous, and that knows the risk of hoping too hard for anything.

The first Democratic debates, held on two consecutive nights in June 2019, were a Babel of issues and logistics and name recognition. Even the moderator panel was sardine-packed, with a first-night NBC "Decision 2020" team that rotated at the halfway mark, so many open microphones that an impromptu commercial break was needed to sort out a commentator's audio feed talking over top of the onstage Q&A.

With the cattle call of candidates, the Democratic National Committee had determined that twenty would qualify, with each ranked by either their polling numbers or their grassroots fund-raising totals. Ryan was one of five who made the cut by polling numbers alone, clinging to the minimum of 1 percent. As the debates neared, Joe Biden and Bernie Sanders were the strong frontrunners, with previous national campaigns under their belts, serious donations rolling in, and poll numbers in the double digits. There would be ten candidates onstage each of the two nights; Ryan was selected for the first night. The participants would be arranged by their polling numbers, with the highest-ranking candidates at center stage and the rest fanned out in descending order. Trying to harness the jumbled cast of characters, Vox.com (mission statement: "Vox explains the news") ran an infographic with an illustration of each night's stage layout. The headline over night one's graphic read "Warren, O'Rourke, Booker, Klobuchar, and the rest." Ryan's podium was second from the left, placing him decidedly among "the rest."

Adding to the confusion of an event that looked more like the opening night of *America's Got Talent* was the range of issues and the question of which topics would maintain and gain prominence as the protracted election season unfolded. Each candidate, especially those lesser known, would need to distinguish himself or herself as quickly and succinctly as possible over the course of the two-hour, internationally televised event.

Ryan, dressed in a dark suit, white shirt, and powder-blue tie, was one of five white males on the stage; the biggest name that first night was Elizabeth Warren, who at the time was polling fourth among the Democratic hopefuls. She got the first question, and the show was on, the candidates pogoing briskly from economic equality to prescription drug costs to the environment to free college to women's rights to the ability to speak extemporaneously in Spanish.

Fifteen minutes passed before Ryan got a chance to pipe in; he was the last candidate to have a question directed to him. He was called on by NBC moderator José Diaz-Balart: "Congressman Ryan—President Trump promised that manufacturing jobs were all coming back to places like your home state of Ohio. Can you make that same promise?"

Ryan began first by telling the story already well known in Northeast Ohio, of the four thousand lost auto plant jobs, of the unfairness of a General Motors tax cut and bailout, of the corporate giant's subsequent decision to manufacture a new car model in Mexico. In an imploring voice, he said this has been going on forty years, that the bottom 60 percent of working people haven't seen a raise since 1980. And finally, and forcefully, he said he wants America to dominate the growing electric vehicle and solar industries, drawing one of the biggest audience cheers of the night thus far.

But it was hard for any candidate, especially those trying to climb from the ranks of the relatively anonymous, to gain momentum. Nearly a half hour more passed before Ryan got a second question; over the course of two hours, he was able to comment intermittently on a topical buffet that included immigration, gun violence, the Democratic Party's connection to the working class, and Afghanistan. He didn't get a chance to address a question about the opioid crisis, despite the fact that Ohio's overdose statistics were among the nation's very worst.

It was Ryan's closing statement that resonated most, drawing from hard-earned experience and reflecting why Ohio is not a story unto itself but rather a grassroots archetype that can speak for vast parts of the country and its people, a statement from the man who a few months before had proclaimed himself the voice of the flyover states:

There's nothing worse than not being heard, nothing worse than not being seen, and I know that because I've represented for seventeen years in Congress a forgotten community. They've tried to divide us—who's white, who's black, who's gay, who's straight, who's a man, who's a woman—and they ran away with all the gold, because they divided the working class. It's time for us to come together. I don't know how you feel, but I'm ready to play some offense. I come from the middle of industrial America, but these problems are all over our country. There's a tent city in LA, there's homeless people and people around our country who can't afford a home. It's time for us to get back on track—the teacher in Texas, the nurse in New Hampshire, the waitress in Wisconsin—all of us coming together, playing offense with an agenda that lifts everybody up. I will only promise you one thing: when I walk into that Oval Office every morning, you will not be forgotten. Your voice will be heard. Thank you.

The second debate, in late July, began with Ryan again positioned second from the end, between Marianne Williamson and Amy Klobuchar. He again tuned his opening statement to the voiceless and forgotten, declaring, "America is great, but not everyone can access America's greatness." Forty minutes would pass before he got a chance to speak another word.

Ryan forged on through the summer and into the fall, but his polling numbers didn't improve and his fundraising was modest at best, totaling only $1.3 million, a tiny fraction of most of his competitors' coffers. He kept pushing his focus on the needs of the working class, but the message alone wasn't enough to qualify him for two debates in the fall, including one that was held in Ohio.

In late October, he announced he was dropping out, turning his attention to a run for reelection to his congressional seat. In his video announcement, he said, "I got into this race in April to really give voice to the forgotten people of our country: the workers who have been left behind, the businesses who have been left behind, the people who need health care or aren't getting a quality education, or are saddled by tremendous debt. I'm proud of this campaign because I believe we've done that."

The announcement drew a tweet from @realDonaldTrump:

So Congressman Tim Ryan of Ohio has finally dropped out of the race for President, registering ZERO in the polls & unable to even qualify for the debate stage. See Tim, it's not so easy out there if you don't know what you're doing. He wasn't effective for USA workers, just talk!

@TimRyan responded with a photo of the empty parking lot at the Lordstown plant:

This is the view from where I live Mr. President. Empty parking lot. Used to be thousands of jobs. All on your watch. You said not to sell our houses. Same with FoxComm, Carrier. You don't care about us. Put your phone down & start doing some work for someone other than yourself.

Congressman Ryan, sporting a one-day stubble and arriving straight from a local union meeting, made a casual entrance into the Youngstown Business Incubator conference room, sliding a ceramic coffee mug onto the table and dropping his six-foot-four, broad-shouldered frame into a chair, pulling one ankle up over the opposite knee. His brown suit pants paired with an orange tie prompted me to suggest that with the presidency no longer an option, perhaps he might consider the position of Cleveland

Browns general manager in the wake of a recent front-office house-cleaning, a nearly annual occurrence for the most dysfunctional franchise in professional sports.

"Might be more money," the old quarterback cracked.

"Yeah, but less job security," I said.

The conference room window overlooked the Federal Street plaza where Ryan had launched his campaign nine months earlier. On a frigid morning in early 2020, the mostly empty street glittered with crushed road salt, a dirty crust of snowplow remains clinging to the curb. Ryan had an office in the incubator, a small-business haven whose type has become standard in middle-American cities still trying to reestablish their economies and identities in the wake of manufacturing decline. A week earlier, Democratic candidate Mike Bloomberg had made a campaign stop at Akron's version, the Bounce Innovation Hub, a tire-factory-turned-business-honeycomb for start-ups and entrepreneurs to gain resources, commiseration, and momentum and a symbol of the fact that people in such cities need one another to succeed.

Nearly three months after pulling his hat out of the ring, Ryan was still replaying the campaign in his mind, thinking about what he could have done differently, what had gone well, what he'd learned. The day after his kickoff rally, he'd boarded a plane to Iowa, beginning a monthslong grind of airports and hotel rooms, the early-season ground game of midwestern farm towns and southern black churches, northern union halls and New England cafeteria forums, tweets and speeches and FaceTime goodnights to his wife and three kids back home.

He got in it to win, he insisted, and not just to raise his national profile, as some observers suggested. Before declaring his candidacy, Ryan's name recognition beyond Ohio was confined mainly to a 2017 attempt to unseat venerable House Speaker Nancy Pelosi. He failed but remained committed to his message that the Democratic Party's old guard had lost touch with the spirit of the middle and working classes. Having entered the race before Joe Biden, and believing the former vice president would not run, Ryan felt confident he could establish himself as the candidate for the working people, someone who could galvanize voters of all races and backgrounds.

"I was uniquely situated to talk about the loss of these jobs for the last thirty years, to talk about the ways the party has gotten away from the middle of the country and the South and become a coastal party," he told me. "I was very uniquely situated to do that, given my geography, who I was, and where I was from."

But in a historically crowded field, one that soon would be joined by Biden, he found himself precast, especially by the coastal media and political strategists, as "the white guy." His tweets didn't get nearly the traffic of those of his higher-profile opponents and he had to scrap for media exposure and donations. With so little money to spend, he found it hard to get his voice—which he knew could speak for a vast, frustrated, forgotten populace—heard.

It came to a head during the mid-broadcast commercial break in the first Democratic debate. Ryan, who'd barely gotten a word in, left his podium to stretch his legs and get a drink of water. Even all these months later, the color in his face rose as he recalled crossing paths with NBC moderator Chuck Todd.

"I was behind the stage, and I said, 'Chuck, get me in the fucking *game*. This is bullshit.' I was mad. Here I am from one of the states—loss of manufacturing, loss of this, loss of that—we feel unheard, and here we are on the debate stage and it's forty-five minutes in and I'm just getting the same eyepiece. Like, this is the problem!"

Being from Ohio, Ryan knew from long experience how it felt to be ignored. But he also knew that he came from a place where people were raised to be polite. And he knew how easily he could invoke an unwanted stereotype: the angry, disenfranchised, industrial-state guy separated by one degree from the protest voters who handed Ohio to Trump.

"With millions of people watching, you don't want to come off as half-cocked, like—'That's why we don't pay attention to you. Cuz you're nuts.'"

So he kept his cool and delivered his message as well as he could, in fact finding himself fueled by the challenge when he finally delivered that impassioned closing statement, a drive that carried into the second debate, where his performance prompted MSNBC analyst Lawrence O'Donnell to conclude that among the moderates, Ryan "had the best night by far."

Away from the lights, though, is where he found the real connection, as he moved outward from home, into places he'd never visited as a politician, and found his Ohio-bred themes resonating, sometimes profoundly. He said:

Just the idea that there are a lot of people that are struggling, that have the same kind of suffering. It takes different forms, but you boil it all down and it's suffering. One of the things that surprised me was the real similarity between rural and urban. I spent a lot of time in Iowa, and the top five issues in rural Iowa were loss of manufacturing jobs; consolidation of wealth—who owns the seeds, who owns the fertilizer; a diminishment of some kind of health care; drug problems—in rural Iowa it was meth, here it was opiates; and no investments in downtown. In Iowa, you've got ninety-nine counties, ninety-nine courthouses, ninety-nine downtowns, ninety-nine places with open storefronts and an old theater that hasn't been renovated in thirty or forty years. It was just consistent. And then I think of my district, which is Youngstown, Akron, Warren, you know: loss of manufacturing, opiates, consolidation of corporate power, downtowns. So I really thought I was connecting to them on that level.

In the South, Ryan said, he found similar resonance, "people who were making a higher wage and now are making a mid-tier wage, and the suffering that comes with that, the anxiety that comes along with that."

In the wake of his run, Ryan hoped that he was able at least to bring a greater understanding to his party that it needs to adapt, to reconnect to the everyday people in the middle of the country, many of whom were drawn to Trump in a way that perhaps shouldn't have come as such a surprise. He told me:

The danger has already happened. The 2016 election is the end result of, I think, Democratic neglect. We clearly didn't frame our party as "We're for this group and the Republicans won't let us help you." There wasn't a national campaign in areas like this. And so the working-class people here, whether it was a diminishment in the African American vote or it was people who went and voted for Jill Stein or Donald Trump, it was because of our neglect. When Trump started talking about NAFTA, how Bill Clinton did NAFTA, I was like, "Oh boy, we're in trouble." I mean, we had a sense that we were gonna lose Ohio, but I never thought we'd lose Michigan and Wisconsin.

Ryan urged his party to return to an understanding of this part of the country, to remember how important the industrial Midwest is, and how important it is to listen closely to the nuances.

"The unsophisticated approach to this is you've either got to be pro-trade, or you've got to be anti-trade. Well, a lot of us are anti-trade when you're not gonna deal with any of the downside. Who's addressing the downside? Because in the aggregate, it doesn't work for Youngstown, or Akron, or Cleveland, or Milwaukee. The aggregate doesn't mean shit, because we're on the downside."

He urged not just his party but all of America to understand that the natural gas industry has had a profoundly transformative effect here, bringing good jobs back to the region gutted by the collapse of the American steel industry. He urged his party to balance its green energy ideals with the reality of families and communities regaining their dignity and their power—economic and political.

"It's like, look, you don't have to take money from the fossil fuel industry, you can look as independent as you want, but there are working-class people that are making a really good living," he said. "These are probably some of the best jobs in the country when it comes to a union job. The steelworkers aren't making that much money. Fifty percent of the man-hours for the labor union, national man-hours, are in western Pennsylvania and eastern Ohio. That plant out there—their payroll is $10 million a day. So it's like, do you guys not think maybe we should talk to someone like that?"

He urged his party to balance its gun control ideals with the reality of middle-class sportsmen and -women, hunters and target shooters who identify their hobby as a wholesome family activity. Invoking an ad from 2016, he urged his party to go after Trump as anti-worker, not as someone who is bad for our children because he uses foul language. That was a misguided approach by a party that has drifted too much toward its coastal elitism, he said, that has lost touch with the real people in Ohio, which, according to a 2013 study that more than a few of us still claim as an honor, was determined to be the most foul-mouthed state in the union.

"I hate to say this, but I swear in front of my kids," Ryan told me. "I don't want to, I wish I didn't, but at times I do. I don't know what it is around here, but sports, and mills, and the legacy of factories—people say bad words."

Ryan said his party needs to understand that to many Americans, the coarse, bullying, locker-room-talking guy in the ill-fitting suit—"he looks normal":

He looks like a normal guy. He looked different in an environment where Democrats have neglected us, Republicans don't get us either, and this guy looks like a pretty independent-minded guy. He's rich, so he's not taking anybody's money. I mean, he *was,* but the perception was that he wasn't. And I get the appeal. Especially as he was saying, "I'm gonna raise taxes for the rich, I'm gonna expand health care, we're gonna do an infrastructure bill, were gonna rebuild the country—that's what I do, I build things." I get the appeal. He is masterful, how he was able to do it. Now, it was lie after lie after lie, but whatever. I get the appeal. And we gave a demagogue like him the opening, because of our neglect.

Listen, Ryan urged, again and again. Listen to us. Because whoever does might find what's been lost.

6

SUFFRAGETTE CITY

Tucked under the stairwell outside the front door to Lacie Cheuvront's apartment in Hilliard, Ohio, is a child's plastic playhouse, pink and purple, real life in microcosm, the size of imagination. The ruler of that tiny domain, Rosalie, was four years old and playing in her bedroom on the Friday morning in January 2019 when her mother slipped out the door, past the playhouse, and into the waiting car of her friend Mitzie Whelan. The pair, along with Mitzie's mother, Kathi, were off on a pilgrimage of solidarity, bound for the streets of Washington, DC, to join who knows how many more for the third annual Women's March.

This was a rare adventure for Lacie, a divorced single mom working two jobs, tied to the grind of getting through each day and beginning the next. A shelf in her kitchen was filled almost entirely with travel mugs, prime weaponry in any working parent's arsenal. But breaking away for this excursion was important to her, for the same reason as pretty much everything else that was important to her: Rosie. She wanted to experience the power of this new women's movement so she could pass it along to her daughter. All children in their own way are vessels of hope. For Lacie, this little girl with the wild blond hair signified a demarcation, as though her birthdate—represented in the numbers on the spines of a book stack tattooed down Lacie's left forearm—was a delivery from the mother's own difficult youth and into the American sisterhood's next loud wave of progress.

Mitzie's Jeep carried them some four hundred miles from the heart of Ohio, across Pennsylvania, through Maryland, and into Virginia. They found parking, checked into their downtown hotel, got settled, and caught some sleep. They awoke eagerly the following morning, peeking through the curtains at the nearby National Mall, pockets of marchers already gathering on the street below, pink hats and placards under a cold, colorless sky. They quickly bundled up in their winter clothing and headed down through the lobby and onto the sidewalk, three women from Ohio merging into a collective formed by similar journeys from all over the country and paralleled by other such gatherings in locations around the world.

By objective measure, this was the least monumental of the three iterations of the Women's March, a downscaling in numbers and energy and urgency, dulled in part by questions and controversy. Like much of the women's movement that had gestated simultaneously with Hillary Clinton's ceiling-shattering run as the nation's first female mainstream presidential candidate and in protest of Donald Trump—who will likely be the only American president to have the terms *pussy* and *porn star* attached to his legacy—the first Women's March in January 2017 developed organically, beginning as a Facebook event and growing into an unexpected, unprecedented, and undeniable spectacle, drawing two hundred thousand demonstrators to the nation's capital and equally large numbers to other locations, totaling an estimated four million participants across the country in what is considered the largest single-day protest event in US history. The emotional spontaneity of the march played like a counterpunch to the man whose ascendancy they opposed and like jet fuel to a movement that had been inspired by his female opponent. Its power was captured in live images of a throng darkening the streets of Washington, whose mass outnumbered that of the presidential inauguration ceremony.

The second annual march, in January 2018, confirmed a momentum that manifested in that year's fall midterm elections, when record numbers of women ran for governorships and for the US House and Senate. That November, an unprecedented thirty-six women were newly elected to Congress—including the first Muslim, Native American, and Palestinian American females, as well as the youngest woman—to join sixty-six incumbent women who had won reelection. Sixteen women ran for governor that year and nine won, including first-ever female governors in South Dakota and Guam. In Lacie's home state of Ohio, a record number of females—eleven—ran for US House seats, and though only three (all incumbents) won, their presence added to the national momentum. (It's important to note that most of Ohio's female candidates were Democrats running in one of the most Republican-friendly gerrymandered states in the nation.)

As the third march on Washington developed, however, its purpose was tested. The statement had already been made; change had occurred. What would this one be about? In the months preceding the event, the Women's March founders came under fire for their association with Nation of Islam leader Louis Farrakhan, known for his frequently controversial anti-Semitic remarks. That factor, coupled with a cold, sleety weather forecast and two years of adjustment to the initial shock of a Golden Rule–trampling president, led to speculation of a diminished turnout, which in turn led to the questions of whether this spectacle had lost its shine and what that might mean.

Lacie does not like crowds; she suffers from anxiety, and the thought of being packed into a throng of strangers had given her pause, but as she and her friends found their way into the flow of the morning, she felt euphoric. Whatever clouds might have moved into the cultural conversation had nothing to do with the reality of this one woman fresh from her small Ohio suburb—daughter of a strong mother, mother of a smart, curious daughter.

More than six months later, she still became emotional as she described the experience.

"It was amazing. Oh my God, it was indescribable," she said. "There were old women, young women, kids, babies, there were men. Grown men, young men. It was very humbling. I cried, like a little baby. . . . I think because we were all there for the same reason, it wasn't like a concert where everybody's pushing or whatever—we were all unified. Amazing. I just got chills telling you about it. I wish that as a country we could all do that, but it's just impossible at this point, unfortunately."

The day warmed slowly; the mass of bodies grew. Acquaintances were made, phone numbers exchanged, Facebook friendships requested. In the end, the Washington crowd, estimated by the Associated Press at one hundred thousand, was indeed smaller than the previous two marches. But a hundred thousand was more than three times the population of the town Lacie had left the morning before, plenty big enough to make its impression.

The group made a simple four-block parade down Pennsylvania Avenue, ending at Freedom Plaza near the White House. Lacie joined in on the spontaneous chants: "Tell me what democracy looks like—*this* is what democracy looks like!"

There were handmade signs on poster board, lofted overhead:

Women's Rights Are Human Rights

She the People

I'm a Girl, What's Your Superpower?

IT'S TIME TO OVARY ACT

An illustration of a resolute Lady Liberty reaching up to one ear: GIRL, HOLD MY EARRINGS

The demonstration lasted into the afternoon and then organically wove its way outward, into the texture of the city, into restaurants and bars, cafés and shops. Lacie and Mitzie went to dinner and then, joined by a friend who lives in DC, went out barhopping, energized by the day they'd just experienced, dancing and celebrating. The evening progressed, the nightclub filled with bodies and energy, music and voices, the clinking of glasses and bump of bass. As Lacie enjoyed herself on the dance floor, she felt something strange, something pushing against her backside. She turned to see a man with his penis exposed. She recoiled and quickly made her way to the bar to alert the staff. She got the attention of a female bartender and told her of the assault, insisting that the man be removed. She made her way back through the low-lit noisy confusion of the bar only to find the perpetrator now standing behind the friend who had joined them.

"So I turned around again, and I found a male bartender. And as soon as I said what happened, he had him gone, in a heartbeat," she said.

On that day—so recently departed from a life-affecting spectacle where she'd taken video of a placard that read LET IT NOT BE SAID THAT I WAS SILENT WHEN THEY NEEDED ME—Lacie felt violated in a way she never would have expected.

"It was really disheartening to say to a woman what just happened and she just stared at me. I was more angry at her than I was at him. This is why we do what we do. This is why we have to. Because there are people out there, for one reason or another, that they think that's OK," she said.

Even more troubling was that she couldn't separate the stranger's audacity from the example set by candidate and president Trump.

This guy—Trump, that is—comes out and says, "Grab 'em by the pussy," all this bullshit, and then we elect him as president. There's one guy at Rosie's day care who has a daughter that Rosie loves, one of her best friends, and he has a Trump sticker on his car. And every time I see it, I just get pissed. I'm like, so you're OK with a guy who makes those comments, and you have a little girl? I don't get it. I don't get it. So, yeah, I absolutely believe that putting that shit in the center, then giving him all this power—yeah, I think that does add to it.

On the early evening we sat talking in her neatly kept living room, surrounded by the whims and dismissals of eight cats, Rosie played quietly in the next room with her father, Lacie's ex, with whom she had an arrangement based on necessity. He stayed in her apartment, sleeping on the couch, so he could help with child-care as she worked full-time as a patient access coordinator in the psychiatric unit of Ohio State University's Wexner Medical Center and part-time as a night server at a Buffalo Wild Wings restaurant, trying meanwhile to figure her way into nursing school. Two jobs, she noted with a sarcastic smile. No wonder the unemployment rate was so low. And what part of the then-booming stock market accounted for the undergraduate student loans she reckons she'll be paying for the rest of her life? A struggle, for sure.

Rosie peeked from behind the bedroom door where she'd been playing—not shyly but rather strategically, emerging to say hello to the stranger who'd been asking her mom questions. She approached and introduced herself, then the family cats.

"That's Hermione," she said, pointing to the one stretched out on the floor. "That's Gracie right there. And that's Kupo. And that's Alice. And some of the kitties are hiding somewhere. Sometimes I try to catch them."

And with that, she strode back into her bedroom.

"I want to be the one to change things for her," Lacie said.

To be the father of a daughter is a confounding thing indeed. It's easy for this basic truth to be flattened into the sitcom-dad/women-are-from-Venus trope or the specious "as-the-father-of-a-daughter" disclaimer often used to negotiate gender politics in the same way as "some of my best friends are black." But there is a legitimate, uniquely deep and edifying mystery that begins when a father welcomes a girl-child into his life. A new relationship to the female body begins with her birth; a new engagement with the feminine psyche evolves with her intellect; a new introduction to womanhood emerges with her own (confounding) emergence.

At least that's how it has been for me since the birth of my daughter, Lia, in 1998, a girl who among other things delivered me the pure transcendence of driving top-down in a convertible through the streets of our town, one-upping each other with bizarro-world "yo momma" jokes—respects, not insults—raucously hurled at full-throated volume, not caring who heard us.

YO MOMMA SO NICE...

WHOA—DON'T YOU GO THERE!

YOU MOMMA *SOOO* NICE...

DON'T DO IT!

YO MOMMA *SO* NICE...PEOPLE OFTEN SMILE WHEN THEY ENCOUNTER HER IN PUBLIC!

YOU DID NOT JUST GO THERE! TELL ME YOU DID NOT JUST GO THERE!

Etc.

She was fourteen. My mother had just died. She knew exactly what she was doing.

Few experiences, however, have been more confounding than when she turned eighteen just in time to register to vote in the

2016 presidential election, to be directly engaged in politics for the first time and to find herself blindsided by a bizarro-world showdown if its own, America's first mainstream female candidate pitted against its most outwardly misogynistic one.

I asked her about this in the kitchen one morning, as she stretched her leg muscles in preparation for a trip to the gym. (The daughter of workaholics, she is genetically predisposed to multi-tasking.) She recalled her high school government teacher guiding her and her classmates through the voter registration process, setting the course for their increasing awareness and engagement. She set out to educate herself about the candidates, only to come across the 2004 audio clip in which Trump gave his approval for radio interviewer Howard Stern to refer lasciviously to his then-twenty-three-year-old daughter, Ivanka, as "a piece of ass."

"I mean, I knew about Hillary Clinton's email scandal, but that was nothing compared to him, because of the trust issues. How could you trust someone who would say such things about his own daughter?" Lia said. "This was a choice between a woman and a man who hates women."

Each of her ensuing rites of passage into adulthood was then paralleled and colored by Trump's concurrent emergence as the national leader. She had just begun college at the University of Akron when she cast her vote for Clinton in 2016. She recalled the day following the election as "perfect" in its cold sunless funk, demarcated by a series of texts and social media exchanges between her and her friends, commiserating "like someone had died."

Until then, she had been vacillating between two career goals: *Saturday Night Live* writer or emergency room doctor. (What a thing, to be eighteen!) But the affront to her own emerging sense of identity pushed her in a different direction.

"This is who our president is?" she recalled thinking incredulously. "It definitely kicked in then. I started to think about becoming a lawyer because of that. I wanted to fight for the rights of women. That was the only reason I wanted to be a lawyer."

An avid runner, she joined a campus club called CHAARG (Changing Health, Attitudes + Actions to Recreate Girls), which combines fitness with women's empowerment. The group's motto—"Liberating Girls from the Elliptical"—is a reference to the double standard of the gym, where a woman's place, she explained, is on the cardio machines. Women are rarely seen among the free weights; she told me about a recent Snapchat she'd sent her friends as she prepared to take on the squat machine at the campus rec center, prompting one of her girlfriends to respond, "How do you get over your fear of going into that area?"

In 2019, Lia was promoted to the head of her campus CHAARG chapter and invited to a national leadership retreat in Chicago. The experience gave her a new sense of confidence and independence—"there was definitely a feeling of girl power in the room"—feeding a growing sense that her new womanhood was its own kind of power.

None of the young women who gathered from around the country that weekend talked directly about politics, but as they repeatedly walked together in a large group back and forth from their hotel to the retreat center, passing the Trump International Hotel & Tower each time, a spontaneous, unspoken ritual began—raised middle fingers to the surname on the side of the silver skyscraper.

The National First Ladies' Library occupies two historic buildings, both saved from the wrecking ball, in downtown Canton, Ohio, just around the corner from the landmark Bender's Tavern, a clubby turn-of-the-twentieth-century steak house, darkly clad in marble and tiger oak, whose private upstairs meeting room is where the National Football League was conceived and whose website proclaims it a harbor for those "flush with victory and success in efforts of physical prowess or battles in courts of law or the front lines of business and commerce, others weary from the toil of healing the sick and succor of mankind." Girls are allowed, certainly, but you get the point.

Less than twenty-five years into its existence, the neighboring First Ladies' Library found itself in 2020 in the midst of an organizational and philosophical overhaul at the same moment of generational change in everything that defines it—gender, politics, technology, and decorum. The institution was founded by an old-school politician's wife who understood how to operate in a man's world, launched as an online venture when a dial-up modem could barely squelch out its information onto what then was called the "superhighway," a cultural entity that dropped square into the after-burn of what Douglas Coupland had just declared our "accelerated culture," and was championed by a sitting First Lady whose own role has now upended the tradition of women and the White House.

The First Ladies' Library was the brainchild of Mary Regula, wife of Ralph Regula, a prominent Ohio Republican congressman who served eighteen terms and was a major champion of the National Park Service. Mrs. Regula was a powerful figure in her own right, a Democrat who nonetheless was a strong political partner to her husband. She was a staunch feminist, well connected to money and influence. In the mid-1990s, she began organizing support for a depository of bibliographical materials related to American presidents' wives, in part because she wanted to cast greater light on the legacy of women in the White House and in part because she wanted to leave a mark that was her own, and not simply that of "the Congressman's wife." Then First Lady Hillary Rodham Clinton agreed to be cochair of the project and the library soon established its primary presence on the newfangled World Wide Web. First Lady Clinton was granted the honor of making the first site-click from a computer in the East Room of the White House. That was February 23, 1998. No one could have imagined that in less than twenty years, the First Ladies' Library would be having legitimate discussions about how to address the prospect of Mrs. Clinton's husband becoming America's first-ever—what?—First Gentleman?

The library's website, a sprawling, clip-art-illustrated potpourri of calendar listings, lesson plans, digital card catalog, First Ladies trivia, tour information, and so on, was truly innovative when it premiered at the dawn of the digital age. But in 2020 it looked exactly as it did in 1998—more like a historical reenactment of a vintage website than the virtual front door of a serious research library. Its most recent blog entry was in 2016; an archive of news articles ended in 2011. When, during a visit, I described the site as "quaint" to the library's president and CEO, Jennifer Highfield, she wryly thanked me for being kind. She called it "archaic" and said the staff was preparing for a complete overhaul to make it a fully modern tool for scholars and visitors.

Highfield repeatedly referred to the library as a feminist institution, yet understood that tourists in the visitor center expect to see traditional lady stuff—fancy dresses, dinnerware, and jewelry—and that nonacademic researchers are more likely interested in obtaining Nancy Reagan's pot roast recipe than, for instance, the text of Lucretia Garfield's remarkable 1881 letter insisting that a female doctor be paid the same as male counterparts who had collectively tended to her husband for the eleven weeks he lingered toward death from an assassin's bullet.

Highfield took over the operation in 2018 amid a major reorganization of the library's personnel structure, which was entwined with the National Park Service, a result of the Regulas' acumen for connecting public and private resources. She had the delicate job of transitioning from a strong-willed founder's original vision

(Mary Regula died in 2018 at age ninety-one) to a historical resource with modern relevance.

The library's Education and Research Center is housed in Canton's former City National Bank building, which was donated in 1999. Its ground floor was the bank; its upper floors were law offices. Its basement was a bathhouse, where—like that meeting room at Bender's—attorneys and judges could meet for a steam and get business done, man to man. On the day I visited, the first-floor displays included a tiny-waisted dress worn by First Lady Anna Harrison. Michelle Gullion, the library's archivist and curator, pointed out the gown's exaggerated hourglass contours, which would have been facilitated by the tight corsets worn by Mrs. Harrison and other women of her day, forcing unnatural change in the human form that often led to injury, illness, and miscarried pregnancies. At the same time, women with diseases such as tuberculosis were treated not for a cure but to maintain the condition because of its correspondent weight loss. In front of that same display, Highfield pulled back a floor covering to reveal the building's original glass-block floor, a design element to allow natural light to filter into the bathhouse below, the building's very architecture illustrating its explicit purpose as a male domain.

"I love that we transformed it into a women's museum," Highfield said.

The other building owned by the institution is the Saxton Mc-Kinley house, a Victorian brick mansion that was the home of Ida Saxton McKinley, wife of President William McKinley. The house is where the couple lived when they were in Ohio. Saxton's family was far more prominent than McKinley's. The Saxtons, a founding family of Ohio's Stark County, owned most of the buildings in downtown Canton, the county seat. Ida's grandfather founded *The Repository*, Canton's first newspaper—still in print—and her father was a prominent banker. Yet the family home is relatively small and modest, and its fortunes fell with those of Rust Belt Ohio. The building underwent spells as a bar and restaurant, a boardinghouse, and a brothel, its ornate façade covered up, its interior altered. When the First Ladies' Library took over, the Regulas, as they had done with the neighboring bank building, raised millions of dollars for a meticulous restoration. The house reflects a certain tension of power. Though it was the true home of the once and future First Family, it is much more the Saxton home, a remnant of the First Lady's family power more than that of the president who lived there.

But for all the nuance, visitors want to see dresses. Callers ask for Lucy Hayes's recipe for Roman Punch. Tourists are drawn to Ronnie and Nancy Reagan's his-and-her house slippers and Hillary Clinton's Christmas nutcracker. The lobby on the day I visited had nineteenth-century gowns and White House china on display in tall glass cases, artifacts of female domesticity.

"There's still very little serious research on First Ladies," Highfield said.

Much of this stems from the official role of the First Lady, which is defined with a single word—*hostess*—with no further exposition or context. Perhaps more than anyone else in the president's circle, the First Lady has to find her own way, but quietly, a highly public figure who has relatively little agency to define her public identity.

"A First Lady gives up her career. She gives up her life," Highfield said.

As the institution's leader, she has taken issue with criticism of Melania Trump, a First Lady who has been reticent and who has remained mostly in the background since her husband took office. Highfield said she sympathizes with a woman she's certain never had an inkling she'd be in this position one day and who has been defined by, and sometimes derided for, the life she lived before any hint of what it would become. When nude photographs of a young fashion model become nude photographs of America's First Lady, they beg for a context and a complexity that do not exist.

"People said she wasn't doing her job. She *was* doing her job—being a mother," Highfield said, reiterating that she is in fact historically denied any other "job."

Highfield contrasted the Melania narrative with its equal and opposite (and just as frustrating) counterpart—the shocked reaction when President Jimmy Carter dispatched his wife, Rosalynn, whom he called a "steel magnolia," as an envoy to Latin America. A female diplomat in the 1970s may have been somewhat unconventional, but because that female was married to the president, it was as scandalous in its way as Mrs. Trump's modeling photos. This is why the Shakespearian notion of what almost happened in 2016—the former First Lady becomes president; the former president takes on her previous role—resonates so distinctly among the library's leaders. They have a unique understanding of what his male presence would likely have done to a role that has not been allowed to change for some 230 years.

This museum, then, serves as a nuanced archive to how women can, and have, asserted their independence and self-identity even in a position so restrictive and scrutinized as that of First Lady. An Education and Research Center display of White House china designed by First Ladies revealed Lucy Hayes's choice of a wheat motif to celebrate her family's midwestern pride. A Mary Lincoln–designed dish was rimmed in purple, her favorite color. (She was criticized even for this, accused of pretension to royalty.) They expressed themselves as much as they could, within highly restricted roles.

In 2016, throughout the presidential run of one of the First Ladies' Library's initial champions, the institution's leaders were struck by the coded sexism in terms used to describe Clinton, in the undue focus on her appearance and her health, in the analysis of her body language—terms and observations never applied in the same way to male candidates. They heard over and over some version of the resistance, even among seemingly open-minded females: "I just would not vote for a woman."

They also know enough to correct the declaration that Clinton was the first woman to run for US president. The first, in fact, was a woman from Ohio, Victoria Woodhull, who ran as an Equal Rights Party candidate in 1872. She was soon followed by another female candidate, Belva Ann Lockwood, who ran in 1884 and 1888.

So the world of women and politics was in a state of historic advancement and uncertainty in 2020. In addition to the coming presidential election, the library staff that year was busy with the institution's reorganization. It was also preparing programming related to that year's centennial celebration of women's suffrage, a movement that had a major stronghold in Ohio, in great part a result of the state's large Quaker population, which championed women's rights and other liberal causes. Many influential suffragettes came from Ohio, including Harriet Taylor Upton, a protégé of Susan B. Anthony, and many others came here to campaign for women's right to vote. Sojourner Truth's rousing "Ain't I a Woman" speech, delivered at the Ohio Women's Convention in Akron in 1851, stands as one of the movement's defining statements.

Mary Regula found the voice she needed through all these historic women, Highfield told me as we toured the library's buildings. With the founder's passing, the institution was finding its next voice, one likely to ring much differently.

Both Regulas lived into their nineties, political partners throughout, despite their differences. The last presidential election for both of them was in 2016.

Ralph voted for Donald Trump.

Mary voted for Hillary Clinton.

A reporter from the Massillon, Ohio, newspaper asked about her choice.

"It's time for a woman," she said.

So much of this began in the digital underground, email connections made, Facebook groups formed, Instagram photos and memes shared from user to user, women at their work computers, on their phones, waiting behind the wheel at the after-school pickup line, retweeting other women's comments after placing an online pizza order—a new kind of coalition and a different route toward action for a population that still generally held down the domestic fort, that worked all day for less pay than men, women of the elliptical who had their own set of concerns in a disconcerting time.

The day after the third presidential debate in 2016, a woman named Libby Chamberlain created a secret Facebook page for thirty of her friends illustrated with a photo of Hillary Clinton, with the group description: "Wear a pantsuit on November 8—you know why." That was the beginning of one of many grassroots movements, one that took hold immediately, shared from person to person, gaining twenty-four thousand followers in its first twenty-four hours, even as it remained "secret." Women mostly, but men, too, from every stripe of the American experience began joining in droves, posting statements of their personal experiences. By the end of Election Day, the group had more than three million members, drawn magnetically to a virtual rally for rights and expression.

Just as organically, the collective mobilized into grassroots political action, raising money, organizing phone banks, providing connections between people who needed rides to their polling places and neighbors ready to help. When the voting ended, Pantsuit Nation did not. A book of that same title was published a few months after the election and the ensuing Women's March, with photo portraits and short narratives from group members. A Texas daughter of immigrants told of her young children helping teach their grandparents how to vote. A North Carolina woman described her young daughter volunteering as an usher at a Michelle Obama speech. A Michigan woman who'd received an anonymous letter objecting to her rainbow flag recounted her neighbors' collective response, unfurling flag after rainbow flag in solidarity. A white man from Ohio posed in a Black Lives Matter T-shirt. And Hillary Clinton herself contributed, expressing thanks to a community that "represent[s] the best of America: people of all backgrounds and beliefs who share a vision for a brighter future for our children, who have each other's backs."

Pantsuit Nation has evolved into a broader network of state and international chapters, with membership approaching four million in 2019. The Ohio chapter, to which Lacie Cheuvront belongs, had more than sixteen hundred members in 2019. Its purpose, too, has evolved, joined by other online, female-centric communities that represent a network of safe spaces where people can interact, ask questions, test their opinions, and organize. In 2019, the Pantsuit Nation founders helped in the formation of a new gender equity advocacy group, Supermajority, whose name derives from the fact that women represent 51 percent of the US population, and whose goal is to "build an inclusive national membership of women who are connected, empowered, and taking action—moving up the ladder of civic participation and advocacy and voting in record numbers."

Harnessing all these communities became an important political objective in 2020. As that election season dawned, Elizabeth Walters, the Democratic Party chair in Ohio's Summit County, told me she believed white women would be the deciding factor in the presidential election. She broke down her party's female population into three key subgroups: (1) women of color, who always have been and remain the strongest activists, (2) older white women, who she called the "ERA sisters," skilled at organizing rallies, and (3) white urban women, a more difficult demographic to mobilize.

As she explained it, Ohio, like the rest of the Midwest, has been losing white working-class and rural voters to the Republican vote. With middle-aged, white, suburban, college-educated women already strongly in the Republican column, the difference would need to be made up with urban women from that same demographic. Much of the political calculus following 2016 focused on niches—who sat out, who rejoined the electorate or joined for the first time, which subgroups could affect the margins. Democratic organizers and candidates in other midwestern states seemed to be doing a better job than Ohio in identifying and engaging white female voters from their cities.

"They're like the unicorn," Walters said.

They also could make the difference in turning Ohio blue, she added.

Meanwhile, Ohio has been the testing ground for what Walters called "some of the most extreme legislation in the country" in terms of women's issues. In 2019, Ohio governor Mike DeWine signed into law a "heartbeat bill," prohibiting a woman from getting an abortion after a heartbeat has been detected in the fetus, even though polls showed most Ohio voters opposed it. The law, which represented one of the nation's most restrictive abortion bans, made no concessions for incidents of rape or incest, and it included criminal penalties for doctors who violate it. It was blocked by a federal judge before it went into effect, on the grounds that it was likely unconstitutional, left in a state of limbo that reflected the larger moral, legal, and cultural divides.

In the 2018 midterm election, six female Democratic candidates running for the state legislature formed an unusual, potentially game-changing coalition called Ohio Women Lead, joining forces to campaign in tandem, producing a video ad that promoted their shared goals, and collaborating in other ways, including get-out-the-vote efforts and shared yard signs.

"In prior elections, women may have been less likely to talk on the campaign trail about what it's like to be a mom and balance family and work," Kristin Boggs, one of the six, told the *Columbus Dispatch*. "With these candidates, our families have been such a motivating factor about why they've gotten into the election. They are actively talking about it, using it to connect with other women who are just as frustrated with the state of affairs."

Five of the six Ohio Women Lead candidates won their elections, all defeating male Republicans, most by landslides. This emergence of a female force in political races was evident across the country in 2018 and continued into the 2020 presidential campaign. Of the twenty-four Democratic primary candidates who qualified for the first rounds of debates in 2019, six were women, including some of the highest-polling candidates.

Lacie Cheuvront was born in Texas in 1987; her family moved to Carrollton, Ohio, a village of about three thousand residents, when she was six. By the time she was aware of a world beyond her immediate surroundings, she knew she wanted out. She described her hometown as a place with no mall, no movie theater, no Wal-mart, "a dead zone of nothing—we celebrated National Tractor Day by driving our tractors into town."

She remembered seeing a Mexican family being pointedly stared at on the street and recognizing the irony of a new Mexican restaurant not far away, packed every night. "We had two biracial people in my entire town," she recalled one early evening after work, socked feet tucked underneath her on the couch, blond hair pulled back, with a sweep of bangs arcing across the top of her cat-eye glasses, the neckline of her black knit jumper revealing the top of the tattoo in fanciful script across her collarbone: "Never Shall We Die." The line is from one of the *Pirates of the Caribbean* films, referring to the importance of taking a stand.

"I think my hometown was a bubble that needed to be burst," she continued.

Her own home was difficult. Family members struggled with alcoholism and mental health, she said. She suffered from depression and anxiety, cutting herself as a teenager and counting the days till she could get out. She graduated from high school at age sixteen and moved to Columbus, the state capital and the fastest-growing city in Ohio, thirteen days after her seventeenth birthday. Eager at first for a means of expression, she enrolled in art classes, studying graphic design at Columbus State Community College. Her more practical sense of survival turned her studies toward real estate before her true heart—to help others—led her to complete a bachelor's degree in psychology in 2016 through the online Ashford University and take classes toward a master's degree, also in psychology. Meanwhile, she got married, had Rosie, and continued looking for where she belonged.

The city of Columbus and its suburbs form a complicated footprint. Metropolitan Columbus lacks the industrial and post-industrial identity that defines Ohio's other large cities. Its primary identity is distinctly split between its role as the seat of state government and the home of the sprawling Ohio State University campus. Locals bristle at an old nickname—"Cowtown," derived from the city's proximity to farmland and Appalachia (not to mention that in 1926 an actual cow was elected OSU's homecoming queen)—even as Greater Columbus has become home to major household-name American companies—Wendy's, Nationwide Insurance, and Abercrombie & Fitch among them—and vibrant, diverse arts and culture. But every city, not just in Ohio but in any state considered part of "flyover country," has some version of an inferiority complex as part of its makeup.

Columbus's suburbs include some of the wealthiest communities in the region, and that's where Lacie and her husband began their life, in a house in the suburb of Dublin, where you can practically smell the money. But it didn't feel right and was more than they could afford, so when Rosie came along, they relocated to Hilliard, with good schools but lower taxes and a looser vibe, nestled at the edge of cornfields but still with access to the diversity and culture Lacie had craved when she got out of Carrollton. She wanted to raise her daughter in a place that reflected her values of inclusiveness and equal rights. When I asked her what message she would want to give to a presidential candidate, she responded, "We have to take care of people." By "people," she continued, she meant immigrants, elderly citizens, students, children.

"I am one of those crazy people that believes we could take care of everyone," she said.

She was exploring psychiatric nursing programs, hoping to take that philosophy deeper into her career. Meanwhile, she said she wants to do what she can to be heard, to work toward her ideals. She remembered her earliest political action, carrying a sign at a John Kerry rally in Columbus at age seventeen, before she was even old enough to vote. In her busy life now, she remains committed to making time to work for change—"for her," she said, in yet another reference to her daughter, whose Washington souvenir was a child-size "Women's March" hat and who eats her meals at a kitchen table under a wall hanging of Martin Luther King Jr.'s quote: "The time is always right to do what is right." Lacie said she would take an active role campaigning locally for whoever opposes Donald Trump in 2020.

"We have to defeat this guy," she said firmly. "We have to."

7

THE STRUGGLE

A short time after my son Evan enrolled at the University of Akron in 2013 and moved into an apartment near campus, Gina and I went to visit. Parenting is a never-ending series of unforeseen coming-of-age moments, and not only for the child. These revelations arrive obliquely and land squarely, and so it was that day:

My child has purchased a toilet brush.

Gina and I poked around the kitchen, stocked with hand-me-down cookware and gadgets, peeked into the refrigerator (ketchup, beer), smirked at the pinup girl displayed in the living room. I wandered into his bedroom. The walls were bare, except for a small sheet of notepad paper taped above his pillow. On the top line, in his small, careful script, was the word "Goals." Below, a list: personal best in *Madden NFL,* bench-press max, find someone to love. And then:

"Save someone's life."

He was studying for a degree in emergency management with the intention of becoming a firefighter/paramedic, something he'd wanted to do ever since he started watching *Rescue Heroes* as a toddler, inspired by the square-jawed, gear-laden Billy Blazes. When *Jay Jay the Jet Plane* came along with a fire engine character—Revvin' Evan—bearing his own name, the die was pretty much cast. He became a catcher in Little League, I'm certain, because of the heroic allure of all that heavy protective armor. (There's no other explanation for volunteering for a position otherwise distinguished by knee pain, heatstroke, and high-impact collisions.) At his high school graduation awards ceremony, the baseball program honored him with the Coach's Award for high character and teamwork. In announcing the winner, his coach said that if his house was ever on fire, the person he'd want to respond was Evan.

He began college about as career certain as anyone I've known, and by the time he began studying for his paramedic certification, he was already working part-time as a firefighter for a small village near Akron. Fire calls were few, but many shifts were busy, and almost always with the same dispatcher's directive. Overdose.

Hop in the ambulance, rush to the address, administer naloxone injection. Repeat.

By the time he turned twenty-one, "save a life" was no longer an ultimate goal but rather a matter of routine. On a single shift, he might save two or three lives between the time the sun went down at night and rose again the next day.

When Evan began working at the firehouse in 2016, Ohio was in the throes of an opioid epidemic, among the worst in the nation in its onslaught of overdoses. The southern part of the state, joined by its contiguous neighbors West Virginia and Kentucky, represented a larger Appalachian region ravaged by prescription and street drugs, with overdose rates at the highest levels in the United States. The term *opioid* had become inseparable from its new suffix, *crisis*. The following year, 2017, Ohio posted the second-highest rate in the United States of opioid overdose deaths—4,293 died that year—well over twice the national average. Prescription drugs were the most common killer, but synthetic narcotics, most notably fentanyl, were on the rampage. It was all over the streets. Public health workers, statisticians, journalists, and government officials scrambled along with first responders to keep up with this runaway new phenomenon in crime, public health, and civic worry. The target kept moving—first oxycodone, then heroin, then carfentanil. Users were warned not to trust what they were buying; the dose they thought would get them high might be enough to kill an elephant.

Obituaries with photographs of young men and women— smiling, beautiful, yearbook faces—began appearing with unnerving frequency in the newspaper, along with a frank new kind of death-notice rhetoric addressing the illness of addiction, some tinged with hurt, others with warning. A close friend had to compose the obituary for his twenty-five-year-old son, a smart, bighearted kid who'd played with Evan as a child, and who, my friend wrote, "tried hard to break away from the chains of opiate use, but the drugs, as they too often do, ultimately killed him." The notice ended with a prayer that he was finally at peace; a brokenhearted family could only hope the same for themselves.

It was, in every way, close to home. Gina and I lost three generations from a single branch of her family tree to overdoses—her sister, that sister's son, and that son's son—within six years of each other. The genealogical order of the deaths is as devastating as the struggle to understand a disease that could hold such power over them: the mother died last, having first lost a son, then a grandson, then finally the battle to kill her own pain.

Everyone in Ohio, it seemed, knew someone who had been affected. And everyone in the country, it seemed, knew Ohio as the epicenter of this new epidemic. Much of that public association derived from J. D. Vance's 2016 book *Hillbilly Elegy,* which dropped into the national consciousness and onto the bestseller lists just as a previously overlooked demographic—disaffected poor people—were lumped together into what was becoming known as "Trump country."

Vance's memoir tells the story of his upbringing in Middletown, Ohio, a rural community in the state's southwestern corner, a place that had sunk into hard times after the loss of a steel mill, a common narrative across the region. He recounts his mother's ongoing struggle with addiction, a story line that culminates in a particularly desolating passage, in which Vance returns to his hometown to put up the money for his homeless mother's stay in a seedy motel. As he approaches the building in the dark, "The streetlight revealed the silhouette of a man sitting halfway in his truck—the door open, his feet dangling to the side—with the unmistakable form of a hypodermic needle sticking from his arm."

In his book, as well as in his ongoing public discussion, Vance draws a linear connection between economic hardship, personal and communal hopelessness, and addiction. The book's subtitle—*A Memoir of a Family and Culture in Crisis*—drives home the point that his own firsthand case study can help place the larger phenomenon in context.

In a 2016 interview with *The Rumpus,* he said, "The more I wrote, the more I realized that the most powerful way to look at the issues was to talk about what I knew, both in terms of family history and personal experience. So, what started as an effort to explain Middletown, Ohio, to the world evolved into a very personal reckoning."

Such personal narratives hold great cultural value. They invite empathy; they allow insight into experiences otherwise shrouded by shame, fear, suppression, ignorance, or apathy. The first line of Pantsuit Nation's vision statement, outlining its purpose in showcasing women's stories, reads as a socially conscious memoir-ist's manifesto: "We believe that stories are an essential part of activism. The empathetic potential of first person narrative to create social change is widely recognized and yet often dismissed as less effective than data driven approaches. The power of emotion, authentic connection, and socially reinforced empathy to shift our understanding of how abstract policy affects individual lives and to create a sense of urgency to engage with our democracy is at our fingertips."

When Tim Ryan described his home state as a place where people go unheard and unseen, he was speaking of Middletown as much as the Mahoning Valley. More broadly, he was speaking of Flint, and Fargo, and Gary, and Buffalo, the unconsidered and marginalized places. Too often, these places are known only for a single facet of their personality, and too often for their worst moments or their most cartoonish quirks, so that Flint is associated with its lead-tainted water, Fargo with its exaggerated movie dialect, Gary with its murder rate, and Buffalo with its chicken wings. Cleveland has spent decades trying to overcome the national specter of its burning river.

It is vitally important, then, for the story of a place to be told in native voices, by people who understand truth and its nuances, and who can offset the superficial narratives too often applied to places like Vance's and mine, which I believe are like most places. Vance's book, with its honest illumination of his Ohio family and neighbors, advances the narrative; its value is that it was told from within. Upon its release, *American Conservative* columnist Rod Dreher wrote, "His book does for poor white people what Ta-Nehisi Coates's book [*Between the World and Me*] did for poor black people: give them voice and presence in the public square."

Vance has been criticized for the fact that he wrote from his perspective as someone who got out, having begun the manuscript while a law student at Yale and completed it in San Francisco, where he'd taken a job with an investment capital firm. He moved back to Ohio in 2017 and started a nonprofit intended to fight the opioid crisis. But for once, at least, the story was told by someone who was from here, who was *of* here, rather than by someone who had come from elsewhere to try to explain us. We get enough of that every election cycle.

But one story can only carry so far. Many Ohioans worry that the only image some Americans have of our region comes from Vance's high-profile account. More than once as I traveled around Ohio, people implored me to balance that image, to visit places like Yellow Springs, a bucolic college town not far from Middletown where, among other anomalous things, comedian Dave Chappelle lives with his family, or to balance the Rust Belt stereotype with narratives of postindustrial revival and success. A varied chorus is needed. And across Ohio, a varied chorus repeated that need to me.

In 2018, Elizabeth Catte, a writer and historian from East Tennessee, published a sort of counternarrative to Vance's memoir, a book called *What You Are Getting Wrong About Appalachia*. Catte felt that her experience had been narrowed by the national impression of her place cast by *Hillbilly Elegy*. Her response intended to expand the portrait. In 2019, West Virginia University Press published an anthology of voices, *Appalachian Reckoning: A Region Responds to Hillbilly Elegy*, which was billed as "a retort, at turns rigorous, critical, angry, and hopeful, to the long shadow *Hillbilly Elegy* has cast over the region and its imagining." The collection of essays, poetry, and photography, contributed by a diverse group of creators, aimed to "provide a deeply personal portrait of a place that is at once culturally rich and economically distressed, unique and typically American."

*   *   *

What will become of him? What will become of his hope? These were questions I had to ask myself about a son who'd set off with a list of ideals and was quickly met with a reality that all but mocked them. As his burgeoning career developed, Evan boomeranged back home for a spell, took the Akron Police civil service exam, and was accepted into the academy, still working part-time as a firefighter/paramedic. At the time, he said he wanted to be the cop who plays basketball with kids at the public park. As Gina and I sorted through a litany of worries amid this new path, we also worked to recalibrate our new role as the parents of someone becoming his own person. The boy we didn't even allow to play with squirt guns was now a man spending hours at the shooting range. Had we taught him enough to carry him through whatever might confront him on the streets? Could he rise above stereo-types on both sides, tensions set by past incidents of brutality and racism? Would the streets change him?

The day he was sworn into the police force, the department posted a picture of its new rookie class on Facebook. A woman commented, "Let's hope they got the training of not pulling out guns on brown and black men just because they felt threatened."

I knew better than to respond, but I did anyway, writing, "Their training was excellent. One of them is my child. I share your concerns, and I'm confident Akron is sending rational, morally grounded officers into our neighborhoods."

I believed this but could only guess at how it might be tested.

The first night on the job, he and his partner arrested a veteran criminal, who, handcuffed, gave Evan a knowing once-over and observed, "You're a rookie, aren't you?"

As Ohio became the national focus of the opioid crisis in 2017, Montgomery County, whose seat is Dayton, became its cause célèbre, with the highest rate of overdose deaths in the state and one of the worst in the country. The *Huffington Post* referred to Dayton as "America's 'Overdose Capital,'" and NBC News called Montgomery the "most opioid addicted county" in America. The *New Yorker,* CNN, the *New York Times,* Reuters, and many others parachuted into Dayton to document the city's dilemma, so much that the *Dayton Daily News* found itself reporting on the very phenomenon of the reporting.

Facebook cofounder Mark Zuckerberg weighed in with a post: "Everyone in Dayton is affected by this. One woman told me her daughter, who is a recovering heroin addict, got promoted to hostess at the restaurant where she works because the last hostess overdosed in the bathroom. Another woman whose husband is a police officer said her family hears overdose calls coming over the radio every night. The Dayton police department once responded to 29 overdose calls in a single day. She's worried it's all going to seem normal to her young daughter."

One after another of the reports made anecdotal reference to a coroner's office so overwhelmed with casualties that it had to rent refrigerated trailers to store the bodies. Between *Hillbilly Elegy*—Middletown is just twenty miles from Montgomery County—and all the media coverage, the area was burdened with a stigma of civic shame on top of the human tragedy. The nation knew plenty about what was happening but less about what was being done in response.

Nan Whaley took office as Dayton's mayor in 2014, amid the escalating crisis. She and Ohio's then governor John Kasich began working together to address the problem and helped set a template for other communities. In 2011, well ahead of the national curve, Kasich established the Governor's Cabinet Opiate Action Team, which took a wholistic approach, gathering state and local resources and attacking the growing crisis from multiple angles—legal, medical, social, and political. The initiative worked to promote safer drug use, to combat the opioid trade, to focus on drug-use prevention, and to expand access to treatment. New laws made it easier to distribute naloxone kits, used to reverse the effects of opioid overdose; in 2016, the state reported that distribution of 10,477 kits resulted in 907 overdose reversals. Recognizing the public health concern, Kasich expanded Medicaid under the Affordable Care Act in 2015, allowing some seven hundred thousand low-income Ohioans access to addiction and mental health treatment.

Whaley, too, took a proactive approach. She was one of the first American mayors to declare a state of emergency in the wake of the crisis, a move that allowed her to raise awareness, fast-track a needle exchange program, and facilitate the distribution of naloxone to anyone who needed it. In 2017, Dayton was among the vanguard in taking on pharmaceutical manufacturers, distributors, and physicians, becoming the fourth city in the country to file a lawsuit against "big pharma."

As this struggle continued, the narrative began to change. In late 2018, the *New York Times* returned to Dayton to report on a 54 percent decline in overdose deaths from the previous year.

"Dayton, a hollowed-out manufacturing center at the juncture of two major interstates, had one of the highest opioid overdose death rates in the nation in 2017 and the worst in Ohio," wrote national health correspondent Abby Goodnough. "Now, it may be at the leading edge of a waning phase of an epidemic that has killed hundreds of thousands of people in the United States over the last decade, including nearly 50,000 last year."

A generation before, Ohio, ever the bellwether, was at the leading edge of industrial decline and in the aftermath has provided case studies for recovery. In a similar way, its difficult position as the epicenter of the opioid epidemic has also made it a test case for strategies to combat the crisis. In 2019, the National

Institutes of Health chose Ohio as one of four states to participate in a study intended to reduce overdose deaths. A federal grant of nearly $70 million was provided to analyze and improve efforts in nineteen of Ohio's eighty-eight counties. The NIH noted that Ohio was chosen specifically because of how well its varied regions represent a microcosm of the nation overall, an echo of the "five Ohios" political map. The state's lead investigator, Dr. Rebecca Jackson, director of Ohio State University's Center for Clinical and Translational Science and associate dean for clinical research in the College of Medicine, described Ohio's unique ability to reflect the national image.

"We believe lessons learned from these communities in Ohio will not only serve to give us important information so we can stem the tide of the opioid crisis across the other counties in Ohio but, in fact, across the region and nationally," she said in an Ohio News Service interview.

In 2019, Ohio legislators proposed two bills to reform drug sentencing, one to offer addiction treatment as an alternative, another to reduce low-level drug felonies to misdemeanors. The *Times,* meanwhile, suggested that Dayton's and Ohio's collaborative effort to reduce overdose deaths could provide an example for other places, particularly in its all-hands-on-deck approach, the combination of Medicaid expansion, naloxone kit distribution and training, needle exchange programs, ongoing cooperation between police and public health officials, and its weaving together of a strong network of addiction support services.

But though the effort in Dayton has received praise and recognition as a potential strategy for other communities, at least some of its tactics have not been embraced, even among the city's closest neighbors. At the same time Montgomery County was seeing the encouraging results of its multipronged approach, the sheriff of adjacent Butler County, which includes parts of Vance's hometown of Middletown, refused to allow his deputies to carry and administer naloxone. In 2017, Sheriff Richard K. Jones cited concern for the safety of his officers, saying revived overdose victims often react violently when snapped out of unconsciousness, as well as the taxpayer cost of naloxone kits, which can run from twenty to sixty dollars apiece. (The State of Ohio helped cover the cost for municipalities.) In Middletown itself, a city councilman proposed a "three-strikes" policy that would deny emergency medical services response for repeat overdose victims.

After a 2017 peak in opioid overdoses, the death rate declined in Ohio and nationally in 2018 for the first time in decades, according to the US Centers for Disease Control and Prevention. Ohio still ranked among the states with the highest death totals, but progress was being measured. Many factors contributed to Ohio's effort to reverse the trend, but in a time of hardened political division, it's worth noting how successfully Whaley, a Democrat, and Kasich, a Republican, worked together, and how important it was to build partnerships and share resources. Collaboration has been at the center of many of Ohio's efforts to address its most complex challenges, from gun violence to urban blight to water pollution to trust between police and the public. It's a lesson well earned in a place where few things come easy. When it works, it's worth understanding how.

8

ROLLING ACRES

To see it demolished was to see it at perhaps its most epic moment: the finally (maybe) definite end of an agonized, highly public decay, prolonged and prolonged, now leveled and laid bare, ready to answer a generational question. I used to refer to Rolling Acres alternately as "my favorite dead mall" and "the gift that keeps on giving." I was a local newspaper columnist then, and there's nothing better in that noble profession than an inside joke that everyone gets and you can keep telling and retelling without it ever getting old. Over a four-year span in the first decade of the twenty-first century, I wrote seven columns about Rolling Acres Mall in Akron, which I'm certain is a higher count than any other single topic I covered, aside from the events of 9/11. I chose the mall as the setting for what would have been my final dispatch before leaving the newspaper in 2008, except Barack Obama got elected president a week later, an event my editor and I agreed was worthy of remark. Rolling Acres, like so many other American shopping malls that debuted in the sixties and seventies, was the epitome of newness for its first decade, a solid go-to for its second, and then, almost imperceptibly and almost overnight, it flipped the way a school of fish goes belly-up in a pond whose chemical balance has suddenly gone wrong. I called it a dead mall for a long time, but it was never quite that. It lingered and lingered, such that it felt as if we, communally, were writing its eulogy in quarterly installments.

I returned to the site on a muggy Sunday afternoon in 2019, not long after it had been leveled, its immense void demanding big American questions, about the wisdom and morality of our voracious consumer culture, about the responsibility to preserve public architecture, even of the ugly 1970s JCPenney sort, about the fate of the hundreds, maybe thousands, of people who'd scraped together a living here, hour by hour, in an era when the "service economy" was the diminished replacement for good factory jobs, and whether anyone thought about them or cared. A few stores and fast-food restaurants still operated at the outskirts of this one-time destination, but on this day the clock ticked slowly without a single car passing by, and the most steadfast man in Ohio was surely the guy at the curb hoisting his sign to nobody:

FINAL DAYS
STORE CLOSING
LaSALLE FURNITURE

The mall's boundless crumbling gray asphalt parking lot was pocked with weeds and strewn with discarded tires, empty save for an unoccupied bus depot near the main driveway and a row of Dollar General semitrailers parked near what was once a Sears. It's existentially disorienting to approach a changed familiar place and try to feel its bones. I was reminded of Scott Russell Sanders's essay "After the Flood," in which he describes returning to the site of his childhood home in Ohio's farmland to find not only the house gone but also the site of all his youthful exploring submerged beneath a man-made reservoir and his tromping grounds turned into a government arsenal, a "paradise of bombs." In that essay, he corrects our modern interpretation of the word *nostalgia* as a warm synonym for homesickness and reaches back to its Greek origin: "return pain." Lost landscapes are part of the definition of America, and what once seemed like progress often becomes dogged by regret, longing, and shame. In some ways, the twentieth-century suburban shopping mall stood like a secular cathedral of our worst traits: superficiality, greed, white flight, gluttony, waste, and unwarranted monograms. Its erasure might seem like a correction. But our social and political responsibilities aren't tested when we save something like an abandoned castle or a town square gazebo. We're tested when we take ownership of our excesses and failings and try again. The dead mall is no different from the block of foreclosed homes or the generation dying of opioids or the pregnant impoverished teenager or the holding cell packed with immigrants. The decisions we make about what to do with them determines our character.

I put my car in park and walked along the boundary where the pavement's end met the immense debris field of the former mall. I thought I'd found the place that was once the main entrance, only to continue another hundred feet or so, where I happened into a still-remaining section of the front walkway, an amorphous pad of synthetic-stone pavers. I pried one up and carried it back to my car, because that's what we do in the Midwest.

I slid back behind the wheel, pulled onto the road, and aimed for home, passing that going-out-of-business furniture store, a giant red sign covering its façade, doubling down on its demise: Liquidator Liquidators.

When you know what it looked like full, 1.3 million square feet of public space can appear mighty empty. For a decade and a half, beginning in the 1990s, Rolling Acres's occupancy trickled downward, stores closing, foot traffic declining, the rambling parking lot growing more and more vacant, the sign hanging above it now serving as an ironic, forlorn pun, inviting tumbleweed imagery: ROLLING ACRES. The mall changed hands from one buyer to another to another, the price falling steadily, but always reported as a figure that was hard for us commoners of the cultural marketplace to reckon. Was the $3.5 million price tag in 2005 a bargain or a fool's wager? And then which was correct—the $1.7 million purchase price a year later, or the $4.9 million the new owner was asking (but never even sniffed) when he immediately flipped it back onto the market? And the public—those of us who no longer went there but who nonetheless harbored a curiously potent investment of nostalgia—we developed a longstanding parlor game, suggesting new uses for the place. Skate park? Casino? Retirement complex? Some thought it could be reinvented for a new kind of retail—an outlet mall, a flea market, or maybe one of those newfangled renovations of old malls in hipper cities, where the roofs were cut off and the store entrances turned outward, creating a public plaza. Yeah, an outdoor mall. In Ohio. Where the oldest joke says if you don't like the weather, just wait ten minutes; it'll change.

As a local newspaper columnist, I was constantly presented with such suggestions, but never once, in all the emails and phone calls and grocery-store-aisle small talk, did anyone suggest tearing it down. I've always wondered about that. My Ohio hometown, like a lot of middle-American cities on the back end of the industrial age, had a mixed record when it came to the preservation and reuse of its architectural icons, be they Gilded Age mansions or shopping malls. In our case, this legacy was immortalized in song by native daughter Chrissie Hynde, who left Akron for London in the 1970s, formed her band The Pretenders, and recorded one of its most enduring songs, "My City Was Gone," whose lament for her hometown's lost places includes the line "The farms of Ohio / Had been replaced by shopping malls."

But here was a populace that, at least by the limited sample size of my voicemail and inbox, was intent on finding a new use for this shared icon of consumerism and its role as a middle-class public gathering place. Folks were just as likely to recall the afternoons they spent playing Ms. Pac-Man in the concourse, or the day they met their future mate while on a work break from Fashion Bug, as they were to recount their purchases. (When I think of Rolling Acres, I specifically think of my first guitar, procured with birthday money at the Sears anchor store, and a tinny tri-gold ring I bought for Gina at a kiosk the first Christmas we were married.) The mall was oddly personal, but even more, its potential razing seemed enormously wasteful. Its fate would say something about us as a community, something large. But still—this was not our property, and it was not our money. It was just a bunch of corporate-owned chain stores, right? That's what left me curious: why it mattered. One of the first and ultimately most popular T-shirt slogans concocted by the local Rubber City Clothing Company in the early aughts carried the plea: Save Rolling Acres.

The king is dead. Long live the Chess King.

Among the policies Andrew Yang promoted during his campaign for the 2020 Democratic presidential nomination was something he called the "American Mall Act," aimed at addressing the giant voids created when shopping malls fail. "When a mall closes down, it hurts the local economy, sends a signal to those considering investing in the area, and becomes a source of blight," he wrote on his campaign website. "We need to do all we can to find productive uses for the hundreds of American malls that are going to close in the next four years. Offices, churches, indoor recreation spaces, anything we can do to keep these spaces vital and positive is an enormous win for the surrounding community. We should provide incentives and funds to help more developers reinvent these buildings and spaces."

Across the country, as bigger-than-life shopping malls were losing traffic amid retail evolution toward different destinations, both real and virtual, the public deliberations had to do with more than mere architecture. If the shopping mall said something about who we were as a culture in the second half of the twentieth century—and boy, did it ever—then whatever became of its uniquely conspicuous edifices would say just as much about who we were becoming at the dawn of the twenty-first. What I heard when I tested that question in my own struggling-for-identity "legacy city" was an echo of urban visionary Jane Jacobs, author of the classic *The Death and Life of Great American Cities.* Her oft-repeated philosophy—"new ideas need old buildings"—had unique urgency in cities where old buildings were not just old but also very often emptied of an activity that had once sustained and defined us. Just about the time Rolling Acres and other middle-American shopping malls were losing their relevance, an urgent question of legacy and permanence loomed over the sooty, redbrick industrial campus of the former BF Goodrich world headquarters, which occupied seventy-five acres right in the middle of my downtown.

The complex was a mix of mahogany-paneled office buildings and small and large manufacturing spaces that collectively told the story of a company that established the American tire industry in Akron in 1870, then grew its footprint within that same locale as it expanded into everything from golf balls to garden hoses to space suits, some ninety buildings employing tens of thousands of local workers. By the time Goodrich was finally acquired by the French company Michelin in 1990, most of the manufacturing space was dormant, and when the foreign corporate owner finally pulled up stakes for good and relocated the headquarters in Nashville (all our departed corporations beelined to southern, nonunion "right-to-work" states), the empty complex was sore on both the eyes and the soul. For a spell, it was transformed (ironically, in this context) into a giant flea market. That failed. A Hollywood publicist floated a request to implode one of the old factory buildings to promote the film *Demolition Man*. Didn't happen. The company name imprinted down the giant round smokestacks loomed like a damning oxymoron, as the landscape below was no longer GOOD nor RICH. But in a dramatic stroke of eleventh-hour acquisition, a private buyer rescued the complex from a real estate operation that had been dubbed "Operation Greengrass"—it was to be leveled and seeded into a seventy-five-acre vacant lot. Instead, the new owner transformed it into a mixed-use honeycomb of small businesses called Canal Place. By the end of the century, it was at full occupancy, praised in the national business press as a model of adaptive reuse. It represented a civic victory, a symbol not of collapse but of reinvention.

It wasn't so hard, then, to understand a public mind-set that focused on a new use for an old mall. But you can't resurrect something when the damn thing won't die. I visited on an August afternoon in 2004, walking from one end of the mall to the other, trying to count the empty storefronts. I lost track, so I walked back, counting people instead. Twenty-five bodies in the entire main concourse.

Months and years dragged on, with the newspaper's business reporters interviewing retail experts about the percentage of occupancy that would signal certain death. But even as the interior storefronts turned one after another into closed-cage mannequin mausoleums, the anchor stores at the various external corners continued to stay busy. I returned the week after Christmas of 2007, looking to tell the story of everyday life inside the technically still-open mall, but there was little life to find, even in a week when other retail outlets were bustling with returns and postseason sales. The passageway from the mall concourse to the JCPenney Outlet store had been walled off, suggesting it no longer had need or desire to associate with its decrepit conjoined twin. From a frigid concourse in which "It's Beginning to Look a Lot Like Christmas" warbled Muzak-style from the speakers, I watched a mailman approach a beauty supply store whose entrance was covered with a plastic sheet intended to conserve warmth. He lifted back a makeshift door cut into the plastic and affixed with duct tape, looked inside quizzically, then, seeing no one, entered and left the mail. When he reemerged, I asked him what it was like coming back here day after day.

"A lot of places, you come in one day, and they'll be gone," he told me, waving a slim stack of mail in evidence.

The only place I found open that afternoon was a menswear store, itself in a going-out-of-business sale. There was one customer inside, sorting through a rack. The store manager told me coming to work each day made him feel like a character in *The Andromeda Strain*. By then, only about a dozen tenants remained, and half the time the owners didn't even bother to show up and open shop. A mall advertising poster across the way boasted WITH MORE THAN 85 STORES, ROLLING ACRES MALL HAS EVERYTHING TO MAKE YOU LOOK GOOD AND FEEL GREAT. I wrote at the time that although the complete demise of the mall had for several years seemed like a foregone conclusion, "Now, it seems like it's time to start counting the days."

The non-anchor tenants held on for most of the following year, then, in a cruel twist, those who'd stuck it out under the owner's promise to reinvigorate the space by converting it to a mixed-use facility were informed on a random Monday morning amid the Great Recession that they were evicted, effective immediately. They scrambled together their remains and lit out.

But it still wouldn't die. The standalone department stores continued to operate. Another year passed, and another. Then, finally, the anchors pulled out. The exterior became a public embarrassment; the postapocalyptic interior became a destination for urban explorers, skateboarders, graffiti painters, ruin-porn photographers, and other, darker souls. In 2011, a man died of electrocution while trying to steal copper wire. That same year, a serial killer stashed a body in the woods behind the hulking edifice. In 2016, the City of Akron acquired the property through foreclosure and razed most of the structure, but the flattened landscape didn't answer the question of what would become of a place we still called Rolling Acres.

Modern mass-retail commerce can be broken down into three eras: the downtown department stores that represented the boom of American cities in the first half of the twentieth century, the suburban shopping malls that coincided with the outward movement of the middle class, and the online shopping that has exploded in the digital age. Each successor has been blamed for killing off its predecessor, and nostalgia has remained robust for the lost forms. Few scenes are more evocative of midwestern romanticism than the Parker family's visit to the holiday department-store window displays (where Ralphie first spies that coveted "official Red Ryder, carbine action, 200-shot, range model air rifle, with a compass in the stock and this thing that tells time") in *A Christmas Story,* which, though set in a fictional Indiana town, was filmed at downtown Cleveland's Higbee's department store. That nostalgia fueled a certain derision for the suburban mall, which in turn is now warmly sentimentalized (see: *Stranger Things*), with new blame placed on Amazon's uber-dominance of American mass retail.

But here's where the story finds its next strange twist. Over the past few years, Amazon has begun buying up dead American malls and repurposing the properties as "fulfillment centers," strategically placed warehouses that help the online retailer get packages quickly to customers. The vast size of the mall properties and their proximity to either population centers or highways make them uniquely attractive for this new use. And Ohio has found itself at the epicenter of this strategy. In 2019, Amazon was in the midst of an aggressive move to buy up dead malls. Ohio, with its abundance of failed retail properties, relatively cheap real estate, a transportation infrastructure that was built to the hilt during the manufacturing heyday, and a nationally central location, had a lot to offer.

A 2019 analysis by CBRE, a real estate research firm, showed twenty-four projects nationally since 2016 in which former retail space had been converted to "industrial/logistics space"—facilities like the Amazon warehouses. Of those, seven were clustered around the Great Lakes, and four were in Ohio. In 2016, Amazon did not appear on the list of the one hundred largest employers in Ohio. By 2019, it had rocketed to No. 25 with a bullet, employing 11,500 in the Buckeye State, up from 6,000 in 2017 and 7,700 in 2018. Two of Amazon's newest facilities were built on the site of former shopping malls in the Greater Cleveland area—Randall Park Mall in North Randall and Euclid Square Mall in Euclid. It was impossible to observe the trend and not recognize how Rolling Acres might fit the pattern.

Euclid, Ohio, is a sturdy inner-ring suburb of some fifty thousand people, spitting distance from Cleveland, with a low skyline anchored by machine shops and warehouses and workaday office buildings. People here are employed mainly in manufacturing and health care. The population is 60 percent African American, aging, and has been shrinking steadily since 1980. It used to boast a popular lakeside amusement park, the site of which is now a city park with a gorgeous view of Lake Erie at sunset. Its best-known natives are towel-chewing basketball coaching legend Jerry "Tark the Shark" Tarkanian and third-generation Kiss drummer Eric Singer. The city is the namesake of the Euclid Beach Band, which in the 1970s produced a regional novelty hit, "There's No Surf in Cleveland," whose Brian Wilson–esque harmonies played an ironic counterpoint to the song's "we'll make do with what we've got" sensibility, embracing the sort of polluted humor that has helped the region through its hard times. (In fact, there *is* surf in Cleveland, but Lake Erie's waves only get big enough to ride in the winter, just before the water freezes, annually drawing a handful of dedicated, wet-suited surfboarders who ride in hardcore defiance of the Beach Boys' easy warmth, and this is pretty much all you need to know about how we get by.)

The city's municipal complex is neatly centralized, with City Hall and the police department and the public library all clustered in a tight formation of buildings that also includes the "Polka/ Softball Hall of Fame," the combination of which is also pretty much all you need to know about how we get by.

This is where I met Jonathan Holody, who became Euclid's director of planning and development just about the time Euclid Square Mall was reaching the danger point between oblivion and possible salvation.

Holody was born about forty-five minutes south of here, in the picturesque New England–style village of Peninsula, nestled in the Cuyahoga Valley National Park. His hometown has capitalized on its relationship to its environment, fostering a tourism industry via its proximity to the park system, its scenic railroad, its historic buildings, and the like. This, in part, is what led Holody toward his interest in the role and welfare of American—and particularly Ohio's—cities. He earned his bachelor's degree at Ohio University, then continued to Cleveland State University for a master's in urban planning, design, and development. A question persists in this part of the country regarding people like Holody—talented, well-educated, young, and with the mobility to move to a place that faces fewer challenges and offers more glamour and opportunity than Euclid, or more broadly Ohio, or even more broadly the Rust Belt region, which candidate Trump in a 2016 Ohio speech decried as "rusting and rotting," an invective that stung then and that few of us have forgotten.

Holody had remained committed to his hometown, serving as board chairman of the Peninsula Foundation, which "preserves the heritage and vitality of the Village of Peninsula, Ohio and the Cuyahoga Valley through education, music, and ownership of over 20 historic properties." But that's a more obviously easy task than steering the well-being of Euclid. Then again, it's easier to surf in Malibu than Cleveland, but people still do. Holody said he sees his job as making Euclid a place people feel good about living in.

When he began his job here in 2013, he knew that Euclid Square Mall was in steep decline, and that its condition and fate—in one direction or the other—would be yoked to the civic identity. Maybe not completely, but certainly prominently, Euclid would be seen internally and externally as either the place with the dead mall or the place that figured out a solution. In 2013, the major retail tenants had departed and the space was transitioning to churches and what Holody termed marginal tenants—an auction house, a truck driving school. It was privately owned, but publicly perceived. The city had a stake in its welfare.

"I think it definitely was a visual eyesore, and it was an indication that things had changed," Holody said. "Even though maybe I understood that retail has changed, it doesn't feel good to have that right in your community. There was a weight on the public."

People around Euclid knew that the diminished mall meant the incremental loss of upward of a thousand jobs. These weren't the kinds of jobs that are lost when a factory closes, and their trickling away didn't carry the kind of bomb-blast impact of GM suddenly deep-sixing a major production facility. Instead, they represented the kind of erosion that can grind a place down.

Holody recognized the decline of Euclid Square Mall as part of a trend, one borne more of regional migration patterns than the evolution of retail habits. Ohio has more dead malls than other places, he said, because people have moved away from the places where the malls were built. And new people have not moved in to replace them. Twenty years ago, regional planners already recognized an excess of retail space, and folks like Holody have been working to address the inevitable abandonment, which in Euclid Square's case occurred in 2016. That year, the city's building inspector and fire department evaluated the property and condemned it as a hazard. It was vacated and sat empty for two years. In addition to the stigma of desertion, the city lost property tax revenue, this coming on top of the lost income tax revenue that the retail jobs had once provided. Holody, still relatively new in the job, eyed the property carefully. He knew the 642,528-square-foot property was being marketed by an industrial land broker. "That was encouraging, because that had been my thinking all along," he said. The property was across the street from an industrial park, and its potential echoed that of other successful transformations in the region. Soon, the magic word was being whispered around town:

Amazon.

There was a time not so long ago when it seemed all but certain that the internet, with its newfangled electronic mail and virtual paperwork, would replace our old letter-writing society and put the US Postal Service out of business. Now that seems laughable, as our mail carriers arrive more often than ever, with stacks of online-ordered packages, their delivery vans even cruising neighborhoods on Sundays to ensure fulfillment of Amazon two-day delivery.

The paper industry, too, was presumed to be doomed by these new forms of communication and literature, with newspapers migrating online, tablet readers replacing bound books, and websites supplanting pamphlets and brochures. American paper mills were reducing production or closing altogether in the early twenty-first century, creating serious economic voids, especially in Wisconsin, the nation's leading paper-producing state, where small towns rose and fell on its fortunes. And then came Amazon and its e-commerce brethren, packing cardboard boxes as fast as they could and firing them out to all of us former mall shoppers. A 2019 *New York Times* feature (which, for the record, I read online) told the story of a 128-year-old small-town Wisconsin paper mill slated for closing in 2017, only to be revived at the eleventh hour by shifting production from white paper to brown, to supply the material used for cardboard boxes. Since 2014, the *Times* reported, "e-commerce has fueled demand for billions more square feet of cardboard."

Amazon, so often derided as a new kind of despotic corporate overlord, has its imprint all over these unexpected, welcome revivals. With its emergent trend toward reclaiming dead mall spaces, replacing blighted real estate with shiny new facilities, and creating hundreds of jobs to help make up for the ones lost when all those stores closed, the complexity of Amazon's cultural role is increasing along with its economic might, especially across the Great Lakes region.

As work neared completion on the Euclid Square property in 2019, Amazon's growing interest in Ohio had many wondering if Rolling Acres, with all its open space and excellent highway access, might be next. For months, the rumor swirled around Akron that the online giant would be building its next fulfillment center here, even as the company and city leaders refused to comment. A cloak-and-dagger intrigue carried on for months. An *Akron Beacon Journal* reporter got hold of a classified set of blueprints for something cryptically dubbed "Project Carney," identifying the old mall site as an "Amazon World Wide Real Estate Transaction." Its construction timeline of late 2019 through early 2020 was described in an accompanying document as "subject to change but…directionally correct." Amazon, as it had with other such projects, maintained absolute secrecy. When asked at a public appearance if Akron would be landing the Amazon facility, Mayor Dan Horrigan coyly smiled and said he'd answer by quoting the title of his favorite Oasis album: "Definitely maybe."

With Amazon interested in the Euclid Square property, local leaders lined up support. Euclid made clear that if the project was right, it would change zoning to allow an industrial use. The city offered a property tax abatement and assistance in permitting and hiring. City administration worked with Amazon to raise about $1 million in government money for roadway work, most from the state, and the rest from the county. The regional transit authority suggested extending a bus line that would reach nearly to the facility's front door, giving Amazon a nice perk to offer workers, and making it more possible for those without cars—perhaps those who need it most—the hope of landing a job in the new facility.

The deal was struck. Amazon would build a three-level, 1.7-million-square-foot facility and was committed to hiring a thousand full-time, year-round workers, with the likelihood of seasonal expansion during the holidays. The construction followed closely on the heels of the October 2018 opening of Amazon's North Randall fulfillment center on the site of the demolished Randall Park Mall, a 2.3-million-square-foot facility that employed two thousand people year-round.

"I think it's a phenomenal thing," Holody told me. "I think it's tremendous that we're recycling land, instead of going out to a farm and taking that land. And we're keeping the jobs closer to the people who could use a job like this."

The facility opened in late 2019 with two thousand new employees, double the initial estimate. Holody said public response to the project was overwhelmingly positive. In addition to the question of the mall's fate finally being answered, residents recognized that their housing values would improve, that more of their neighbors would be working, always a key concern in places like this. People even inferred (probably incorrectly) that they might get their Amazon packages more quickly with the warehouse right up the road.

Johnny Joo remembers running young and with abandon through the old mall, Rolling Acres, when it was at its most confused, its concourse a free-for-all where his friends cruised and kick-flipped on skateboards as he photographed the ruins—the leaking sky-light and dead fountains and an untended centerpiece display once known as "The Court of the Twelve Trees"—while meanwhile JCPenney shoppers gazed from the other side of the portal, that strange thin opening between the dead place and the still-operating appendage of a department store.

He was a kid at the dawn of the twenty-first century in a part of Ohio that perpetually raised the question of whether this was a place beyond salvation or a place worthy of being saved. He wasn't asking those questions yet. He was just a teenager with a Myspace page, a camera, and a high school art-class assignment that led him into an abandoned farmhouse. What he found there—evidence of a life that no longer existed, a story of its own—led toward a growing consumption to see and understand places other people were trying not to look at or think about. The more he explored, the more he recognized the abundance of decay around him. Nature retaking the built environment, edifices of success that had backslid into failure. From his home in Mentor, at the edge of Lake Erie, he began entering and photographing abandoned places around Ohio and the surrounding region—Mike Tyson's decadent, deserted mansion in Southington, Ohio; collapsing greenhouses and barns; Cleveland's blighted Victoreen factory; a forlorn amusement park; and the growing number of dead malls. He started a blog, then began compiling and self-publishing books of his work. In the process, he became one of the last people to walk through the corridors of the Euclid Square, Randall Park, and Rolling Acres malls.

At the same time Amazon was establishing its foothold on the reclaimed ground of Ohio's shopping malls, Joo was approaching age thirty, growing in his understanding of what all this meant, and preparing to release his fifth book, *Ohio's Forgotten History (Part 1)*, whose parenthetical addendum implies the story is unfinished and whose pages included many images of the malls in their final stages before the next phase had begun. A snow-covered escalator, a darkened concourse littered with fallen ceiling tiles, the rows of empty red seats in a shopping mall movie theater.

For all the impactful emptiness of the images, Joo's greater imperative has been reclaiming the stories of the life that once existed in the same spaces, the people and their relationship to their places. As a child of the nineties, he was thrilled to realize that, technically, *SpongeBob SquarePants* wouldn't exist without that Victoreen factory, which produced most of the equipment used in the Cold War–era Bikini Atoll undersea nuclear tests, whose post-atomic seascape inspired "Bikini Bottom," the fictional spawning ground of SpongeBob and his crew. More to the point, his photographs have led him to connect the past to the present and help inform the future. To tell the story beyond the frames of his pictures.

"Younger people now have nostalgia for stuff we didn't experience," he told me in 2019. Inside the malls and other locations, he felt like part of a lost generation, trying to re-create its context from within the psychedelic diorama in which a woman peers through a hole in the wall of a department store into a shadowy corridor of caged-off storefronts and finds the lens of his camera looking back, each of them as quizzical as the other.

He looks at his photos of Randall Park, once the biggest mall in America, now reclaimed by Amazon, and he wonders whether the lesson of history will take hold. In a YouTube spoken-word commentary titled "Our Future," he talks of empires and future building as he walks through the ruins that have become his work: "As a community we will someday have to explain to future generations that this was once part of a big dream, but that was as far as it ever got—a dream, denied."

"We need to see what we did wrong," he told me.

I asked him about our political moment, about how all this fit in. He pondered his answer for a long time before saying the question felt too big, too distant, lost in our talk of history and a decision that was then more than a year away, finally offering this: "I would like the exact opposite of what we have now."

On July 22, 2019, after long months of secrecy and speculation, Amazon confirmed that it would indeed be building a seven-hundred-thousand-square-foot fulfillment center on the footprint of the old Rolling Acres Mall, bringing fifteen hundred new jobs to the site of colossal blight. *Business Insider* magazine's headline that day referred to Rolling Acres as "America's most infamous abandoned mall"; in a news conference, Mayor Horrigan called the new facility "the single largest job-creating project we have undertaken in a generation." Even though the announcement was expected, the reversal of fortune felt immediately spectacular. The city was abuzz. New roadways were already under construction to handle the anticipated increase in truck traffic; the old mall site was fenced in, yellow construction vehicles at the ready.

The new jobs would pay $15 an hour plus good health care and benefits, with hiring and the facility's opening anticipated in late 2020. On the same day as the Akron announcement, Amazon also revealed a new facility to be built in the Toledo suburb of Rossford, bringing another thousand jobs. Amazon said it had invested more than $5 billion in Ohio since it began doing business in the state. Between those new jobs and a hiring surge amid the online buying spree during the 2020 pandemic, the total number of what the company calls "Amazonians" in Ohio would approach twenty thousand, making it the state's eleventh-largest employer.

In the so-called Rust Belt states of Ohio, Wisconsin, Michigan, and Pennsylvania, certain aspects of the culture are consistent and certain messages resonate. One of those was Trump's drumbeat of 2016, his insistence that he would revive our factories and bring back the good-paying manufacturing jobs of the past, the same jobs that begat the American middle class, which begat the shopping malls, which now are turning the tale in a new direction.

So far, in Ohio, those factory jobs were not returning, and in fact the ones we had were continuing to migrate elsewhere, often out of the country entirely. Plenty of concessions were made by our cities to complete the Amazon deals, but the fact is that our communities—Euclid, North Randall, Akron—found a new sense of agency, a way to stave off the stigma of public failure while at the same time bringing new jobs, new construction, and new relevance to places where such things are not taken for granted.

To see it now is to see the way a big American narrative pushes forward, to see the grand pattern that human experience—itself a daily chaos—craves. I've often described the postindustrial Midwest as the place where we call things by what they used to be. These new buildings have Amazon's name on their fronts, but I can guarantee that in Akron we'll still be calling it "Rolling Acres" for a long time. We remember.

Whether Amazon is the right answer to the old mall's long-looming question is not really the point. It is *an* answer, which always means a new question, and that's enough to go on.

9

WORKING THE LAND

I drove the length of Northwest Ohio's Great Lakes Plains on a mid-June Friday in 2019, passing mile after flat mile of patchwork green-on-brown, the ordered landscape eerily vacant under a rare sunny sky, one that yet again would boil up with rain by day's end. Again. The rain. Not a farmer in sight, no tractors patrolling the fields, no pickups cruising the access roads. Pools of water, some big as ponds, shimmered darkly in the middle of the muddy terrain, some fields seeded and prayed over, others left frustratingly untilled. All the farmers could do in those long weeks was tinker in their barns amid the idle scent of diesel and seed, or sit at the kitchen table with another cup of coffee, maybe paging through the *Farm and Dairy* for a spot of good news or scanning the long-term forecast for any final hope. The few workable days had been precious and exhausting, all hands on deck, predawn till after dark, frantically planting seeds and shoots into the mud, hoping they wouldn't drown.

In 2019, when farmers in Ohio said they wanted to drain the swamp, they weren't talking about Washington. They were talking about their land. But they *were* talking about Washington, too,

145

throughout that agonizing, sodden spring and summer, as the historic rains coincided with a trade war with China that was killing their business, meetings far away from the carefully worked plains that sustained them and far beyond the control of these families, many of whom had tended the same land for generations, each of which had angled to endure challenges that change every year, but never cease.

Arranging to meet with a farmer in times like that was a squirrely proposition, often requiring last-minute phone calls to see what the morning forecast might hold. I called Jerry Suter, a produce farmer in Putnam County, an old acquaintance I wanted to reconnect with that year, a man whose good sense I trusted, to get his take on the state of our nation when much of what I consider good sense seemed twisted and dismissed. We'd arranged for me to make the 150-mile trek to visit him on a late-spring day, but when I checked in the evening before, he said the morning promised a narrow break in the weather and he was sorry, but he needed that day desperately, and could we put it off?

"Sure," I said. "When do you think we can reschedule?"

"Winter?" he suggested.

So, I would try back in November when, we both hoped, he'd have made it through another set of seasons. Each farmer's year is calibrated uniquely on established patterns that perpetually shift within themselves, the way children all look generally alike from a distance but exhibit their own quirks and variations when examined individually. And this farmer's year, in Ohio and beyond, was every bit the problem child.

A few weeks later I set out for Delaware, in central Ohio. The radio weather forecast, as had been the case for weeks, was framed by agricultural concerns. *More rain coming,* the announcer said; *still no hope for Ohio's farmers.* As I left the northern cities behind me, navigating south and west, the terrain flattened and the vista grew longer. The character of Ohio's surface geography and the qualities of its soil owe mainly to events of the past two million years, as the slow grind of mile-thick Pleistocene Ice Age glaciers advanced from Canada to the state's southern border. Their passage flattened most of the state, ending at the unglaciated Appalachian Plateau, whose choppy hills and hollows form a rugged ridge along the state's southeastern edge. The massive glacial melt resulted in the Great Lakes—inland oceans, really—the largest cluster of freshwater lakes on the planet, containing more than 20 percent of the Earth's fresh water. The fourth-largest of these, Lake Erie, defines Ohio's northern border as well as much of its aesthetic and lore. The eastern and southern borders are just as prominently girdled by the Ohio River, itself a product of the glaciers. Much of Ohio's economic and cultural fate was determined by those massive, unfathomable ice formations. Lake Erie and the Ohio River offered transportation routes and power-generation resources vital to our early industry, in addition to substantial, lucrative recreational enterprises. Sand, gravel, and clay deposited by the glaciers provided raw materials for concrete, pottery, bricks, and other products. And the Ice Age graded the lowlands, leaving abundant groundwater and the rich, thick soil that defines the Great Lakes Plains across the state's northwestern edge and the Till Plains that sweep across much of its western half, where Ohio feathers into the true Midwest. This land has been farmed since the pre-Columbian Adena people planted sunflowers and squash; its fields and pastures defined the first century of our statehood as profoundly as smokestacks and assembly lines defined the second.

Soybeans most of all, but also corn, winter wheat, berries, tomatoes, and greenhouse plants, remain important components of the state's economy, as do poultry, cattle, and hogs. According to the Ohio Soybean Council, there are twenty-six thousand soybean farmers in Ohio, with the state ranking sixth in the nation in soybean production, creating an annual economic impact of $5.3 billion. The Ohio secretary of state's website has Ohio ranked first nationally in the production of swiss cheese, second in eggs, and third in tomatoes and pumpkins.

And yet, knowing all this, it's still an adjustment for a life-long dweller of the citified north to cross the imaginary line into another of the "five Ohios." This land is corporeally different, as are the human traditions, questions, and concerns. There are more than seventy-five thousand working farms in Ohio, nearly all of them run by families and individuals who share an intense pride in independence and utilitarianism and perseverance. There's no question all this rain was causing despair, but there's also no question that these families would fight their way through, as they always had before.

As I continued down I-71, the sky in all directions was laundry-white and wrinkled with gray. I passed Grandpa's Cheesebarn, a regional landmark whose name, I would hope, begs no further explanation (it involves a grandpa and a barn and a lot of cheese), and this is where one can feel almost in the loins the trace of those glaciers, the way they scraped the high ground and filled the low, creating a sublime averageness of terrain, an effect so deft that Ohio's highest point, Campbell Hill, is in the exact middle of the Till Plains and feels not *high* but rather *whole,* the attuned center of a vast plane, where Ohio finds a oneness of elevation that I'm sure a farmer could express in far more functional terms than these.

There on the highway, a hundred miles from the Mahoning Valley, I passed a car whose driver's door advertised an audiology center and whose rear quarter panel bore a message spelled with stick-on letters: SUPPORTING THE LORDSTOWN GENERAL MOTOR'S PLANT. More than three months after the assembly line shut-down, no new promise had come for the facility's revival. Families continued to despair, with many of the idled workers uprooting from Ohio to start over at another GM plant, the local economy struggling through the loss of spending power, and the initial national attention fading even if the gravity of the plight was not. Across Ohio, people were feeling the effects of forces beyond their control, and that feeling was not good.

I approached the town of Delaware on a state route flanked by broad stretches of fields bordered at the far ends by tree lines, a few dancing with yellow wheat, others stamped with a low, deep green, but many distinguished only by the same broad pools of water I'd seen previously in the northern farmlands. I'd recently heard about a desperate farmer who imprudently tried to plant his crops, only to bury his tractor up to the axles in a field too muddy to accommodate its rescue and there it sat in full view, a metal beacon of caution. The US Department of Agriculture had just reported that by mid-June only 50 percent of Ohio's corn crop had been planted, and much of that far later than normal; a year before at the same time, 96 percent of the crop was in the ground. Never before had Ohio's corn gone in so late. The state's usual yield—three-plus million acres of corn—could be slashed by as much as half.

It's impossible not to be fixated on such concerns in Delaware County, where virtually everything in the landscape is informed by its agricultural use—the rocket-topped silver silos, the neat, low brick houses set near the road so as not to occupy more land than necessary, the HORSE XING sign, the grain elevator along-side the railroad tracks, the street names: Buttermilk Hill Road, Milo Street.

I eased up the gravel driveway toward a metal-sided barn, the headquarters of Bret Davis Seed, the namesake of the man I was there to see. He'd recently sold the company, along with its adjacent farmhouse, to a young couple just getting started in the agriculture business. Selling the seed business didn't make him any less busy. Davis, a sixth-generation family farmer, maintained thirty-five hundred acres with his stepson, Wade McAfee, and also served as secretary of the American Soybean Association and a board member of the Ohio Soybean Association. In fields stretching beyond the visible horizon of the flat landscape, Davis Farms plants soybeans, corn, and winter wheat, with a significant amount of the yield sold overseas.

The inside of the barn was dominated by a large piece of equipment, a seed conveyor, offset by pallets stacked with seed corn. A workbench was backed by a corkboard with a series of charts identifying the contents of various bins, its surface bare save for a box of shop towels and an open case of duct tape rolls. Bret Davis arrived dressed for a meeting he'd attend later in the day with the state soybean council, khakis and a blue plaid shirt, no need for boots and jeans on a day when the fields would again have to wait. Sporting a neatly trimmed white beard and an easy smile, he offered a meaty handshake and a seat at the small conference table inside the barn's office. One thing about Ohio—talking about the weather is never the lame icebreaker it's perceived to be in other places. Here, in a region of meteorological curiosities and extremes—a state where half the city of Xenia, occupying land known to the Shawnee Indians as "the place of the devil wind," was infamously leveled by a 1974 F5 tornado—it's often the most fascinating topic available.

So, I'd barely finished my opening question before Davis's head began nodding in affirmation.

"I've never seen anything like this before. Ever," he said. "I've had people in their nineties talk about 1947 being like this, but me as a farmer—I've never seen anything like this. We've had record rainfalls for ten months; really it started back in October. We had trouble getting crops out last fall."

At that point, he said, he felt fortunate that he and his stepson had "mudded in" 90 percent of his corn crop and 80 percent of his beans, noting, "the things that we planted, we shouldn't have been there." Already, 20 percent of that planting had been lost to flooding, and what remained was not growing.

Many farmers hampered by heavy rain were turning to a vital emergency resource—crop insurance, which covers losses from "prevented planting." Along with the historic precipitation, experts were predicting record insurance payouts. The money is a kind of life support, enough to pay the bills, but no more, and only increases the anxiety-tinged hope that the following year would be better. You can't bank on optimism, but you can't farm without it.

"So it's a little bit of a desperate year this year," Davis continued in what may have been the understatement of the season, extending that word—*desperate*—spontaneously and seamlessly into the topic of equal concern, the tariffs that China was charging American exporters in retaliation for President Trump's imposition of tariffs on Chinese goods. China is the world's largest buyer of soybeans and until 2018 accounted for about a third of American farmers' business.

"We've spent forty years building this relationship with the Chinese," Davis said. "They've been our best customer; we've given them exactly what they want. In fact, I have a group of Chinese that come here every year, that are traders that physically go out in my fields and look at the soybeans to see what kind of crop we're going to have. So we've developed a great relationship with them."

As a result of tariffs, Davis said, only about 5 percent of the American soybean crop from 2018 ended up in China.

American farmers were already weakened by a low-profit year when the rain and the unresolved negotiations dragged them down further, like twin cement blocks tied to their ankles. As the trade war

continued, the nation's growers were saddled with both the continued high cost of the tariffs (Trump claimed, falsely, that this burden
was borne by China) and the fact that China had turned to suppliers
from other countries. Even if a deal was reached, it might be too late
for American farmers to regain their most important customer.

And then there was the third prong of this scepter—the
government bailout. President Trump had already made subsidy
payments to farmers to help cover the losses suffered in the trade
war and had promised another round of relief for this year's crops.
But a farmer can only be reimbursed for crops that went into the
fields, and with all the rain, many farmers in Ohio and across
the Midwest had only managed to get a small percentage of their
acreage planted, if that. No seeds in the ground would mean no
relief payment. And even that—the bailout, which amounted to a
welfare check—struck directly at the self-reliance that is the very
bedrock of the American farmer.

"We don't want the payment," Davis said. "It's denigrating. You
feel awful taking it...we don't want that."

The necessary mind-set of the farmer could be described as
pragmatic optimism, a belief that things will turn out, but an
instinct to leave nothing to chance. It's no mistake that farmers
buy duct tape in bulk. They're used to fixing things on their own.
And so this spring was a deep test of will, a season in which nature
and government, two forces entirely out of their control, dictated
their fate, day after day after day, betraying the constant lookout
for a ray of hope.

"You can't control anything. It's a completely lost feeling," Davis
said. "We're farmers; we can do everything right that's under our
control. But it used to be the weather that predicted what kind
of crop we're going to have. Now the weather predicts and also
politics predicts where we can sell it and where we can't sell it. So
the Ohio farmer is very frustrated right now."

Heavy rains in 2018 meant that many farmers barely scraped by, only compounding the effects of 2019.

"It's devastating, because you just made it through a crop last year, and now you're sitting here with basically no income for another year. You talk about the psyche of a farmer—this is one of the most depressing times that I've seen."

Trade talks with China had dragged on for weeks. Davis, in his advocacy role with the American Soybean Association, engaged with state and national leaders, speaking for farmers whose lives are so busy that they need someone like him to convey their concerns, to make them understood. Davis figured he spent about half his time in that role, the rest back on the farm. In 2018, he met with federal lawmakers to champion the cause of crop insurance and other measures to protect farmers from bad years like this one; the resulting farm bill, which he described as "workable," indicated that Washington had listened. But in a more recent trip to the nation's capital, "we were assured that we were *this* close," he said, holding his thick thumb and forefinger an inch apart. "We told them, 'Get it done. Get something done. This is serious out here. We can't work on the unknown.'"

By late spring, farmers across the country who'd been squeezed nearly dry by the tariffs thought that promise would finally bring a resolution, reopening the market they hoped would still be there for them. And then "*this* close" moved again. Talks broke off and, said Davis, "farmers' stomachs dropped out."

When I asked him if he believed the president understood his situation, if he thought he was truly working in the farmers' best interest, Davis smiled and answered slowly.

"I believe people in his cabinet understand the situation."

He had met with US Secretary of Agriculture Sonny Perdue and trusted him enough to keep his faith that the ultimate strategy was sound. Short-term, though?

Davis quoted a farmer friend he'd recently talked to, who was resigned to taking the long view necessary for survival in a vocation that can't afford pessimism: "He said, 'I'm just about done with this year. Let's worry about next year.'"

A farmer has to keep two minds at all times, balancing the daily urgency of the work with the long game. It can be easy to become consumed by the moment—a sick calf, a rare sunny day that triggers a marathon session in the fields, a blown hydraulic line—and lose sight of the yearslong planning that keeps an operation on track. The perpetually repeated process of watching a seedling grow by tiny increments to a full-grown plant certainly seems like good training for that duality. So does the farmer's unique notion of time, the way a family farm's longevity is measured in generations and the day's length is measured by its labor. Says Davis, "We don't work in hours. We work in acres." A career, too, is calculated by the length of a life. Farmers don't retire.

The land that Bret Davis and Wade McAfee tend now was first planted by Davis's ancestors after they migrated from Wales in the nineteenth century. Each generation has carried it forward, watching for the right traits to emerge in a son or daughter who seems like the likeliest one to step next into the role. Bret, who grew up on the farm and had never lived more than a half mile from the spot where we sat talking, took easily to the sensibilities and rhythms of what was then about five hundred acres farmed by his father, Everett Davis, and an uncle. The farm then was a mishmash of livestock and crops, an operation whose bottom line was augmented by his father's side business building storage bins and selling them to his fellow farmers. Bret participated in 4-H and Future Farmers of America activities, and by the time he finished high school, he knew how he wanted to spend the rest of his life. Even so, he came to recognize the privilege and responsibility associated with succession; more than once in our conversation, he said not that he made the decision but rather that his dad and uncle "allowed me to come into it." They had to be sure that he was not only capable but also committed for a lifetime, and committed to the understanding that he in turn needed to identify and groom the next generation. That as much as anything explains the deeply personal pride farmers take in their vocation and the reason they're willing to persevere even in years as difficult as this. It is their blood.

Davis described his father as a micromanager, someone who did everything himself and therefore maintained an operation whose scale was limited to his personal capacity. Farming, for him, was more a way of life than a business. His workday started at five a.m. and ended after dark, seven days a week. Bret bypassed higher education—but takes pride in the college-level math skills and the general hard-knocks lessons the farm has taught him—and began working alongside his father and uncle. As he took over the operation, his longer view of the business led to the acquisition of more land and a more streamlined set of crops. Though he didn't attend college, he has kept up a constant education on new methods of growing and selling; early in his career, he studied agronomy and became a certified crop consultant. He gleefully showed me an app on his smartphone—a map of Davis Farms with all the fields labeled and pinned, allowing him to tap any one of them and view information on its current conditions, its history of crop yields, and the like. But for all his tech-savviness, his executive acumen and industry organization leadership, he maintained the pure, dirt-level pragmatism that, for instance, leads him to scoff at buying a sixty-dollar pair of Levi's when he can just as easily get muddy in a no-name pair of ten-dollar jeans from Target.

Davis and his wife, Janie, raised a blended family of seven children. Plenty to choose from, but he watched carefully over the years to sense which, if any, might be right to bring into the fold. It was his stepson Wade, who, although he didn't move to the farm till age ten, connected with the lifestyle and who also, as he matured, exhibited a talent for management, which eventually allowed Davis the flexibility to travel to the state and national capitals, advocating for his people. Meanwhile, as he neared age sixty, Davis was keeping a close eye on the grandchildren, looking for the traits he knew would be needed, just like all the fathers and grandfathers before him.

The long view and the short view. Never were they needed more than this year, when all perspective was strained and jumbled.

The corn, in blatant mockery of the old rhyme, was not knee-high by the Fourth of July. Ohioans in 2019 were more aware than usual of the travails of agricultural life because of the daily news, and perhaps more attuned to its economic implications as the trade war threatened to raise food prices. Most years, though, most of us don't think much about the farmers or the land; our food, it might seem, is produced in the back room of the supermarket. We don't see the loading dock or think about the trucks that arrive there or where their cargo came from.

But this changes when the local farm markets open. Produce farms are abundant across the Midwest, and that's certainly the case in Ohio, where, I will argue, the best sweet corn in the known universe drops into our reach every midsummer. So when word of the delayed and diminished planting spread across the region, I couldn't help but wonder selfishly how this would impact my family's late-summer dining, when the pleasures of sorting through a farm-market bin of corn still warm from the field can make up for all the snow shoveling and spring road construction and August humidity of the Ohio year. Through the precious weeks of the harvest, Gina and I feast on local corn almost every day. I have a homesick West Coast cousin who annually tries to make it back to Ohio during corn season. My mother used to bite into a fresh ear with such rapture that I believed no greater human pleasure existed. My grandfather, who planted a small crop each summer, would boil a pot of water, head out to the garden, pull an ear and shuck it hurriedly as he jogged back to the house, where he dropped it, still warm from the sun, into the water and ate it as soon as it cooled.

How long in the water? This is a question of literally and figuratively heated debate among those of us from corn country. Three minutes? Five? Six and a half? Cut the heat when the corn goes in, or keep the rolling boil? Sugar in the water? Salt? Or is it better grilled? And if cooked over coals, do you soak it first, or do you peel back the husks and slide butter inside?

And then the eating: Back and forth across the rows, or rolling it in circles as you go? Rotated across a stick of butter? Salt or no salt?

"I think I do a row and then I work sideways," said Douglas Katz, the corn-loving chef-owner of Fire, a farm-to-table restaurant in Cleveland. "I eat, then turn a circle, and that gives me an open spot to go left to right."

These are important cultural questions, no doubt about it. My friend and colleague Jane Snow, a longtime food writer for the *Akron Beacon Journal* who now writes an e-newsletter, *See Jane Cook,* used to go into breaking-news mode each summer on the day the first wagons of local corn rolled in from the fields.

"To me, fresh corn on the cob is the essence of summer," she wrote in her newsletter in July 2019, lamenting the season's low yield. "It would be on my bucket-list last meal. I love it so much that I think I talked Northeast Ohio into making it the symbol of summer, too. A new managing editor imported from Miami once expressed surprise that my 'corn is here' story appeared on the newspaper's front page. On reflection, he decided that in Ohio, the opening of corn season probably was big news."

Katz told me the excitement over the annual corn crop offers an opportunity for people not normally in tune with the land to think about what they're eating and where it comes from in ways that have more to do with ethics than economics. Eating local offers the same personal and political power as shopping at the downtown independent bookshop or being mindful of where your automobile was assembled.

"I think there are so many reasons that's important," he said. "Safety, what you're eating, how it affects your body. I think, too, the networks, the relationships with local food—you're creating a real neighborhood around your needs, providing for ourselves. If every neighborhood had to grow its own food, we would be more sustainable."

The corn did arrive. In late July, Gina and I drove out to our favorite farm market in the country and sorted through a big pile of fat, green-husked goodness still in the wagon that had hauled it from the adjacent field, taking home the first half dozen ears of what would be a steady but ever-fleeting haul, savoring the temporary pleasure of summer.

At season's end, a survey of the eight Corn Belt states revealed that Ohio had suffered the worst from the heavy rainfalls, with a yield nearly 20 percent below normal, the worst harvest in more than a decade.

The land. The water. The question of progress. When Ohio's native people occupied this space, nature dictated the direction of their lives. The street I live on is called Portage Path because it traces the route the Indians took when they carried their canoes overland, portaging the eight miles between the Cuyahoga and the Tuscarawas Rivers, a path that predated even them, forged initially by wildlife treading the same course. The Cuyahoga gets its name from the Mohawk Indians, derived from a word meaning "crooked river."

At the same time Ohio's farmers were fighting nature in mid-2019, environmentalists and others were commemorating one of the state's lowest moments, the fiftieth anniversary of the Cuyahoga's notorious conflagration. On June 22, 1969, the chemically contaminated river caught fire. It wasn't the first time, nor the worst. But this instance was reported on by *Time* magazine and coincided with growing environmental awareness, enough to spark the beginning of change.

During the industrial age, the many urban rivers, which initially had been an attractive resource, were reduced to industrial sewers, all manner of poison and trash dumped into their waters. The Cuyahoga, tracing along Northeast Ohio's industrial valley, was the worst of all, identified as the most polluted river in America. A long stretch between the cities of Akron and Cleveland was so fouled that no animal life existed there. Along Cleveland's industrial Flats, the final passage before the river vomited itself into Lake Erie, factory workers described rats the size of dogs floating dead in the blackish flow; those who worked in its vicinity were warned to seek immediate medical attention should they ever fall into its water.

The river was a doglegged oddity from its very Ice Age–carved inception, the "crooked" part referring to its trajectory as it flows southward eighty-four miles from the state's uppermost edge until it arrives in Akron, where it makes an abrupt hairpin back north, returning to Lake Erie. As a native of Akron, it's hard not to be insulted by this harsh retreat.

It might be ugly, but it's ours, and its postfire legacy goes a long way to explain the ethos of a place that has embraced its hard times as a matter of face-saving and acknowledgment that, for a while there, we didn't really have much else *to* embrace.

The embarrassment of the river coincides with the beginning of the end of the state's industrial heyday. The Cuyahoga became a national punch line, and not just the river, but everything that extended from it: ultimately, *us*. We were the punch line. Randy Newman wrote a song, "Burn On," in which "the Cuyahoga River goes smokin' through my dreams." R.E.M. took a turn with "Cuyahoga," a mournful lament for the human manipulation of nature that ends, "We'll burn the river down." But one thing downtrodden survivors learn is how to take ownership of the insults. The reason Clevelanders have such a sharp and dark humor is because they've perfected their habit of delivering the punch line before someone else has the chance to. So as the river—a poster child for the Clean Water Act and a significant factor in the formation of the Environmental Protection Agency—was slowly brought back to life, a generation found a sort of bluesy poetry in its struggle and disrepute. The godfather of Cleveland's heralded craft brewing culture, Great Lakes Brewing Company, produces a popular Burning River Pale Ale. In Northeast Ohio, "Burning River" is the name of a coffeehouse, a guitar repair shop, a kayak rental, and a hundred-mile endurance run.

Fifty years after its most humiliating event, the river was being celebrated in 2019 as a triumph of environmental intervention; simultaneous with the anniversary, the EPA declared that fish from the Cuyahoga were finally safe for human consumption again. During the commemoration events (which included a paddleboard race called "Blazing Paddles"), a conservancy group arranged for a flaming torch to be carried the entire length of the Cuyahoga, lit amid Native American ceremonial blessings at the headwaters and undergoing an Olympic-style series of handoffs as it made its journey to the river's mouth, where it was extinguished.

Seven months later, the Trump administration cut deeply into the Clean Water Act, dramatically reducing the number of waterways that received EPA protections, allowing pollution to flow without regulation, a move that alarmed environmental scientists, the EPA's own advisers, and the advocates and volunteers who'd worked so hard to repair our harm.

As much as anything else, the awareness represented by the half-century saga of the Cuyahoga River's abuse and restoration was a reminder of how disconnected modern Americans are from the same natural forces and resources that formed and sustain and enrich us. The question of humanity's role in climate change was rising in scientific urgency and the national consciousness, and it was certain to be a topic as the presidential election drew nearer. A United Nations report released in 2019 warned that a million plant and animal species were at risk of extinction as a result of human activity, more than at any other point in our human existence and potentially threatening the survival of our own species. President Trump, meanwhile, routinely dismissed widely accepted scientific findings about climate change and our human role in it, at one point tweeting, "The whole climate crisis is not only Fake News, it's Fake Science." But as rain continued to pound farm fields and the rest of the Midwest at a historic rate—the twelve months from June 2018 through May 2019 were the wettest on record in Ohio—many wondered if the increased precipitation was a result of global warming and rising sea levels, while others pointed out the effects of man-made infrastructure that inhibits absorption and natural runoff patterns.

I was reminded of another wild Ohio summer, that of 2006, when a wicked storm, not officially identified as a tornado, but close enough, ripped through the middle of the state. Its path of widespread damage included Malabar Farm, which had been established some sixty years earlier by its owner, Louis Bromfield, as a sort of experiment in conservation and environmentalism. I knew enough about his philosophy and his work there to wonder how well his ecological foresight had held up to this onslaught of wind and rain. I traveled there on a July day, passing through a state park littered with the jagged yellow trunks of snapped-off trees, vistas ripped through the forest by the gusts, fields flooded, and roadside ditches ravaged by water and debris that had rushed through. When I arrived a few days after the storm and first surveyed the grounds of the farm, now managed as a state park in Richland County near the city of Mansfield, I saw snapped and uprooted trees, torn-off roofs, and roads and fields that had been overwhelmed by rainwater rivers. But for all that, and considering what I'd seen in the landscape leading to the farm, I was most struck by how minimal the damage appeared to be.

Why didn't the ground squish underfoot? Why were those vast cornfields still standing tall? How was the place already reopened to visitors? The answer could be traced in the legacy of a man who'd died fifty years before.

Louis Bromfield was born in 1896 on a farm not far from Malabar. He studied agriculture at Cornell University, then went on to a distinguished literary career. His third novel, *Early Autumn,* won the 1926 Pulitzer Prize; several of his books were made into successful Hollywood films. (The title of his most famous novel—*The Rains Came*—carried an unfortunate echo on that summer day in the twenty-first century.) But Bromfield was drawn back to his beginnings and in 1938 reestablished himself in Ohio on Malabar Farm, where he immersed himself in the study of agriculture. He wrote extensively about conservation and farming with environmental sensitivity, and he used his nine hundred acres as a testing ground for organic gardening, soil conservation, and other techniques that respected and responded to the land, rather than trying to force it to conform to human will. The farm was an extension of his intellect, and vice versa. He didn't completely leave Hollywood behind, however. His friends Humphrey Bogart and Lauren Bacall were married at Malabar in 1945.

The landscape I toured fifty years after Bromfield's death in many ways proved not just his theories but also the importance of ecology, and not just to farmers but also to human progress and survival. His fields employed the technique of "contour plowing," in which furrows follow the profile of the land rather than running in straight lines. The result, evident in the post-storm landscape, was greatly reduced soil runoff. As I stood at the center of the farm and looked around its perimeter, I could see how the strategically planted woods created a windbreak. Malabar Farm lost about fifty trees in the storm, but the thousands still standing protected the crops and livestock. And Bromfield had created a series of sediment ponds, which helped control erosion. Even when I found myself at the lowest point in the vast landscape, where I might have expected to encounter a temporary lake, the ground was dry, thanks to a man-made wetland whose informational sign explained WETLANDS PREVENT FLOODING BY HOLDING WATER LIKE A SPONGE.

As I made my way back up a gravel road, passing uprooted trees and splintered limbs, I came upon a small cemetery where one section of white picket fence had been knocked over in the storm. Inside was a small handful of gravestones, including those of Louis Bromfield and his wife, Mary Appleton Bromfield. The inscriptions seemed to confirm the deep understanding of this land that now held them, and read almost as a prophesy.

On hers, a quote from the biblical book Song of Solomon: "Many waters cannot quench love, neither can the floods drown it."

And on his, a quote from William Cullen Bryant: "To him who in the love of nature holds communion with her visible forms, she speaks a various language."

*   *   *

The first Democratic presidential primary debates were televised a week after my visit to Bret Davis's farm. I watched and, probably like most people, I listened to the voices of those twenty early candidates for evidence of someone who seemed to understand me, my concerns and best hopes, and I wondered if that was even possible. In Ohio, where laid-off autoworkers were feeling burned for believing the promise of a manufacturing boom, and where despairing farmers were still waiting for a trade deal they'd been told was "this close," and where women were reeling from the recent passage of a "heartbeat bill" that aligned our state with Georgia and Alabama as standard-bearers for increasingly restrictive abortion laws, and where people scavenging a living wage by working two or three jobs were frustrated by boasts of low unemployment, the question of who understood us—who understands *me?*—was momentous.

For his part, Davis felt alienated by a message of prosperity measured primarily by stock market and employment statistics, one that failed to account for the nuance and disparity of many Americans' situations.

"Here we are struggling while the rest of the economy is growing," he told me.

Davis voted for Donald Trump in 2016, as did most farmers. An October 2016 poll commissioned by Agri-Pulse Communications and the American Farm Bureau Federation showed 55.4 percent of respondents favoring Trump, with Hillary Clinton coming in a distant second, at 17.8 percent. Ohio led all the states identified as "battlegrounds" in that poll, with 68 percent of farmers supporting the eventual winner. Delaware County, where Davis and many others farm, voted 55.6 percent for Trump, with Clinton receiving 39.5 percent of the vote.

"I believe the reason farmers voted for Mr. Trump is he's a businessman, he's not a politician, and so he approaches problems differently," Davis said. "And in the same way the farmer is a businessman and we look at a problem and—let's fix it, let's not just talk about it."

Although some farmers had become pointedly outspoken about their change of heart as they suffered massive financial losses due to the unsuccessful tariff war, Davis said he believed most still backed Trump. With more than a year before the next election, he wasn't ready to commit to anyone. Regarding Trump, he said, "He hasn't soured me. But he hasn't earned it. He's doing what needs to be done; I don't know if he can accomplish it."

Davis, seated in an office surrounded by reminders of the hands-on nature of his livelihood—a tractor battery on a work-bench, a framed DEKALB Quality Seed Corn sack serving as a wall decoration, a pair of Duluth Trading work pants slung across a chair—was hard-pressed to name a politician who he thought really understands the American farmer. Most, he said, have never been in the real world, and whatever their message might be, once they get into office, their main job becomes getting reelected. Some have visited his farm. He tries to educate them, hosting "farm-to-fork" dinners where guests are served food grown on the same land where they sat enjoying it, as he tries to reinforce awareness of where our products come from and who makes them. When I asked if any president in his lifetime stood out as pro-farmer, he thought a long time before finally answering in the negative. The worst, he said, invoking the 1980 grain embargo, was Jimmy Carter—a farmer.

So, it's easy to understand why he spends so much of his precious time advocating for a profession that, like all family businesses and vocations tied to generational succession, goes well beyond the bottom line. More than once that day, Davis repeated his motivation: longevity.

"The reason I farm is not for me, or my stepson, who's my

partner. It's for my grandkids that can be the partner and keep this going as a generational farm. We're very proud of what we're able to attain, and we work hard towards keeping it going."

One might not expect a Republican farmer and a Democratic union leader to arrive at the same bottom line, but that's exactly what I found when, at different times and under very different circumstances, I asked Bret Davis and David Green, Lordstown's local UAW president, the same question—what they would want our presidential candidates to understand about them. Their answers were identical: be aware of where your products come from and support the American way of life when you choose what to buy.

"The consumer today in America has the most expendable income. We don't think about where it was made," Davis said, later adding, "I would like them to understand, inside the belt of DC, what it takes to grow the food they consume and appreciate what the normal businessman does out here, whether it's run a comics shop or a farm. It still comes down to what you put into it is what you get out of it. You don't go live on somebody else's money."

A politician might be able to understand the business side, but only the words of a farmer can really explain why they do what they do, despite it all.

"It's to plant that seed and understand what it takes to grow that seed and to see it blossom every year. One thing was told to me about ten years ago and it stuck with me: a farmer usually has forty to fifty years to plant a perfect crop. And it's what *you* do to make it a perfect crop. That's your reward for this. That crop of beans is your Academy Award."

His perfect crop, he told me, had come just last season, a beautiful yield of soybeans harvested just months before, an experienced farmer's triumph over the daunting trials of nature and one whose hope would have to carry him through.

10

THE DRUMBEAT OF THE
DEMAGOGUE

He was a bullying populist outsider with a bird's-nest comb-over and a blunt, spontaneous rhetorical style, adversarial with the Washington establishment (he told the FBI to "go fuck yourself" and called the IRS "a bunch of political prostitutes"), dogged by legal probes throughout his years in office, hostile to the media yet a master of using it, a man at odds with his own party but supported by a deeply loyal base that confounded convention.

When Donald Trump emerged as a presidential contender, folks around Ohio looked at one another with a shared, uncanny sense of déjà vu. We'd seen this guy before. His name was Jim Traficant. I don't think anyone around here thought we'd ever see the likes of him again. But as soon as Trump arrived, everything—from the hair to the locker-room talk—took us straight back to the man we called Jimbo.

Aside from the circumstances of his birth—Traficant was the lowborn son of a truck driver; Trump was, well, not—the Ohio congressman's unlikely rise and his fierce popularity, especially among people who felt left out of the American equation, shed a lot of light on the Trump phenomenon. As an October 2016 *USA*

Today headline put it, "If Trump wins Ohio, he should thank Jim Traficant, who wrote the roadmap." Other headline writers cast the two as "soulmates" and "twins." Although Trump was a Republican candidate and Traficant ran as a Democrat, the Venn diagram of their supporters has a very large overlapping center. When I asked Eric Murphy, who coproduced and directed a Traficant documentary, where I might find some of Traficant's old groupies, he suggested going to an Ohio Trump rally. "You will probably see folks still wearing the Traficant shirts or buttons," he said.

Traficant was born into a working-class Youngstown family in 1941. A star quarterback at his Catholic high school, he won a football scholarship to the nearby University of Pittsburgh, where he was a teammate of hard-nosed, eventual NFL legend Mike Ditka. Upon graduation, Traficant was selected in the late rounds of the 1963 NFL draft by the Pittsburgh Steelers. He tried out for both the Steelers and the Oakland Raiders, an appropriate candidate for two of the most notoriously bare-knuckled teams of the era, but didn't catch on with either and instead returned to college and earned master's degrees in administration from Pitt and in counseling from Youngstown State University. In his early career, he lectured at colleges and public agencies on drug and alcohol addiction, eventually becoming executive director of the Mahoning County Drug Program.

His political career, as well as his larger-than-life mystique, began in 1981, when he bucked the Democratic Party establishment, which refused to back his candidacy, and was elected Mahoning County sheriff. Youngstown, equidistant between Cleveland and Pittsburgh, was in both the grip and the cross fire of mafia families in both cities. The remarkable influence of the mob is detailed in Murphy's captivating film *Traficant: The Congressman of Crimetown*. The documentary was released in 2015, coinciding with Trump's ascendancy and drawing immediate parallels to the contemporary political moment, with a marketing blurb that began, "Before Trump or Bernie, Congressman Jim Traficant was the original bombastic populist."

In a video clip from the era, the Mahoning County Democratic Party boss declares outright, "Everybody takes money from the mob." All the way back in 1963, the *Saturday Evening Post* had profiled Youngstown as "Crimetown, USA," a variation on the city's other nickname, "Murdertown, USA," and its waning designation as "Steeltown, USA," a reputation now preserved only as the title of a book about the tragedy of deindustrialization. The hitmen's weapon of choice—the car bomb—is still referred to in local colloquy as a "Youngstown tune-up." Interviewed for the documentary, former mayor Pat Ungaro describes the nuances of a political system totally intermeshed with mob influence: "Money came my way, yeah," he says, "I seen $50,000 thrown on a pool table."

Traficant, the unequivocal outsider, came swaggering into the middle of all this, sometimes wearing a cowboy hat atop his outlandishly unstylish bell-bottomed suits and skinny ties, pointing his umbrella like a gun, firing threats northward toward Cleveland and southward toward Pittsburgh, calling out the ruling mob families by name. At the same time, he made headlines for refusing to serve foreclosure papers to families in a region where regular folks had been economically decimated by the collapse of its defining profession—steelmaking. He was charismatic and particularly skilled at tossing off one-liners and sound bites, sometimes sounding like Dirty Harry, sometimes, Robin Hood, a heroic paradox: the sheriff who urged local judges to suspend all sheriff's sales and who refused to be a party to their service. This refusal prevented the county from collecting unpaid taxes but saved down-and-out residents from forfeiting their homes. There was a political brilliance in positioning himself as the foe of the establishment—the partisan machine, the mafia puppeteers, the legal system—while simultaneously endearing himself to the masses as the champion of the downtrodden, an adjective of identity that applied to just about everyone else in the region. For his refusal to carry out sheriff's sales, Traficant was convicted on ten contempt-of-court charges and sentenced to ten days in jail for each case. The news footage of him being booked into his own county jail and his continued statements from within its walls—refusing to back down from his choice to protect broken-down people from losing their homes—cemented a bond with his base, the momentum of which would carry him through the next chapters of a political narrative that otherwise can't be explained.

In 1983, an FBI investigation of a mob hit uncovered tape recordings of Traficant in a room with Charles and Orland Carabbia, a.k.a. "Charlie Crab" and "Orlie Crab," brothers in the Cleveland mob family said to control half the gambling racket in the Mahoning Valley. The recordings captured a conversation in which Traficant clearly refers to a quid pro quo, receiving $60,000 from a rival Mafia family and $103,000 from the Carabbias in return for his protection.

"You don't worry about this fuckin' family here," Charlie Crab says. "You be honest with us and you got the strongest mother-fuckers around right here. That's a fact."

"In the area, you can go wherever you want," Orlie interjects.

Charlie continues: "You put this in your mind, and when you go to sleep tonight, don't you worry about this family here."

To which Traficant responds: "We're like family now."

Seemingly caught dead to rights, Traficant handwrote and signed a confession to the FBI. He was brought up on racketeering charges in Cleveland Federal District Court. If convicted, he'd be staring down a possible twenty-three-year prison sentence.

In the face of overwhelming evidence against him, Traficant made a move that seems straight from the "fake news" playbook. Refusing to step down as sheriff, he began a "deny, deny, deny" counter-attack, claiming his signed confession was "a false and fraudulent statement" created by the FBI and that he'd been framed.

The documentary includes archival footage of an interview with local Democratic Party chairman Don Hanni saying, "Y'know, you have to remember that Jim Traficant doesn't always tell the truth, and one of Jim Traficant's styles is to throw confusion into the situation, and then suddenly descend down from the heavens and solve all the confusion."

Prior to the beginning of the trial, Traficant didn't reveal the name of his lawyer. When he arrived at the federal courthouse in Cleveland the morning the hearings were to begin, he was alone. He would be representing himself.

If you live in Ohio, it's easier to understand how people who feel left out, powerless, or abused can become galvanized by a figure who gives them a voice, someone who represents them when it seems no one else will and who uses their shared language to tell them what they want to hear, true or not—even someone who from the outside seems repellant. Ohio, especially its formerly industrial communities, closed ranks in the 1980s as nationally projected images of the burning Cuyahoga River, narratives of political corruption, the "brain drain" outmigration of our youth, the emergence of our Rust Belt persona, and a general habit of being used as a punch line put the state on the defensive. When Traficant arrived on the scene as a congressman, *Washingtonian* magazine fired a cheap shot at both Traficant and the state he represented, describing his notorious hairstyle as "a creature from Lake Erie before it was cleaned up." We were used to such jabs; the more we were marginalized, the stronger we bonded.

Stories of disenfranchised voters gathering in support of Trump echo the way the Mahoning Valley rallied around the maverick

Traficant. His greatest political talent was his ability to convince a marginalized constituency that he understood and cared about them in ways his opponents did not. Ohio congressman Tim Ryan, who began his career as a Traficant aide, recognized the Trump parallels but also asserts a foundational difference.

"Jim Traficant really gave a shit about average people," Ryan told me in 2020. "That was not a show. And he was a showman, no question. But he gave a shit about people. He would have never gotten to be president and then cut taxes for the top 1 percent and for corporations. I think, in his heart, he was in it for the people, and Trump in his heart is not. Trump is in it for Trump."

Traficant's claim of being railroaded by the FBI coupled with a "Traficant vs. the World" message in his decision to act in his own defense played a finely tuned note among his base, his people, one likely not picked up on by the federal prosecutors.

At the opening of the trial, Traficant asked to have the venue moved from Cleveland to Mahoning County, where his hometown, Youngstown, was the county seat. The request was denied, so he then petitioned to have the jury include members brought in from the Youngstown area.

"It's a unique animal," he said of his hometown while being interviewed outside the courthouse, "and in a unique jungle, unique animals function differently."

It worked. When the jury was seated, half of its twelve panelists were from Youngstown. They listened as Traficant began a defense in which he claimed that he'd strategically "impregnated" the mob, gaining their confidence so he could break their power. Accepting the bribe money was part of a sting operation, he said, boasting of his success. He claimed the signed confession was a forgery, that the FBI surveillance tapes had been doctored, that this was all a witch hunt. In his closing remarks, again playing to the Youngstown underdog mentality he understood so well, he told the jury, "Stand firm—like a junkyard dog in the face of a hurricane."

They found him not guilty.

The following year, Traficant ran for Congress as a Democrat against three-time incumbent Republican Lyle Williams. As Murphy's documentary illustrates, Traficant had a habit of positioning himself so that he loomed over Williams, who was a foot shorter, whenever they were together, reminiscent of Trump's prowling presence behind Hillary Clinton during an October 2016 debate, a display of alpha-male body language the British politician Nigel Farage famously praised as the demeanor of "a silverback gorilla."

Traficant won and entered the halls of Congress in January 1985, the only newly elected Democrat to make it through the Ronald Reagan–led Republican tsunami, unhumble and conspicuous. He reveled in his outsider status and loved the political stage, which gave rise to his catchphrase, "Beam me up, Scotty—there's no intelligent life down here," which quickly became a T-shirt slogan back home. To this day, the Youngstown Clothing Company markets a shirt with an illustration of Traficant's signature hairdo framing the words BEAM ME UP.

Blunt and profane, he riled his House colleagues and jousted with reporters, once blurting to a media throng, "Get outta my face, don't bother me, or I'll kick you in the clutch." He was uncouth, sporting that grayish toupee (yes, it was fake) whose sweep across his cranium seemed to defy direction, parted neither left nor right but rather gathered at his crown in a chaotic bouffant, and a garish outmoded wardrobe that led *60 Minutes* to portray him as Washington's "ugly duckling." He spoke crudely in the halls of government, called newscaster Connie Chung "you little TV vixen" during an on-air interview, and baselessly accused Attorney General Janet Reno of having an affair with a call girl. His legal troubles loomed throughout his Washington years—after all, while he'd beaten those racketeering charges, he never denied having accepted all that bribe money. But he met the investigations with defiance, at one point declaring, "The IRS has turned into a bunch of political prostitutes—and I want to apologize to all the hookers of America for having associated them with the IRS."

And he was reelected again and again, eight times over, in landslide after landslide, with margins of 75 or 80 percent.

Meanwhile he fought for those who idolized him, publicly calling out President Bill Clinton to keep a campaign promise to build a defense accounting center in his district, which would create thousands of jobs. When Clinton instead assigned the center to the state capital of Columbus, Traficant attacked him publicly and privately, to the extent that he once had to be physically removed from the presidential limousine by Secret Service agents. He kept pestering until finally Clinton granted millions of dollars to upgrade the district's air force base and built two new federal courthouses in the Valley.

Even as he was easily elected to his ninth term in 2000, the legal heat surrounding him was rising, as was criticism for his increasingly unhinged and erratic behavior. He was decried for his vocal, ongoing support of John Demjanjuk, a retired Ohio autoworker who was involved in a protracted legal battle following his conviction in Israel on charges that he was "Ivan the Terrible," a Nazi guard at a World War II concentration camp. Several of the congressman's hometown associates were accused and arrested for corruption amid a mafia probe, and the trail led closer and closer to Traficant. His congressional colleagues iced him, stripping him of committee assignments. In 2002, he was indicted on ten counts of racketeering, fraud, and bribery and was accused of filing false tax returns as well as forcing aides to work on his Ohio farm and on the houseboat he kept near DC. Again, he chose to act as his own legal counsel, another display of hubris against the urging of his advisers. His mockery of the charges and the ensuing proceedings played out with remarkable similarity to Trump's bold defiance of investigations into his campaign and his 2019 impeachment.

"Most people have trouble with a fly on their face," Traficant said at the time. "I have an elephant eating my ass."

In answer to the charges against him, he pleaded "not guilty by reason of sanity."

As the legal drama grew, the House opened an ethics hearing, during which Traficant behaved like a petulant high school rebel threatened with expulsion, at one point standing up, turning his back to the ethics panel, bending over, flipping up the tails of his sport coat, and thrusting his buttocks toward them.

He was expelled from Congress, the first member to face such punishment since the Civil War, and only the fifth in the nation's history. The vote was 420 to 1. The only no came from California representative Gary Condit, who was at the time embroiled in his own scandal—the unsolved disappearance and death of intern Chandra Levy, thirty years his junior, with whom he'd been carrying on an adulterous affair. Though he was never charged, Condit's vote placed him and Traficant in conspicuous allegiance.

Traficant was convicted on all charges and sentenced to seven years in federal prison. In her sentencing statement, the judge declared, "The truth, sir, is rarely in you....If you repeat a lie enough times, over and over again, some people are going to believe it...and that's the drumbeat of the demagogue."

As Traficant was booked into federal prison, he had to surrender his hairpiece, the first time most of us realized the coif was not his own, prompting Ohio journalist Vince Guerrieri to quip in the documentary, "he *paid* for that hair!" But any suggestion of a Sampson analogy was immediately steamrolled by Traficant, whose first act behind bars was to announce himself as an independent candidate for the congressional seat from which he'd just been expelled.

Traficant was hard to figure, and so was the psychology of those who continued to support him despite behavior that reflected negatively not only on himself but also on them. Ohioans have a hard enough challenge controlling and conveying our story, and some felt a need to correct the impression that we all must be uncouth, loudmouthed small-time crooks. (Traficant's wardrobe did little to squelch the unfortunate term "full Cleveland," used to describe a leisure suit paired with white patent leather belt and shoes.) For a *Washington Post* piece about Traficant's prison-run political campaign, Mark Leibovich interviewed Youngstown *Vindicator* political columnist Bertram de Souza, who said, "He never polls well because no one admits they're going to vote for him." In the same piece, Traficant campaign office manager Carol Tigert explained, "A lot of people are angry at what happened to him. They plan to vote for him to make a statement."

And plenty did. Traficant lost, but the imprisoned candidate still earned 17,294 votes, 15 percent of the total.

The winner of that 2002 race for Ohio's 17th district was the young former Traficant aide and political newcomer Tim Ryan, who seventeen years later would begin his run for president.

Jim Traficant served all seven years of his sentence and returned to something of a hero's welcome in Youngstown, where he resumed public life, speaking at dinner events and club meetings, repeating his old stories, charming the aging fan base that had stayed with him throughout his battles. He was invited to speak at Tea Party events, his antigovernment rants playing to the heart of their philosophy. In 2009, he ran again for his old seat, again as an independent, facing Ryan, whose star was rising in Washington.

He lost, though his vote total was still a noteworthy statement about the loyalty of his base, considering that 29,969 of them—16 percent—cast their lot with an ex-convict who'd been heartily booted from Congress.

After that defeat, he retired to his farm where, in the early autumn of 2014, his tractor rolled over on top of him, asphyxiating him. He never regained consciousness and died four days later. There was no public funeral.

There are a lot of places in America like the Mahoning Valley, where people feel like no one is listening to them, places that have suffered social and economic losses with no apparent way to recover, places that will rally around someone who pays attention to their plight. It happened when Bruce Springsteen wrote a song called "Youngstown" and in return received the key to that city. It happened when Donald Trump came to the Valley and promised to restore the factory jobs that had once defined every aspect of life here, their residue literally seeped into the pores of the populace. Trump began a 2017 rally speech in the Valley by saying, "Tonight I'm back in the center of the American heartland, far away from the Washington swamp, to spend time with thousands of true American patriots." He was rewarded with a resounding cheer.

One of the most dramatic Ohio statistics in the 2016 rise of candidate Trump came in the Mahoning County primary, where more than half the ballots in Trump's eleven-thousand-vote victory were cast by Democrats and Independents who switched their affiliation to Republican. That November, Clinton squeaked past Trump by only 3 percentage points in Mahoning County, which four years before had delivered Barack Obama with 63.5 percent of its vote. Trump beat her handily in neighboring Trumbull County, which hadn't voted for a Republican for president since 1972.

It's been said again and again that Jim Traficant couldn't have happened anywhere else but in the Valley, where people seemed to understand him in a way no one anywhere else did. The truth, and perhaps the warning, is that he could have come from anywhere. Traficant wasn't unique to working-class Ohio. He was an example of what can happen when people feel like no one else will speak for them.

One unintended beneficiary of the Traficant phenomenon was Youngstown's *Vindicator* newspaper, where the man in the toupee and cowboy boots endured for decades as a recurring character in the daily narrative. Columnist de Souza, a critic equal to Traficant's bluster, covered the politician for the entirety of his career. He recognized Traficant's political talent but also recognized—and publicly called out—the danger of someone who operated as a demagogue. In Traficant's district, de Souza was more often than not the lone voice of caution.

In a 2002 profile of de Souza focusing on his contentious journalistic relationship with Traficant, the *American Journalism Review* recounted an incident that occurred at the victory celebration for Traficant's first congressional election in 1984. De Souza was there to cover the acceptance speech.

"A few of Traficant's supporters began screaming at de Souza, which Traficant encouraged by verbally attacking de Souza and the *Vindicator* during his speech," the *AJR*'s Rachel Smolkin wrote. "As de Souza departed, two 'huge oak trees of men' stood in the doorway blocking his path, forcing him to squeeze through to escape."

The attack offers another obvious parallel to Trump, at whose rallies such upbraiding of the press is routine. Traficant's public browbeating of the journalist continued throughout his time in Washington, as did de Souza's watchdogging of both the politician and his unquestioning supporters. When the congressman was convicted on his corruption charges in 2002, the columnist issued a warning to those he knew would still vote for Traficant even as he sat in federal prison. "Traficant is a two-bit criminal who used his public position for personal gain," he wrote.

It seems certain de Souza's warnings informed and influenced at least some of Traficant's constituency. And even if they didn't, his service as a member of the fourth estate achieved the perspective and check on power that democracy crucially needs. The *Vindicator,* with its avenging name, had long stood up to dangerous forces, from its reporting on local Ku Klux Klan activities in the 1920s through its exposure of mafia crime, political corruption, and abuses of corporate power.

Bertram de Souza outlasted Traficant, but the *Vindicator* didn't outlast Trump. On August 31, 2019, after 150 years of publication, the financially struggling newspaper issued its final edition, leaving the city and its surrounding communities without a daily print news source. This continued a troubling trend; since 2005, according to a study by the University of North Carolina's School of Media and Journalism, more than one in five American newspapers have folded, leaving communities across the country in a dangerous void, a lost connection to everything from daily death notices and high school sports scores to local editorials and investigative journalism, the disappearance of a voice and moral compass.

In response to the news of the closing, Tim Ryan, still occupying the House seat once held by Traficant, tweeted,

> The *Vindicator* has been a pillar in our community, and its reporters and staff have always been unwavering in their commitment to truth and transparency. Local newspapers are critical to our democracy. We need to support them.

In his Sunday column that same week, editor Todd Franko acknowledged the friction sometimes caused by the *Vindicator*'s watchdog journalism. "But over the course of a year and a lifetime, it was way more right for the Valley than it was wrong."

11

TRANSLATION

So much of navigating this part of the country requires knowing things by what they used to be. When defining economies disappear, when touchstones are repurposed and gentrification whitewashes old-boned neighborhoods, when the native dialect is lost in exodus, translation becomes necessary.

I thought I knew what I was looking for in Cincinnati, but I didn't know exactly where to find it, or how to recognize it when I did. Cincinnati is one of the most racially complex cities in America. It has been through the kinds of hard times that leave lessons behind, scars and monuments, stories passed down, many of them faded or obscured by evolution. So I thought I knew what I was looking for, but I knew I'd need help.

Among the rocks and weeds of the Ohio River bank, I was looking for the place where the South ends and the North begins, where in 1856 a woman named Margaret Garner crossed over from slavery, escaping to an even darker fate. In the Over-the-Rhine neighborhood, I was looking for the alleyway where in 2001 a black teenager was shot dead by police while trying to pull up his droopy trousers. Among the handsome refurbished town houses on Dayton Street, I was looking for the home of an African American family that transcended its Civil Rights–era expectations and transformed Ohio politics, tucked into a block where that same family couldn't afford to live now.

Toni Morrison died the week I traveled to Cincinnati. She was born in Ohio, up north in the working-class city of Lorain, and while she isn't so often defined as an "Ohio author," her frequent choices of settings in her home state reinforce its unique adaptability to the American story as well as the inextricable importance of any artist's native place to the spirit of her work. Morrison has always been one of my most valued translators, gifting me with her insight into the black American experience, into womanhood and parenthood and poetry as political power. Her 1987 novel *Beloved,* for which she won the Pulitzer Prize, and which vaulted her into the prominence she held for the rest of her career, was based on the real-life story of Margaret Garner, who, along with her husband and their four children, made a harrowing escape from their Kentucky slave owner, crossing the Ohio River to Cincinnati, where they were then led to a safe house. They were soon tracked down by a team of slave catchers and US marshals who rode into Cincinnati on horseback, intent on apprehending them under the Fugitive Slave Act, which mandated that escaped slaves be returned to their owners upon capture. Confronted by her would-be captors and recognizing the renewed inhumanity her children would face, a panicked Garner killed her daughter with a butcher knife and maimed her other children. The question her act raised, and which *Beloved* deepens, is whether there are fates worse than death, whether hers was an act of motherly protection or ungodly transgression. Its darkness and inscrutability mirror the unsettled question of a nation still at odds with the implications of its original sin.

So the place where the Garner family arrived is important not as a matter of literary curiosity—I scoured *Beloved* for an exact location, but couldn't identify one—but rather as the pinpoint of a deep agony, a scar in our landscape that warns us that an imaginary line between bondage and freedom is a false comfort. Cincinnati, once the first stop on the Underground Railroad's northern side, is no more or less free than any other American place.

Thanks to a historical marker on the Kentucky side, I knew where the Garners' final crossing began. In the city of Covington, at the corner of Sixth and Main Streets, a brown plaque with gold lettering begins SLAVE ESCAPE, followed by brief details of the incident. But directly across the river, there is no apparent next point of the passage, no marker. On a quiet, sunny afternoon, I scanned the riverbank from the railing of the John A. Roebling Suspension Bridge, the slow-moving, green-brown water gently rippling below, birds chirping, a distant mower droning across the kempt landscape of Smale Riverfront Park, where families and couples strolled the walkways of a public space nestled between the Reds' Great American Ball Park and the Bengals' Riverfront Stadium. The rocky shoreline was tufted with willowy green weeds and strewn with driftwood. At the river's edge, a man cast a line into the water and settled into a lawn chair to watch the bobber.

But somewhere in this psychic landscape is deep unresolved pain. Nearer the surface is the ghost of a recently dangerous downtown; only two decades earlier, this park had been installed in an effort to recover from a depression of crime and neglect. Follow a straight line from Covington's Sixth and Main, across the river to here, and continue up Vine Street, just over a mile, and there is the alley where that young man was killed. That location, too, is no longer what it was.

So begin at the beginning. Where, precisely, did Margaret Garner arrive?

*   *   *

"She crossed here. *Right* here! It's been vetted."

Carl Westmoreland set his light-brown fingers firmly on the surface of the conference table as though to place the incident within his very reach. The table was in a small meeting room in the research wing of the National Underground Railroad Freedom Center in downtown Cincinnati, overlooking where the Roebling Bridge completes its span from Kentucky to Ohio. Dr. Westmoreland is the museum's senior historian, and he said it's just as important to know the place where the Garners' story enters Ohio as it is to understand that their crossing was not the end of a struggle but the continuation of one.

Look at this building, he told me. They wanted to make it out of marble, smooth and pretty, but he, one of the people consulted on its location and design, resisted. He wrote a letter to the planners expressing his objection. "There's nothing about the black experience that's soft and smooth and nice," he said. And so the exterior is made of rough stone, intercut with raw copper panels that have been allowed to darken and bleed with age and exposure. This was never a permanent stopping place, never safe enough for that, and so its exterior layout includes curving, shadowed pathways, hiding places that open into the next vista.

On the afternoon of our visit, Westmoreland told stories that cascaded one into the next, a long lifetime of unsettled experience. He had lived his eight decades in Cincinnati, whose population of three hundred thousand is 45 percent African American, and whose core identity is itself unsettled. Persistent development and redevelopment have pushed black neighborhoods around like chess pieces. When the route for Interstate 75 was planned in the mid-twentieth century, it cut through the middle of Cincinnati's West End neighborhood, where half the city's African American population lived, resulting in the largest urban-renewal displacement of black residents anywhere in the country. In succeeding decades, other historic neighborhoods with strong architectural bones but little social capital have been gentrified, with new, high rents pushing out the low-income minority residents who'd made their homes there. A 2018 Brookings Institution study placed Cincinnati eighth on a ranking of America's most segregated cities. I saw real-time evidence of this trend in late 2019, where a new Major League Soccer stadium was under construction in the West End, on the site of what had been the Taft High School football stadium. The soccer club, FC Cincinnati, agreed to build a new stadium for the inner-city public school, but the displacement reinforced a prevailing perception, expressed this way by one long-time observer: "if white folks want it, we're screwed."

So whatever Westmoreland's sense of freedom—a complicated word here—he has never allowed it to go unchallenged. He told me about his house, a gracious thirty-five-hundred-square-foot home built in 1812, overlooking the river, in what he described as "the hood," the predominantly black Mount Auburn district, where decades of population decline have given way to major recent investments in new and rehabbed housing, which, if the local pattern holds, will again price black residents of lesser means out of their own neighborhood.

"We're the northernmost southern city in America," Westmoreland told me. "I call it northern Mississippi."

He opened our conversation with a discourse on the Ohio Constitutional Convention of 1802, during which the state's founding document was drafted. It prohibited slavery but afforded no other rights to African American residents, most notably the right to vote. Throughout the document, the state's civilizing principles are drawn in terms of "white male inhabitants, above twenty-one years of age." The Black Codes, limiting the rights of freed slaves, were implicit in the state's formation and, said Westmoreland, "my sons and my grandsons have to live with the Black Codes of Ohio."

The Freedom Center is a three-story educational museum. I had taken a self-guided tour the day before, beginning on the top floor, in a round, darkened room where a hummed rendition of "Amazing Grace" floated from the speakers. Small, softly illuminated glass cases displaying slave-trade artifacts were set into the stone walls: shackles, a whip, a slaver's memoir. The walls bore the names of slave ships: *Amistad, America, Black Boy, Le Fortune.* The tour continued through a series of exhibits documenting plantation life, slavery in other cultures, the Underground Railroad experience, abolition, and other related themes. The institution's centerpiece is a log cabin–style slave pen built in the early nineteenth century on a farm in nearby Mason County, Kentucky, which was painstakingly dismantled and reconstructed on the museum's second floor. The pen, the size of a small garage, housed up to seventy-five humans at a time. Outside the only door, their names, as many as could be verified from the slave owner's ledgers, are listed on a display.

The Freedom Center, with its rough walls and unsettled questions, opened in 2004, built at a cost of $110 million, part of an effort to revitalize a downtown that had, like so many other middle-American urban centers, slipped into neglect, with crime and despair filling the void.

"This place sits in what's called 'Little Africa,'" Westmoreland said. "We were killing each other here."

In its early twenty-first-century revitalization, the city donated the riverbank land between the newly built professional football and baseball stadiums, foregrounded by the public park, also new, with its fountains and walkways, and, Westmoreland said, "we built a modern masterpiece," a point he underscored not by celebrating its place in the skyline but rather by noting its wooden floors, installed by local African American women who were once on welfare and who, he said, leaning back and cackling, "ain't on welfare now. They're in the *union*."

*   *   *

In the early morning hours of April 7, 2001, Timothy Thomas left the apartment of his girlfriend and his infant son to buy cigarettes. On the street, he spotted two Cincinnati police officers who, apparently, had spotted him, too. He was wanted on fourteen non-violent misdemeanor charges, twelve of which were minor traffic violations. He began to run. They began to follow.

Thomas, nineteen years old and black, raced through the streets of his neighborhood, the impoverished, drug-and-crime-infested Over-the-Rhine. The officers pursuing him were joined by a young white patrolman, twenty-six-year-old Stephen Roach. Thomas cut into an alley. Roach followed. Thomas's baggy pants started to slip down his hips. He reached to pull them up. Roach thought he was going for a gun. He shot the teenager in the chest. Thomas died before dawn.

Two days later, two hundred protesters gathered outside Cincinnati's City Hall, where the city council was meeting. Joined by Thomas's mother, Angela Leisure, the group's homemade signs and shouts demanded an explanation for the shooting. Though inflamed by the incident in the nearby alleyway, their protest was driven by larger, ongoing allegations of racial profiling and the fact that in the previous six years, fourteen black men had been killed by local police. Council members remained inside the building, offering nothing. Soon, hundreds more gathered outside the local district police station, where they were held at bay by officers on horseback and in cruisers. Members of the crowd began to throw rocks and bottles at the officers. They smashed the station's glass front door, pulled down its flag. Police used tear gas and rubber bullets to disperse the crowd. The next day, and the day after, and the day after that, protests and violence escalated, with open warfare between residents and police, businesses vandalized, white motorists pulled from their cars and beaten. More than 150 people were arrested over the course of the rioting, which caused an estimated $3.6 million in damage and which culminated in Mayor Charles J. Luken's declaration of a citywide curfew and a state of emergency, the city's riot-geared police forces bolstered by Ohio State Patrol troopers. Another 800 were arrested for violating the curfew.

Timothy Thomas's funeral was held a week after his death. A police helicopter hovered overhead. Riot police were stationed nearby. Some two thousand people marched from the service into downtown, a peaceful demonstration that nonetheless ended with police firing bean bag rounds into the crowd. Later that year, Stephen Roach stood trial for negligent homicide. He was acquitted.

The 2001 Cincinnati riots are among the most notorious in modern America's difficult negotiation of racial tension but are hardly the only ones. Timothy Thomas's death was a tragedy and an outrage, but he is but one in a long line of what can only be called an American "type," an unarmed black man shot by police. But Cincinnati, whose uniquely twisted history of race includes a series of abolition-charged riots in the decades before the Civil War and another round of violence following the 1968 assassination of Dr. Martin Luther King Jr., chose not to leave the raw ends of the Timothy Thomas saga hanging frayed. Its experience ran deep, and local leaders decided to look within for a solution.

In the months following the Thomas incident, as lawsuits were filed against the city and protests continued, Cincinnati's leaders and citizens began to engage in dialogue that led to the formation of a panel representing the city's major constituencies: African American residents, social service and religious organizations, businesses and philanthropic groups, police officers and spouses, city officials, white citizens, other minorities, and youth. Their directive was to listen—more than thirty-five hundred residents participated in interviews and online questionnaires—and to develop a set of goals for improved relations between police and the community. In 2002, this culminated in a "Collaborative Agreement," a federally supervised program detailed in a thirty-three-page court document that stated five goals:

1. Police Officers and Community Members Will Become Pro-active Partners in Community Problem Solving
2. Build Relationships of Respect, Cooperation and Trust Within and Between Police and Communities
3. Improve Education, Oversight, Monitoring, Hiring Practices and Accountability of CPD (Cincinnati Police Department)
4. Ensure Fair, Equitable, and Courteous Treatment for All
5. Create Methods to Establish the Public's Understanding of Police Policies and Procedures and Recognition of Exceptional Service in an Effort to Foster Support for the Police

The agreement resulted in significant, concrete reforms in officer training as well as larger philosophical changes in the relationships between the police force and the citizens it serves. In 2008, court supervision of the agreement ended, but a new guide was enacted to maintain the effort. Cincinnati's Collaborative Agreement has been hailed nationally as a landmark and a model for other communities to follow; city leaders have frequently been invited to other municipalities to share their experience. In 2014, after a white police officer shot and killed an eighteen-year-old African American man, Michael Brown Jr., in Ferguson, Missouri, the founders of the Collaborative Agreement traveled there to hand out copies of the document.

"It really was the best of things that could have come out of the worst of things," Mark Curnutte told me. He spent a quarter century covering minority issues for the *Cincinnati Enquirer,* including the Thomas shooting and its aftermath. A collection of his work, *Across the Color Line: Reporting 25 Years in Black Cincinnati,* was published in 2019, when he left the newspaper to teach full-time at Miami University.

But the Collaborative Agreement was not the end of anything. One thing that Ohio knows deep in its bones is that nothing is ever settled, nothing comes easy, nothing works without constant tending. In 2015, when a white University of Cincinnati police officer shot and killed an unarmed black man, Samuel DuBose, during a routine traffic stop, "those scabs ripped right the hell open," Curnutte said. In 2017, recognizing there was still much work to be done and that some of the principles of the original agreement had faded from prominence, city leaders launched a "refresh" of the document, a process of research and assessment overseen by a citizen advisory group that updated and refined the principles of the agreement.

When Mark Mallory was a kid growing up on Dayton Street in the sixties and seventies, he and his friends would race up and down the streets on their bicycles, stopping at the local pharmacy for a comic book or at the mom-and-pop deli for candy. As with many midwestern inner-city neighborhoods at the time, Dayton Street, in Cincinnati's West End, was something in between. It had been developed originally as a sort of nineteenth-century millionaire's row, its sidewalks lined with handsome brick-and-stone Italianate town houses fronted by wrought-iron fences and stone pillars. But as also was the trend in developing cities, the barons soon moved outward from the stink and soot of the industries that were making them rich. In thriving Cincinnati, known in the 1800s as "Porkopolis," Dayton Street was, quite literally, too close to where the sausage was made. The wealthy moved outward and eventually their homes fell into the hands of humbler classes.

The Mallory family, too, was something in between, an African American clan that knew its share of the struggles faced by minorities, but was also a growing force for edification and change. Mark Mallory's father, William L. Mallory Sr., was elected to the Ohio House of Representatives in 1966 and served for twenty-eight years in the Ohio legislature. When he was elected Majority Floor Leader in 1974, he became the first African American to serve in that capacity; when he retired twenty years later, he had held the post longer than anyone in the state's history. William Mallory made a regular habit of taking young Mark with him to local community meetings and to legislative committee sessions in the state capital of Columbus. But back home, Mark was still a kid on a bicycle who, riding with a group of his neighborhood friends one day, heard the siren of a nearby firetruck.

"We're twelve years old. What are we going to do?" Mallory asked me over coffee one morning, when we'd managed to snag the only open easy chairs amid the busy weekday rush at Coffee Emporium, a café in Over-the-Rhine. Composed and understated, with short-cropped hair and a soul patch, gray suit and open-collared dress shirt, he unclasped his hands, gesturing with the obvious answer. "We're going to follow it, of course."

Off they went, in pursuit of adventure. It wasn't long before their game of chase was halted by a police officer who'd pulled alongside and directed them to stop. He asked what they were doing. We're chasing the firetruck, they said. He asked if they'd pulled a fire alarm. The boys looked at one another. No, they hadn't done that. They were each instructed to put out their hands, which were checked by the officer's flashlight for traces of the luminescent ink released when a fire alarm was pulled. Nothing. They were allowed to leave. But not without consequence.

"I'm twelve years old, and I'm thinking, that's ridiculous," Mallory said.

On he went, to and from the statehouse floor, to and from school, off on his bicycle whenever he could. Riding down the street on another day, he was stopped by a cop. You can't ride on the street, the officer told Mark. You have to ride on the sidewalk.

So Mark directed his wheels to the sidewalk and continued on his way. Before long, another cruiser pulled alongside and the officer inside motioned for him to stop. You can't ride on the sidewalk, he told Mark. You have to ride on the street.

It was incidents like these, small in their own right and certainly not isolated to Cincinnati, that persisted and accumulated in the local psyche, hardening perceptions, limiting perspectives, and leading—seemingly inexorably—to a young white police officer seeing a young black man reach for the waistband of his pants and responding in fear of something not that he saw but rather that he believed.

The burden of Cincinnati's history, its habits and prejudices, exploded in the shooting of Timothy Thomas, with the Collaborative Agreement drawn as a map out of the wreckage and hopefully beyond.

It was from this moment that Mark Mallory emerged as the city's first elected African American mayor, in 2005, just four years after the Thomas shooting. By then, his family had become somewhat of a legend in Ohio politics, with his father's long legacy in the state legislature and the children following his path. Mark was the youngest of five boys who grew up in that house on Dayton Street, where they were accustomed to picking up a ringing telephone and listening to questions and concerns from constituents, a home where they were all groomed for public service. Mark's brothers William Jr. and Dwayne both became municipal court judges; his brother Dale became a state representative for the same district once served by their father, and his brother Joe became vice mayor of the Cincinnati suburb of Forest Park.

But young Mark, bookish and reticent, with a degree in administrative management from the University of Cincinnati and a burgeoning career in the city's public library system, had no plans to run for public office. That was until one of his brothers pulled him aside in the late 1980s.

"We think you should run for Dad's House seat when he retires," Mallory recalled him saying.

"I don't want to. I like my library job," he responded.

"No, you don't understand. We've *decided*."

In the brightly lit coffeehouse, Mallory laughed at the memory. "It was like the mafia!" he said.

So, in 1995, at age thirty-three, he was elected to the Ohio House of Representatives, taking the baton directly from his father. It was one thing to continue the family legacy, but another thing altogether to advance it, to become the first black mayor elected by a city so historically, so deeply, and so recently defined by race.

Despite the successful reception of the Collaborative Agreement, Mallory said, "I still felt something was missing. Too much pride was gone. Not enough forward movement for development."

For a long time, Cincinnati's national image had been pecked at by a series of embarrassments, small and large. A blind pedestrian was charged with jaywalking after being struck by a car. A sixty-two-year-old grandmother was arrested and charged with obstructing official business for feeding expired parking meters ahead of an officer who was issuing tickets. Controversy erupted over an exhibit of Robert Mapplethorpe photographs at the Cincinnati Contemporary Arts Center, whose director, Dennis Barrie, was charged (and later acquitted) on obscenity counts, the first American museum ever to face prosecution for the work it displayed. And, much more heinously, the public spectacle of Cincinnati Reds owner Marge Schott, whose racist comments included referring to two of the team's outfielders as "million-dollar niggers."

"All those things drove me to run for mayor," Mallory said.

The Freedom Center had opened the year before his election, part of an effort to revitalize a gutted central city, but the perception of crime and urban grit, much of it tainted with lingering tensions of race, kept many residents from venturing back toward the riverfront.

"I appealed to people's civic pride," Mallory said. "I told people, come back downtown. To compete with peer cities, we had to be able to attract people."

As mayor, Mallory participated in a series of events called "Downtown Hop Around," in which local celebrities—Mallory, Johnny Bench, Jerry Springer, and others—were stationed at restaurants and bars, where visitors could mingle with them. New energy was coming into "Little Africa." The inner city was changing. Over-the-Rhine, a district of crime, violence, and hopelessness at the turn of the twenty-first century, began its gentrification in earnest following the riots, raising the old difficult questions of progress and its cost, as redevelopment money poured in and poor minorities slunk away to other neighborhoods with rents they could afford. Over-the-Rhine now is peopled by young bicyclists in skinny trousers and exfoliated Caucasians in business suits lifting flutes of prosecco under sidewalk umbrellas, its enchanting nineteenth-century Greek Revival and Italianate façades sandblasted of their old factory soot, patina scrubbed and reskinned, retrofitted with a Vine Street juice bar called Off the Vine, a cheese shop called The Rhined, a women's boutique called The Most Beautiful Thing in the World Is. Its core streets bear no resemblance now to those where Timothy Thomas ran away in the dark, just as his streets then had lost all reference to the neighborhood's original ethnic etymology. Over-the-Rhine derived its name from the bridges over the canal that formed the neighborhood's boundaries. The working-class German immigrants who first settled there in the early nineteenth century were reminded of crossing the Rhine River. Long gone, translator required.

In early 2020, the Ohio Legislative Black Caucus Foundation and the University of Akron Bliss Institute of Applied Politics released the results of a poll of black Ohioans, the first of its kind to focus specifically on the views of the state's African American population. State polls of this demographic are rare in general, according to the Bliss Institute, with surveys of minority voters usually focused nationally. With the information gathered, the state's black caucus hoped to better address the specific concerns of this important voting bloc.

Crime, drugs, and jobs ranked as the most pressing problems on the minds of the fifteen hundred adults who responded. Though the numbers reinforced some common perceptions—75 percent of the respondents agreed that "police officers are deployed in some neighborhoods with more effectiveness than others" and 58 percent agreed that "most black citizens who work hard may not be able to get ahead"—the results offer a complex, nuanced, and sometimes surprising profile of the state's 1.7 million African American residents. Black voters skew decidedly Democratic in Ohio and nationwide; a 2019 Quinnipiac University poll simulating a presidential election between Democrat Joe Biden and Republican Donald Trump showed Biden winning 84 percent of the vote to Trump's 8. Even so, there was an unexpectedly distinct note of conservatism in some areas of the survey, elevating its suggestion that old patterns and assumptions should be set aside, that this is a population to listen to with new ears.

Fifty-four percent of those polled reported experiencing no racial discrimination within the previous year. Fifty-three percent were in favor of a citizen's right to own guns. Seventy-six percent supported protecting a woman's right to choose abortion. Seventy percent believed health insurance should be provided by a mix of public programs and private insurance. Seventy-five percent agreed that "strict environmental laws are worth the cost for better health and quality of life." The majority favored taxpayer funding for both public and private schools and public assistance as a route toward financial independence but also supported smaller state government "providing fewer services but with lower taxes." Finally, and in this context, most importantly, the majority agreed that "voting gives black citizens some say in how government runs things."

In announcing the poll, Barbara Sykes, the black caucus foundation president, said, "We want elected officials and candidates for office to truly understand what black Ohioans are thinking so they can make informed decisions when discussing and formulating policies and programs, or voting on critical issues."

Through all its changes, Cincinnati tells the story of America. Its version of events holds important lessons. Its scars reflect wisdom. As mayor, Mark Mallory, who served until term limits forced him out of office in 2013, continued to teach the Collaborative Agreement's example, visiting other cities to remind leaders and citizens of the danger of forgetting.

Over coffee that morning, I told him about my son, the rookie police officer back home in Akron. I asked Mallory what Evan, a young white cop dispatched to neighborhoods with high crime and high minority populations, should understand.

"There are differences, cultural differences, in how races of people respond to situations," he told me. "Black people are verbal, active. Sometimes their reactions can appear to be more aggressive than they really are."

Mounted police, he continued, draw very different reactions depending on one's cultural experience. The sight of a horse and rider is an exciting novelty to some, a thrill for a small child, but not to others. And though he did not himself hearken to *Beloved,* I was drawn directly back to the moment that triggers Morrison's fictional protagonist, as it triggered Margaret Garner herself, to her terrible dizzying spin into an act of desperation: the sight of four horsemen arriving to retrieve the slave owner's property—her children and her—and take them all the way back to the hell from which they'd fled.

There are primal triggers; there are subtle, vital disconnections. A black teenager instinctively ran from the police, a twenty-six-year-old white cop misunderstood what he thought he saw in the dark, he reacted, and everything changed.

"It takes a while in urban areas to understand," Mallory said.

Months after this conversation, having dinner in Cleveland with my friend Jamaal May, a young black man from Detroit, I relayed this story and asked him the same question: What should my son understand?

He answered without hesitation.

"Assume I'm smarter than you," he said.

From the sidewalk, I had to crane my neck and shield my eyes from the sun, squinting to make out the black letters spray-painted on the weathered brick wall above an air-conditioning unit, crude capitals about two feet high, faded almost to nothing:

R I P

"That's where it happened," Mark Curnutte said, pointing from the graffiti down into the alleyway, then tracing a line in the air to indicate the path that had led Timothy Thomas here.

We tried to find our way closer, but the building was surrounded by black metal fence work with sharply pointed finials at the tops of its pickets. Making our way around the perimeter, we found a gate, locked, with a sign anchored across

its center: THIS BUILDING RESTRICTED TO RESIDENTS. TRESPASS-
ERS WILL BE PROSECUTED. ELITE MANAGEMENT SERVICES.

On Thirteenth Street, less than a block from the alley, Thomas
is memorialized in a more public yet still broken way, but even
here, you need to know what you're seeing. It's an impressionistic
painting of a face on a piece of plywood, peeling at its bottom,
screwed to a metal frame like that of a real estate sign, chained
to a tree on the sidewalk. The russet face, which blooms from the
painting's center like a flower amid splashes of amber and green, is
that of Timothy Thomas.

In 2016, Curnutte brought Thomas's son to see it. Tywon
Thomas was three months old when his father died, sixteen years
old when he and the newspaper reporter approached the board
leaning against the tree. Tywon stood considering the face, then
turned to Curnutte.

"It's weird," he said. "It looks like me."

12

BELLWETHER

Walking from my car toward the metal detectors at the Ohio Renaissance Festival Grounds outside Dayton, I found it impossible not to be aware of the shootings. One week before, just thirty miles away, a twenty-four-year-old man had opened fire in a busy downtown nightclub district, killing nine people, including his own sister, and wounding seventeen before police shot him dead. Less than twenty-four hours earlier, a man had opened fire with an assault rifle at an El Paso, Texas, Walmart, murdering twenty-two people and injuring twenty-five more. So an uneasy vigilance nagged at me and Gina as we joined the line of music festival attendees making their way through the security check. I unshouldered my messenger bag and flipped it open, preparing to hand it over to the young woman in the staff T-shirt, wondering. Would they be more thorough than usual? Was it wrong for me to look around and think that none of these people could do something like that? They were young and loose-limbed, many of them overnight campers, almost all of them bearing the cultural markers of peaceability and nonviolence—dreadlocks, cat-ear headbands, a Twin Shadow T-shirt. These are not the ones to fear, I thought, people who'd chosen to journey deep into the green nowhere of Ohio to attend a weekend-long indie rock music festival. Was it wrong of me to pick up the faint skunk of pot smoke and calculate a hypothetical Venn diagram of music-loving stoners and mass murderers with an empty intersection? Or was it wrong for me to look down the line and think, well, OK, maybe *that* guy . . .

I had planned months before to come to the Bellwether Festival in part for its name, that keyword so often applied to Ohio in a political context, and in part for the opportunity to place one of the headliners, Dayton-based indie rock stalwarts Guided By Voices, into a larger metaphorical context. Mostly, though, I wanted to talk to young people and hear what mattered to them. Then that godforsaken kid cut loose with his semiautomatic and it had been impossible to think about anything else. Rolling down the highway toward western Ohio, I'd seen flags at half-staff. At a rest stop, a Dayton Strong T-shirt. News of the events and the investigations and the victims' lost lives and the controversy surrounding President Trump's visit to Dayton had topped each day's newspaper headlines and led all the radio and TV broadcasts.

Another thing nagged at me, too, something I couldn't quite put words to until months later when Democratic primary candidate Cory Booker bemoaned a national "crisis of empathy," urging Americans not to wait till a mass shooting hits close to home before demanding action. It was true that at some level of consciousness, I conceived of the Dayton shootings as "my" event, in the same way El Paso native Beto O'Rourke had simultaneously taken personal stake in the Texas massacre and more broadly the way parents of young schoolchildren had their own version of terror and concern after the Sandy Hook Elementary School shootings in 2012. I'd cared before, of course. But I cared differently now.

Still, it was hard on this day, in this place, with Gina at my side, if not to embrace the optimism and imagination of the scene before me, at least to acknowledge its paradox. Early on a Saturday afternoon, the August sky was pure blue innocence, temperature in the eighties, an easy breeze. The festival grounds, styled for Renaissance fairs rather than rock festivals, were laid out like a high-concept enclave of pre-Elizabethan whimsy, an amusement park for nerds. The entrance was styled like a medieval castle, a long parapet wall punctuated with stucco turrets whose cone-shaped tops were capped with wood shakes and anachronistic Olde World flags. Gina and I passed through the archways onto a gravel path that led into the sprawling, tree-shaded property, with open green meadows and shop-lined walkways bearing names like Troll Crossing and Minstrel's Grove. The first person we encountered was a woman standing at the beginning of a wooden bridge, wearing a bosomy peasant dress and a templer atop her frizzy blond hair, offering a basket of flowers for sale.

The clientele, meanwhile, was decidedly nonfeudal, drawn not by the promise of lutes and tambourines but rather by hipster staples like Beach House, STRFKR, Real Estate, and Cake. Nonetheless, many of the regular shops were open for business, Tudoresque huts and cottages selling handcrafted leather items and gypsy dresses and blown glass, in stubbornly flamboyant contrast to the more conventional festival vendors set up for the weekend in their trailers and tents—Swisher Sweets, Sparkling Ice, State Farm. We spotted a kid at a picnic table gnawing on a big, greasy, brown Henry VIII turkey leg as we made our way from the main Sunset Stage to the smaller Shipwreck Stage, elaborately styled as a Hollywood back-lot pirate ship, with the quarterdeck extending from the left side of the stage and the bow and mast jutting from the right.

We'd made it only halfway across the meadow, though, before being stopped in our tracks by the sight of two men on horse-back charging violently toward one another, one dressed as ZZ

Top's Billy Gibbons, the other as Sir Elton John, each holding a shield and jousting lance. His long beard bouncing in rhythm with his steed, Billy Gibbons made a violent jab at the shield of the Rocket Man, a loud crack splintering the end of the wooden lance. A thick-bearded ring announcer in brown leather pants and long dark ringlets described the action, emphasizing the "Sir" in Elton John's name. After a few more thundering passes, the Rock and Roll Hall of Fame doppelgangers dropped from their mounts, took up swords, and started swinging, sparks flying as their blades connected with a loud clang. Watching from the stage behind them were the two jousters who'd already been eliminated—Gene Simmons and Angus Young—and the reigning "Rock 'n' Roll Joust" champion who awaited the outcome to see who he'd be taking on later in the evening: Freddy Mercury, calmly perched on a throne.

You hardly ever see this at Bonnaroo.

Despite all the aggressive novelty, however, the Bellwether/Renaissance pairing isn't Ohio's only incongruous, high-concept rock-festival mash-up. It shares the annual entertainment calendar with the Inkerceration Festival, a three-day affair that brings heavy metal acts and tattoo artists to the Mansfield Reformatory, a decommissioned prison best known as the setting for *The Shawshank Redemption*. Patrons at Inkerceration 2019 could book an ink session with one of sixty-five guest tattoo artists and roam between two stages featuring a total of thirty-four bands, including Godsmack, Shinedown, and Five Finger Death Punch.

To be in a crowded public space just days after assault rifle bullets tore through unsuspecting bodies is to feel your own flesh, to be aware of your body and the bodies around you, in an involuntarily self-conscious way. Where would I run to? Would I throw myself over Gina? Who are these strangers? Could we today become something together that would define us collectively forever? Or would we go on, forget? Is safety a delusion?

Gina and I remarked on the obvious police presence—after the flower-peddling damsel, the next person we saw was a cop—both of us continuing in our new awareness of their purpose by way of our son's new position, aware of their role—his role—in this dangerous time, and also their own flesh, what the body armor covers and what it does not, and what it would mean to have to pull their own gun. Police in Dayton had been right there in the nightclub district, reacting almost in the instant, shooting the attacker dead thirty-two seconds after he'd opened fire, all of it a blur of instinct and reaction. Then what?

Within the fantastical construct of the medieval staging, the usual humanity of a large musical gathering played out. Groups of friends sat tightly together in whatever patches of shade they could find, beneath trees and the corners of awnings. Couples held hands as they staked out their territory before the stages. Overnighters from the adjoining campgrounds took makeshift showers in the misting tents. A man in skinny black jeans dozed in the middle of a crowd, fedora covering his face, T-shirt riding up to reveal his bare abdomen as Black Moth Super Rainbow pumped electronic beats through the air.

In addition to the main and secondary stages, the festival featured a smaller stage for acoustic sets. Over the festival's two days, twenty-four acts would play, in addition to DJ sets and yoga sessions and the escalating rounds of the "Rock 'n' Roll Joust" and food trucks and tents and postconcert movies at a makeshift outdoor theater: *Wayne's World* on Friday and *The Hangover* on Saturday. There was no center. There was no single target. There was no target at all, or there was no end to them. Everything and everyone were everywhere.

The people I talked to at the Bellwether Festival were uniformly saddened and angered by the recent shootings. My questions were as obvious as their answers, so much that it almost seemed not worth talking about, even though it was at the front of all our minds, the specter of what had just happened right up Highway 35, the choice to come here nonetheless. Most I spoke with were from relatively nearby—Dayton, Cincinnati, Indianapolis, and Northern Kentucky. There was an almost universal ambivalence: yes, people said, they'd thought about it, but no, it hadn't deterred their plans, but yes, they cared and they wanted change—a dynamism of reaction to something that, as one man lamented with bitter syllabic emphasis, "just. keeps. happening."

I spent a long time talking to a group of four friends who'd traveled up from Lexington, Kentucky. Carolyn Spears said that the Dayton shootings had come up in conversation during the two-and-a-half-hour drive, because how could it not, "but we don't live our lives in—I mean, it's there, but we can't let it stop us from living."

Her friend Matt Little cut in: "The fear is there. But *fuck* the fear."

Carolyn smiled, remembering something that had come up in that highway conversation.

"You know you're an adult living in 2019 when you want the police to actually search your car."

The conversation turned to the next presidential election, and the group asked what I thought was going to happen. I told them that after months of listening to so many people in so many different situations, I was less inclined than ever to extrapolate any sort of generality from the experience of any single individual. But I couldn't help being aware that whenever I talked to a Trump supporter, that person's own certainty convinced me at least for the duration of the dialogue that he would win a second term, and whenever I talked to anti-Trump Ohioans, they expressed concern that I was right, even as they couldn't conceive this happening again. To know people who voted for Donald Trump and not to be able to comprehend how anyone could do such a thing is to confront the fact of our divide: a nation of people who cannot understand one another and who are losing reasons and opportunities to do so. A "crisis of empathy." But I never got into this trying to handicap a political game. I just wanted to know what people cared about. And when I asked these three men and one woman, all around thirty, their answers maintained a kind of optimism and idealism that can't be overlooked, even in such cynical, divisive times.

"What would you want to tell a presidential candidate, regardless of who it is?" I asked them.

"That every person is the same. We're all people," Carolyn said.

"Compassion," Matt said. "You can just write that one word."

Two days earlier, Tim Ryan, still in the race for the Democratic nomination and working in tandem with the group Moms Demand Action, led a caravan through the state, beginning in his Northeast Ohio congressional district and stopping in cities along the way—Cuyahoga Falls, Westerville, Dayton, and Cincinnati—before arriving at his destination: the Louisville, Kentucky, doorstep of Senate Republican leader Mitch McConnell. Since the Dayton shootings, Ryan had been a vocal agitator for action, challenging McConnell's resistance to gun background-check legislation, calling for him to "get off your ass, and get something done." His Louisville rally drew hundreds of people, many hoisting protest signs as Ryan declared the country had reached a "stage of outrage."

The day after the shootings, Ohio governor Mike DeWine had traveled to Dayton to address a crowd of mourners gathered in the Oregon District, the neighborhood of restaurants and bars where the massacre had occurred. As he spoke, a man named Bob Mendenhall, co-owner of two establishments in the district, spontaneously mouthed three syllables that immediately took hold as a chant and then a rallying cry: "Do something!"

In the midst of all this, Ohio was at times, and as usual, played as a flyover political pawn. Insult was added to injury when President Trump, two days after the Dayton shootings, declared, "May God bless the memory of those who perished in Toledo."

Dayton mayor Nan Whaley responded sarcastically, "All these Ohio cities look alike."

Democratic hopeful Joe Biden, meanwhile, made a reference in a campaign speech to the mass shootings in "Houston and Michigan," though he did correct himself afterward.

The frustration of not being heard was raw and urgent. The plea to "do something" cut straight through the chaos and posturing; its drum kept on beating. Mayor Whaley immediately took center stage, emerging as an eloquent, heroic voice not just for the victims and her community but also for a growing American populace fed up with repeated inaction in the wake of serial gun massacres. DeWine, urged on by Whaley, seemed to take the directive to heart. Within forty-eight hours of his visit, the Republican, a former state attorney general, announced a package of proposals to address gun violence. The centerpiece was a "red flag" law, which would allow guns to be seized from anyone deemed by the court to be a threat to him- or herself or others. He also proposed expanded background checks on gun sales, including at gun shows and in private transactions between individuals. Within weeks, he took additional action, creating an Ohio School Safety Center that would provide resources to help schools, law enforcement, parents, and others in "preventing, preparing for, and reacting to violence," and launching a program to use state and national databases to strengthen background checks on gun buyers and sellers.

As the year advanced, however, DeWine's initiatives were buffeted by gun control groups saying they didn't go far enough and gun rights advocates saying they went too far. His quick initial response slowed in the muck of legislative gridlock; 2019 ended with virtually no action by the state general assembly. Meanwhile, a database compiled by the Associated Press, *USA Today,* and Northeastern University revealed that more mass killings had occurred in the United States in 2019 than in any other year going back at least to the 1970s. There were forty-one mass killings, defined by having four or more victims, including thirty-three mass shootings, with more than 210 total victims.

"Bellwether" is a tricky bit of verbiage. People often misinterpret its second half as "weather," as though the term is about which way the wind blows, a forecast, which it sort of is, but not exactly.

The *Oxford English Dictionary* offers three definitions:

1. *The leading sheep of a flock, on whose neck a bell is hung.*
2. *A chief or leader. (Mostly contemptuous.)*
3. *a. A clamorous person, one ready to give mouth. b. (Used opprobriously.)*

Various other lexical sources vacillate between connotations of enlightened leadership and less noble implications of piloting a sheeplike crowd.

When applied to Ohio, though, the word morphs into something considerably different—not deliberate leadership, but rather an inherent, unstudied imaging of the nation. So, though Ohio isn't, in this context, a "leader," primarily because few outsiders would perceive us as such, the state does tend to be a leading indicator. Bellwether Ohio can tell us where we're already heading in ways we may not have recognized otherwise. Ohio's other *B* word, *battleground,* derives partly from this bellwether tendency. Because the state has almost always correctly chosen the presidential winner, it is quadrennially considered to be in play. Ohio doesn't decide the winner so much as it appeals as a delicious geographical morsel to anyone who wants to win, because it could always go one way or the other, and because if a candidate appeals to Ohioans, he or she probably appeals to most regular folks. The eighteen electoral votes don't hurt, either. (Ohio: It's delicious and nutritious.)

Ohio's Bellwether Festival, though, has its own take on the word, seizing on its implications of change and optimism.

"It's the hope for something good to happen in the future," Elise Donabedian said, squinting under the bright sun as she paused near the VIP area with her two young sons, Soren and Kieran. She knew the direct genesis of the name because her husband, Bill Donabedian, founded the festival, which debuted in 2018. A musician and concert promoter from the Cincinnati area, he had made his reputation with the success of other such events, including the Bunbury and Midpoint festivals in Ohio. That led to the Ohio Renaissance Festival organizers reaching out to ask him to develop this event on their grounds. Donabedian told an interviewer for Cincinnati TV station WCPO that he'd come up with the Bellwether name several years before, intending to invoke the avant-garde spirit of an Andy Warhol festival in Pittsburgh that never panned out. He registered the domain name nevertheless, and pulled it back out for Ohio.

"I love that word and what it stood for—that idea of being just a little bit ahead of everything," he said.

His wife said the name fit this event because Bellwether is something new for the Midwest, a boutique indie rock festival with a Bonnaroo vibe—the three concert stages augmented by camping and nonmusical activities such as morning yoga, an axe-throwing booth, comedy acts, and a "Dark Carnival Maze."

I asked Elise if she and her husband had safety concerns after the Dayton shootings. She said she didn't, first citing confidence in the festival security, then her personal philosophy: "We can't allow ourselves to live in fear."

When I asked her the question I asked everybody—what she wanted the candidates to know about her—she answered without hesitation.

"We want to be free to make our own choices. We're libertarian; we want the government out of our lives as much as possible."

"And what do you want for them?" I asked, nodding toward her two sons standing at her side.

"I raise them to think for themselves," she said.

"Hey, check it out, kids. We make three albums a year. You know why?"

Robert Pollard cockily bobbed from side to side at the center of the main stage, the only band member not wearing sunglasses against the late-afternoon slant of daylight, head held erect, squinting defiantly and holding the microphone left-handed to his mouth, elbow jutting outward, the right fingers lifting its cord loosely, almost elegantly, Prospero in sneakers, gesticulating an air of command that is the one true constant of one of the unlikeliest forces in the history of American rock music. He was, by some measure, an old man. Here in the broad daylight, the evidence showed: wavy hair gone white and thinning, road lines at his temples and throat, the sixty-one-year-old ex-jock's frame looking vaguely frail in his loose-fitting pinstriped suit trousers and his baggy button-up work shirt, plain gray save for an Ohio state flag patch on the left sleeve. Monsignor of the underground. He lowered the microphone and mugged at the crowd, slapped the air with his right hand, and brought the mic back to his mouth.

"Because it's fun, and we like to do it, and nobody else can."

And then he punched the microphone into the space before him, arm rigid and vertical, and the band started in on the downstrokes, all of them dressed in unstudied black, Doug Gillard spider-legging across the neck of the black battle-worn Gibson Les Paul he bought back in the eighties from a bar band in Akron, an audacious purchase, we thought at the time when we were all just teenagers playing toy instruments together in the same Ohio underground, and Mark Shue, the rangy kid, the worker bee who manages sound checks and teardowns, skinny and shaggy, full of excitement, pointing his bass neck upward with a rising progression, and Kevin March behind them, the muscle, fluidly machining a drum kit with a Zeppelin rigid airship across the red bass head, and Bobby Bare Jr., unlikely as all the rest of this, Nashville son of a country legend, curly-headed, spazzing on the strings of a battered SG with the flower-child decal of a butterfly behind its bridge.

Whatever myth exists in Guided By Voices is an accident. America's tastemakers have always sought and evangelized "authenticity," but they rarely find it in true form (authenticity itself being an accident), and they have so many ways of spoiling it that we don't often get to receive it as a product. (As though to expose, forestall, or accept his own such fate, Pollard wrote a song titled "I Am Produced," singing, "Pressed, printed, stomped, tripped, trapped, tricked, packaged, shipped . . . the prisoner leaves limping.")

The legend, such as it is, unraveled from Dayton a long time ago when Bob Pollard and his brother Jimmy and their drinking fraternity of pickup basketball players and wisecrackers kept trying to make a rock band out of whoever was around them, Pollard seeking a vehicle for all the album covers he'd been drawing in notebooks and a suitcase he kept stuffing fuller and fuller of song lyrics. Channeled through all the ambition and deficiencies of this random collective, the tunes came out as twisted incarnations of the British Invasion melodies, prog-rock grandiosity, and punk belligerence of Pollard's fervent mind. He recorded songs as fast as he could, on cheap, limited machines, developing a sound full of accidents that the tastemakers would soon dub "lo-fi." But not yet.

What happened in western Ohio is that a young man who wanted something badly, who had a passion burning inside him and a hearty ambition but no understanding of how to channel it, and who felt like he was in the middle of nowhere but unwilling or unable to leave for better positioning, was not an unusual man at all. Ohio is full of these.

A hundred years before the Bellwether show, Sherwood Anderson wrote a book filled with versions of that character, citizens of the titular, fictional Winesburg, Ohio, a town based on Anderson's actual hometown of Clyde, 150 miles to the north of these Renaissance grounds. One after another of these people has a passion that slowly corrodes, not disappearing, but distorting within the confines of four walls that become ever more constrictive until the only option is to remain within them and accept, as Anderson wrote, that "Many people must live and die alone," adding with tight irony, "even in Winesburg."

A young woman falls in love with a man who moves away, and instead of pursuing him or moving on with her life, instead she holes up in her room, perpetually fantasizing his return. It never comes. A man with artistic ambition actually does leave town, taking a room in New York City, which promptly becomes a rented relocation of his hometown and its inevitable fate—Winesburg-in-Gotham—this room populated not by a new bohemian community but rather by an imagined gallery of artistic coconspirators whose ghostly presence only reinforces his isolation. He is alone. His ideas have nowhere to go. He tries to find an audience. He tries to find collaborators. He is alone.

And finally, in a remarkably spot-on prototype of Pollard and his lyrics-stuffed suitcase, a doctor fills his pockets with scraps of paper on which he's written "thoughts, ends of thoughts, beginnings of thoughts." But as time passes and he finds no outlet or audience for these ideas, he reaches into his pockets, squeezing the pieces of paper into tight little balls, and finally throws them away.

Pollard finished college, married, took a job as a schoolteacher, became a father, and continued making songs with his drinking buddies, always with aspirations of success, but never with an idea of how to make it happen. And then, as he was about to give up on it completely, a series of marvelously improbable discoveries happened somewhere out in that vaporous elsewhere beyond Dayton. Mr. Pollard, longtime teacher at Lincoln Elementary, was thirty-six years old when the music industry came calling.

The songs were good and the players were interesting. There was never any question of that. And Pollard was driven and hardworking, no question of that either. But all of this was an accident. In a place where things don't come easy, though, we know better than to hesitate. When opportunity comes, we get to work, driven by fear and the hard-won knowledge that it doesn't knock twice in neighborhoods like ours.

Pollard—the only constant in a rotating cast of musicians—accepted the contract offered by the influential independent Matador label, quit his job, and dropped one record after another in the can, producing them as fast as the label could release them. Critics fawned. Audiences were swept up by the live show, communal, drunken, adrenalized marathons of two-minute anthems. Pollard, not taking any of this for granted, audaciously told an interviewer, "We want to be the Beatles on record and the Who live." He punctuated his performances with airborne bounces and high leg kicks, twirling the microphone on its cord and belting out his cryptic lyrics with an iron larynx, meanwhile perfecting a sharp-witted, boozy, braggadocious stage persona dubbed "Your Bobness." The beer cooler on the drum riser was as essential a piece of stage gear as the amplifiers. Buckets were sometimes placed behind speakers for bladder relief. The band was relentless; the shows could go on for three hours or more. This, ladies and gentlemen, is what happens when Ohio gets its chance.

By the time Pollard announced to the Bellwether audience "I'd like to play you a song that's on our next album, it's coming out in October," he'd been well established as one of the most prolific songwriters in the history of recorded music, with more than two thousand (and counting) songs registered with BMI. That October album would be GBV's twenty-ninth studio release since 1987 and its sixth in just over two years. Not to mention Pollard's solo career, which had produced an additional twenty-two full-lengths, plus an ever-expanding series of side projects. Even the most devoted completists in the band's intensely loyal following differ on the exact count of recordings. The converted garage where Pollard cranked out all these songs was around the block from Dayton's Needmore Road, which he took for the name of his publishing company: Needmore Songs.

Near the end of the Bellwether set, a final boast from His Bobness:

"Hey, GBV's got the goods, baby."

To be heard. This may be the most universal, most existential desire of Ohio and its people, of anyone who has been painted with and bristles at the term *flyover*. It seems that we only get asked to speak when our voices serve someone else's purpose, which is a big part of the frustration and the paradox of living in a place that knows it has something useful to say—knows this because we always get asked, but rarely outside the months leading to a national election. It's what drove that bar owner to speak his thought when the governor was there, to feel it inside and say it out loud, hoping this was his rare chance. To be heard. "Do something."

This same frustration has always existed for artists, especially those who tried to be seen and heard in the times before the internet. Prior to the Bellwether Festival show, I asked Pollard what commonalities he perceived Ohio bands and musicians sharing by virtue of being from here. (Though he eschews computers, he conducts interviews only by email, with his wife, Sarah, as the digital go-between, asking the questions and transcribing the answers.) His response was preceded by a long list of his favorite Ohio rock bands: Devo ("They had the greatest concept and the best songs. Songs are the most important aspect of being in a rock band."), The Mirrors, Pere Ubu, the Ohio Express, Death of Samantha, The Mice, Thomas Jefferson Slave Apartments, The Raspberries, and The Breeders. Then he continued:

> Well, with some of the bands I mentioned, we seem to share or express a kind of frustration or boredom in the difficulty of getting anyone to listen to you. I mean, there seemed to be mostly a heavy metal or "Top 40" mentality where I came from and we almost were embarrassed for anyone to even hear what we were doing. Granted, we weren't very good during the early stages. We were just entertaining ourselves in the basement and I think that's what most of the bands were doing. Bands like the Electric Eels and Rocket from the Tombs didn't even release an album. I don't think they believed anyone would give a shit.

There is plenty of nuance to Pollard's work, but the delivery has always been aggressive, the veins in his neck sticking out, that foot kicking high in the air, the working-class deliberation of whatever musicians he surrounds himself with. (There have been twenty-five members in the band's history, according to Wikipedia, but I'm pretty sure that list isn't complete. A friend of mine refers to Pollard as "the Donald Trump of indie rock" for his habit of firing band members and his notorious onstage shit-talking about his critics and rivals. In a 2018 mid-concert taunt, he mimicked a quote he'd heard from the band Weezer: "We could write 100 songs a year like Guided By Voices, but we choose quality over quantity." Pollard smirked theatrically at the audience, threw his hands up, and declared, "My worst song is better than the best song that Weezer ever wrote.")

With a constant rotation of acts among the three stages, the festival schedule was necessarily rigid. Guided By Voices was allotted seventy-five minutes, and as the closing notes of "Teenage FBI"—the twenty-eighth song in its set—rang out, Shue tapped Pollard on the arm and the singer leaned his ear toward him. Pollard nodded and announced that they had time for just one more.

The band jumped into "Glad Girls," three minutes of ringing anthemic power pop that set the audience members pogoing, throwing arms around shoulders, raising their plastic cups of beer in sloshy rock solidarity. Just offstage, in the wings to Pollard's right, a small group of Dayton regulars from way back, members of an informal GBV fraternity that called itself the Monument Club and gathered regularly in Bob's garage, jumped and danced with the same glee as the ticket holders. There was Bob's brother Jimmy, in a red T-shirt and shorts, backstage lanyard hanging around his neck, holding his beer steady as he bounced to the music. Old friend Gary Staiger was at his side, wearing a yellow T-shirt with green lettering that documented Bob's other claim to fame, from his time on the Wright State University baseball team: POLLARD THROWS NO-HITTER—MAY 11, 1978.

The final chord rang out. Pollard raised an arm, thanked the hometown crowd, and he and the band departed.

Backstage was more like a family reunion than a postconcert groupie fest, with picnic tables and a catering tent set up in a campground behind the festival area. Pollard held court at an outdoor table, sitting with his wife, Sarah, and his daughter from his first marriage, Erika. Staiger sipped a beer and told tales from the old days, and the band members milled about, balancing paper plates of food from the catering trays. As the sun began to set, Bob and Sarah said their goodbyes and made their way toward the exit as the band returned to their equipment semitrailer, overseeing the stage teardown.

Gina and I fell into step next to Jimmy Pollard and his wife, Deloris, as we headed back toward the festival grounds from the makeshift backstage. Other than Bob, Jimmy has been the only true constant of Guided By Voices, having played on all the early recordings and cowritten a number of songs and praised by Bob for his musicianship throughout his recent authorized biography, Matthew Cutter's *Closer You Are*. Though he often joined them in the van on road trips—a traveling frat party—and has always been close by, Jimmy told me he never played live with Guided By Voices.

Early in their lives, Jimmy—five years Bob's junior—was the bigger star, a high school basketball phenom who led Ohio in scoring his senior year, averaging thirty-five points a game even as he played in the era before the three-point line. He was given a full athletic scholarship to Arizona State University and may well have been on his way—along with teammates Byron Scott and Fat Lever—to the NBA. But he was sidelined by a knee injury, lost his scholarship, and returned to his hometown, where he eased into a more mundane existence, marrying and taking a second-shift job at the same General Motors plant in the Dayton suburb of Moraine where their father had worked.

Although Bob wanted him to be a full member of the band, the good pay and security of the auto plant job were too much to pass up. Bob's unlikely career trajectory slowly unfolded as Jimmy held steady at the factory, a choice few would have questioned at the time.

But in 2007, as fifty-year-old Bob remained in full flower as a rock star, Jimmy's decision to stay with the stable career choice began to distort. The GM plant where he worked, which by then had been spun off to its Delphi supplier division, would be closing amid a devastating reduction of its Ohio workforce. GM and its subsidiaries had employed close to twenty thousand people in the Dayton area in 1999, the same year Guided By Voices signed its first major-label contract. By 2008, that number had dropped to less than six hundred.

Jim and Deloris Pollard both worked at the Delphi plant. They each accepted buyout packages of $140,000, far from enough to retire on, but enough to pay off their mortgage and regroup. Now, Jimmy said as we neared the backstage exit, the jobs they once held are in Mexico. He's an hourly worker at GE Aviation; Deloris works at Miami Valley Hospital.

In the 1980s, the idea that "rock star" would be a better long-term career plan for a young Ohio man than "GM autoworker" would have seemed ludicrous. Three decades later, Jimmy was feeling fortunate to have gotten out of GM with at least something to his name, piecing together a path toward retirement. And Bob was preparing to release his gazillionth album.

The Ohio night sky was clear and starry above the vast Renaissance Festival grounds, the castle spires jutting up through the haze of a settling dew. Spectators filled the meadow before the Sunset Stage, some sitting cross-legged on the grass, some lying down, tired after a long day in the August heat. Closing act Beach House opened their show, dreamy, low-key pop carrying across the medieval land-scape, the stage dark and smoky, lit in green. Gina and I lingered for a song, then made our way across Minstrel's Grove and down Wander's Way, back through the castle wall and out toward the complicated road home.

13

DREAMING OF HEROES

A fuzzy halo surrounded the white spot at the top of each metal pole, electric moonglow beaming through the cold night sky, illuminating the artificial grass, the shiny white football helmets, the feathered marching band hats and smudged trumpet brass, a shoebox of a press box, backhoe tires and tackling dummies stowed against the end zone fence, tweens scheming beneath the field house awning.

"Fifty-*fifty* tickets! Fifty-*fifty*!"

The air, tinged with ketchup and woodsmoke, smelled the way oxygen smells when it's 45 degrees in October in Ohio with a river close by. Kids in junior-size Purple Riders gear raced in threes and fours along the catwalk at the bottom of the stadium's metal-roofed home cheering section, passing the I beams like marker poles, one of them cutting suddenly right, racing up the gray-painted wooden bleachers, too fast, tripping, down in a heap, frantically regathering the chicken tenders spilled from their red-checked cardboard nest.

"You OK?"

Laughing, embarrassed, not looking back toward them—

"yeah"—he drawled in imitation of a world-weariness he couldn't possibly yet know. And then upright and off again.

My bleacher-mate, Dave Lucas, poet laureate of Ohio, cocked his wool-capped head toward mine.

"How long do you think it's felt exactly like this to go to a high school football game?" he asked. I tucked my cold fingers tight into my armpits and nodded.

"Yep," I said, confirming a question that was its own answer.

Senior Night, Martins Ferry Purple Rider Stadium. Non-conference game versus the Wheeling Central Catholic Maroon Knights. Sets of parents in jeans and hoodies clustered near the goalpost as the pregame clock ticked down, each waiting to hear their boy's name from the loudspeaker, sending them out to the twenty-yard line to greet their purple-and-white-suited son. A handshake and a hug, pose for a snapshot, depart to the end zone, next man up.

Purple Rider Stadium sits across a set of railroad tracks from the water treatment plant that serves this city of seven thousand, a few hundred yards from the Ohio River, across which one can see West Virginia. The football field is nestled among a patchwork of warehouses and light industry—a welding-supply company, a blacktop manufacturer, an RV park, a weed-choked lot filled with empty semitrailers. Beyond the bleachers, the horizon is dominated by a big, weathered, barn-red depot and a regiment of towering white metal cylinders with POLARIS OILFIELD INFRASTRUCTURE stamped on their sides, and beyond that the deep green hills of the Ohio Valley. Further on is a whole lot of forest, and more hills, and the little towns of Yorkville and Mount Pleasant and Tiltonsville and others trailing along the river's edge. The Ohio, whose name comes from the Seneca for "good river," defines this region, stunning both for its natural grandeur and the massive, sprawling power plants, refineries, and fracking rigs that straddle its banks like otherworldly H. G. Wells invaders.

The communities of the river valley found their footing in an industrial era when their proximity to the waterway, as well as the Baltimore & Ohio Railroad and the National Road, gave them their place and their power. People here could make things, and the transportation system favored them, connecting their hands' work to markets far away. Their place and time were factors of fate, serendipities long lost in the hustle of commerce and the constancy of change. The industries along the river determined the places people called home; now those industries are mostly gone, and the people who still call this home find themselves having to answer why. What keeps them here?

The sun set as the game kicked off, a thrilling start. On the second play from scrimmage, the Purple Riders quarterback, Jake Probst, one of the seniors honored before the game, laced a beautifully arced pass that landed neatly in the hands of his receiver, who was gliding full tilt two lengths ahead of the defender, straight to the end zone, seventy-two yards in a single gasp. On Wheeling Central Catholic's first play after the ensuing kickoff, a Purple Riders defender intercepted the ball, returning it to the thirteen-yard line, running straight toward a hand-painted plywood sign mounted in the end zone:

112 YEARS

710

ALL TIME WINS

How long has it felt like this to go to a high school football game?

One of the reasons I'd asked my friend Dave to join me on this road trip into the Ohio River Valley was because of our mutual fondness for the poetry of James Wright, a native of Martins Ferry whose life and work grappled with his hard upbringing here. The poet was born into a rough-hewn, inelegant place, a notion underscored by the deficit of an apostrophe in its name, as though basic punctuation was too fussy for here.

In 1963, Wright published "Autumn Begins in Martins Ferry, Ohio," set at the Shreve High School football stadium, a facility that no longer exists. It's a short poem in which millworker fathers, "ruptured" and "ashamed to go home" to wives they can't satisfy, watch "their sons grow suicidally beautiful...and gallop terribly against each other's bodies."

Here, some six decades later, the fathers sat shoulder to shoulder, dressed in Steelers jackets and Martins Ferry High hoodies, the mothers wrapped in purple blankets, gloved hands cradling Styrofoam cups of hot chocolate, calling out to the field.

"Come on, defense! Come on, Riders!"

"Wrap 'im up!" a man hollered. "That's one of the problems with football anymore. They never wrap 'im up!"

The higher up in the bleachers, the younger and less engaged the ticket holders became. A pair of teenagers down the row from me and Dave cuddled and kissed and giggled. A kid behind us held court, delivering a series of dubious self-affirming claims, including his pending obligation to beat up a kid "who owes me money."

"You like guns?" another kid said. "I'm obsessed with guns."

Below us, someone dressed in a purple gorilla suit and a Martins Ferry football jersey with the name GRAPE APE on the back walked along the sideline fence, waving.

Central Catholic stiffened and hit back; the score was 20–7 as halftime neared, with the visitors driving. The Maroon Knights called a timeout. The stadium announcer's voice echoed across the night air.

"Ladies and gentlemen, a house key was found with a red tip."

Before this, my last visit to Martins Ferry was in 2016, a week before the November election. I had been writing about the presidential campaign, beginning with the Republican National Convention in Cleveland back in the summer, and was curious to see how the story was unfolding in a very different Ohio. I drove the hundred or so miles south from Akron through a cold drizzle, the first time in that political season I'd had occasion to head into that part of the state. A lot was being assumed that month. A lot was unknown. In general, there was a vague sense of something—what?—a barometric anomaly, barely enough to detect, easy enough to ignore.

I'd departed from my home in a reliably blue city, where there hasn't been a Republican mayor since 1983 and the local GOP establishment doesn't even bother to offer a candidate for many races. As I passed through the neighborhoods and continued onto the urban highway, I noted fewer of those blue Clinton/Kaine STRONGER TOGETHER signs than I'd imagined I should be seeing. And as I continued south on I-77, through Canton and into the next territory, where the concrete and rust of Northeast Ohio give way to fields and open bonfires and signs for unincorporated villages, crossing what many of us here recognize as an invisible line from one sort of Ohio to another, the blue banners thinned and gave way to a higher and higher density of Trump/Pence MAKE AMERICA GREAT AGAIN campaign signs. And big suckers, too. Like the billboard size you see in front of campaign headquarters and such, except these were in people's front yards.

In Martins Ferry itself, I found a single, solitary Clinton sign, in the grass strip in front of a Wendy's restaurant. And I could pretty much figure that place was owned by an out-of-town franchisee. A Clevelander, maybe. An outlier for sure.

Martins Ferry was scraping by. The local unemployment rate that month was 6.9 percent, down from a 2016 high of more than 9 percent, but still well above the national rate of 4.7. Twenty-three percent of the city's residents lived in poverty, double the national average, and population had been trickling away every year since 1940, when it peaked at 14,700. By 2016, it was less than half that. The city's most visible economic anchor was the hospital at the edge of downtown, over by the cemetery, its parking lot filled with cars bearing both Ohio and West Virginia license plates, a regional destination the way the Wheeling-Pittsburgh Steel plant used to be. I continued through the center of a small town in which a single block of Fourth Street contains three churches, Presbyterian, Catholic, and Lutheran, plus the headquarters of Mother of God Council 1421.

What promise, I wondered, does a silver-spoon New York billionaire who defies Christian values offer the people who live here?

It's not as though I felt like I'd entered a foreign culture. One benefit of a life lived in the same place is the nuance of understanding. I knew the Ohio Valley. I knew these people. I'd heard the term *Trump country* applied to places like this and I knew what that was supposed to mean to people from the coasts and the big cities. That this was the backward *other* where, as Barack Obama had said during his 2008 primary campaign, people "get bitter, they cling to guns or religion or antipathy to people who aren't like them, or anti-immigrant sentiment or anti-trade sentiment as a way to explain their frustrations." It was Hillary Clinton's "basket of deplorables," the phrase she used to describe half of Trump's voters during the 2016 campaign, or maybe it was the other half, which she characterized as people "desperate for change." Her phrases carried undeniable echoes of Wright's "Autumn Begins," whose men are "dreaming of heroes" and women are "dying for love."

In truth, and especially in light of portrayals like those, as well as Trump's own declaration of this same region as "rusting and rotting," Martins Ferry is more than anything a place where people don't get the chance to speak for themselves. Even James Wright was long gone from here when he wrote those lines, not speaking directly for his people but rather remembering them from his decidedly cosmopolitan New York City, halfway through a career whose work reflected an artist at odds with his origin.

In Ohio, in those final days before the 2016 election, people were mostly just tired of talk and speculation, tired of the probing and the promises from people whose primary interests were their own, not ours. Ohio has something of value in a presidential season, and a lot of people come here to try to take it. When the Republican National Convention was held in Cleveland that July, the prevailing local sentiment was the hope that nothing would go wrong while we were briefly in the international spotlight, that nothing would happen to harsh the precious good feeling of the Cavaliers having just won the city's first major professional sports championship in more than half a century. When the Trumpian circus made camp in the middle of downtown, a friend of mine dubbed it "the Johnny Manziel of conventions." At the end of the convention week, there was a collective civic sigh of relief, the welcome sight of everyone packing up and going back to where they'd come from, and us not having lost anything.

Martins Ferry in late October 2016 couldn't much be bothered with anyone's speculation about its electoral value, instead trying to figure out what to do in the wake of a devastating fire that had just gutted half a block of the small downtown, starting at the True Value Hardware store and spreading to five other businesses. The day I visited, the stretch of old brick storefronts was blackened and cordoned with yellow caution tape that fluttered in the drizzling breeze.

A stronger reality than politics, a stronger message than slogans, had revealed itself spontaneously amid the nighttime flames. Workers for a local fracking company rushed to the scene, filling their tankers with water from the Ohio River to aid the firefighters. Students returning to St. Mary Central School on the Monday following the weekend fire immediately launched a fund-raiser, bringing in $520 in small donations. The owner of the fire-damaged Z's Jewelry, Bob Zilai, flatly told the local newspaper, "We're going to reopen," the kind of statement that defines a region that understands hard times and what to do when they return.

Noting the sign advertising Wednesday night wings at the Elks Lodge on Fourth Street, I left Martins Ferry that day with the distinct impression that, whatever happened the first Tuesday of November, the Elks crowd would be talking the following night about how damn glad they were to be back to their real selves again.

The morning after the football game, the color purple was in evidence amid the flannel and denim of the bustling breakfast crowd at Schlepp's Family Restaurant in the village of Belmont, just up the road from Martins Ferry. The home team had won 27–13, bringing that victory total on the end zone tote board to 711. Dave and I were escorted to a table by his uncle, Dan Lucas, a regular here. The brightly lit diner was decorated for fall, a papier-mâché wreath on the wall pronouncing BE THANKFUL. The dry-erase board near the kitchen listed thirteen kinds of pie. Families and couples filled the tables and booths.

Dan had lived all his seventy-four years among his family here in Belmont County, which he quipped is covered with two things: "Lucases and ragweed." Friendly and soft-spoken, a trim man with a gray mustache and wire-framed eyeglasses, he served as the official historian of his hometown of Bethesda, and its unofficial ambassador, a fact underscored by the number of people who stopped to say hello as they passed our table, many of them dropping inside jokes and references to recent events. Earlier in the week, Dan had moderated a candidates' forum for the local mayor's race, which featured three women, a significant break from tradition. Dan said he could recall only one other female candidate in his lifetime, at least two decades before.

As we looked over the laminated menu, I asked Dan if the term *Trump country* was an accurate description of the place he lived.

"Most of the people I associate with, I would say, support Trump," he said, adding that it hadn't always been that way. "When I was a young man, everything in this county was Democrat."

That was mainly the result of the influence of the unions, which went hand in hand with the steel mill and coal mining jobs that dominated life along the river.

"They sorta told you how you were supposed to vote," he said.

Life was different here then. Dan remembered the Bethesda of his youth as "a really busy little town," with six grocery stores, a car dealership, and "a great hardware store." During the Cold War, he said, the local concentration of steel-manufacturing facilities led many in the region to believe it would be the potential target of a nuclear attack, a feeling at once frightening and powerful.

Now, he said, "we have one service station, we have one restaurant, a bank, a post office, and that's pretty much it."

It's easy to hear that description, and to look at the area now, and to factor in the shift of Democratic voters to Trump, and to assume a fundamental change. But it's not that simple. The impression of a postindustrial exodus, as evidenced by Martins Ferry's population decline, is undermined by the fact that Bethesda has maintained its population of about twelve hundred people for the past century, with little fluctuation. The union jobs are mostly gone, but the energy resources beneath the land have drawn new money to the area, with oil and gas leases going for $6,000 an acre and a major new fracking plant in the works. This has been an underrecognized development. Environmentalists who protest fracking, in which pressurized liquid is forced into underground rock formations to extract oil and natural gas, get far more public attention than the individuals whose economic well-being has been revived. The hotel where Dave and I were staying had a sign outside the entrance welcoming oil workers, along with a cheery request to use the boot-cleaning station before entering the lobby. The hotel had been constructed just a few years before, concurrent with the fracking boom, and its parking lot held at least as many big-tired, mud-spattered work trucks as passenger cars.

"We have a lot of new millionaires," Dan said. "If you have a lot of land, you don't need to do anything."

He joked about his own windfall, a one-twenty-fourth share of a quarter acre of inherited land. Amid the evolution of his home place, his own progression has been slow and steady, his life kept on his own terms. He remembered being certain, from a very young age, that he would never move away from his hometown.

"I'm just small-town, and that's it," he said.

He and his wife, Connie, live in a tidy little ranch in the shadow of Bethesda's old water tower. When I teased him for maintaining an allegiance to the long-beleaguered Cleveland Browns when he could easily root for the much-nearer Pittsburgh Steelers, he responded flatly: "You root for the team from your state."

Retired after a varied career that included teaching school and selling cars, he now spent his free time tinkering in the "playroom" he built in his oversized garage, the historian's headquarters, filled with antique toys and old photographs and advertising signs documenting the region. He was especially proud of the big Coca-Cola sign from Delaney's Grocery, where he held his first job. Through all the years, even during a spell when he was a registered Democrat, he had always voted for the Republican candidate for president, he said, adding without missing a beat, "and Nixon was a mistake."

I'd noticed a sticker, though, on the rear window of his Chevy

Colorado pickup when he pulled into the restaurant parking lot: AMERICA NEEDS JESUS. I asked him how his support for Trump jibes with his personal values.

"Every time he puts out a tweet, I don't always agree," he said. "But general philosophy, I like his conservative ideas because I'm a conservative."

He said his neighbors were drawn to Trump by his promises of a tax cut and more jobs. In a community characterized by religious conservatism, many were swayed by his anti-abortion and freedom-of-religion messages.

"Cleaning up the swamp," he continued. "I think that registered with them."

The week before my visit to Martins Ferry, the *New York Times* published a special section describing a social experiment called "America in One Room." A pair of political scientists, James Fishkin and Larry Diamond, had carefully selected 526 voters to represent the entire spectrum of the nation's political philosophy and brought them together for a weekend of conversation at a Texas resort. Although they were fed distinctly political topics, including health care, immigration, and the environment, they spoke, according to Fishkin, like regular folks, tending to place topical matters into personal terms. According to the report, most of the participants departed the experiment without changing their own views, but with a better understanding of other perspectives. They found common ground and enriching, civil discourse. When I read the report and looked at the photographs that accompanied it—hundreds of headshots in row after row, like a high school yearbook—I felt a sense of relief, a sort of validation. The conversations I'd been listening to all year had given me the same sense, that people are more alike than different, and that personal contact and real communication are all it takes to reinforce that truth, but also that when we are removed from that contact, we quickly become convinced again of our dividedness. I wondered how long those 526 people would remember how they felt when they were in that room.

Dave, who is close with his uncle, the brother of his deceased father, kept mostly quiet during breakfast, allowing me and Dan to talk. He did engage at one point, when Dan asked Dave which candidate he liked "on your side," and Dave acknowledged his status as the family's "token liberal," drawing a chuckle.

When breakfast was finished, Dan invited me to come and see the "playroom." Dave rode shotgun in my car as we trailed his uncle's pickup through the winding backroads from Schlepp's to Bethesda.

"I feel like I can talk to Uncle Dan and we can disagree," Dave said, almost as a revelation.

I told him I had the same feeling about my younger brother, one of the few people in my family circle who I can talk to about our political differences in a way that doesn't quickly devolve into discomfort and division. But those opportunities are rare, and greatly enhanced by a larger, long-established understanding of our commonalities.

When we reached Dan's house, he eagerly ushered us into his garage, narrating his collection of local memorabilia, interrupted first by an impromptu visit by a neighbor and shortly after by Dan's daughter stopping by to say hello, the social reckoning of a man who's lived his life in one place. Dan wanted to show me Bethesda's crown jewel, the local park, but time was running short and Dave and I had to get back on the road.

Weeks later, back in Akron, I met Dave for lunch. With 2020 looming, his two-year tenure as Ohio Poet Laureate would soon be coming to an end, and I wanted to hear more about his travels around the state and to compare his experiences with mine, as we'd been both touring these same roads, talking to Ohio's people during these strange times. The role of poet laureate, as defined by the Ohio Arts Council, is "to foster the art of poetry, encourage literacy and learning, address central issues relating to the humanities and heritage, and encourage the reading and writing of poetry across the state."

Dave, who told me over lunch that "I did not want to be a thin pope," had taken on the role with gusto, driving a total of 13,696 miles and making 115 public appearances, giving readings and talks at colleges, high schools, libraries, community groups, and a prison. In addition, he wrote a regular syndicated column under the title "Poetry for People Who Hate Poetry."

A charismatic speaker with prominent horn-rimmed glasses and a Dylanesque thicket of dirty blond hair, Dave had begun his tenure in early 2018, thirty-seven years old, dressed in a dark suit and tie, reading poems at the Ohio governor's mansion, an event hosted by then First Lady Karen Kasich. From his book with a very Ohio title—*Weather*—the Clevelander read about midwestern cities, "threadbare capitals, lost satellites," and about the burning Cuyahoga River. He then embarked on his statewide journey. He interacted with a lot of Ohioans over those twenty-four months but acknowledged to me that people who attend poetry events tend to fit neatly into the same cultural and political niche.

"Most of the people I talked to were 'poetry people,'" he said. "They and their poetry friends might be the only three liberals in Logan County."

I asked him about what he'd told me in the car that Saturday, about being able to talk politics with his uncle Dan, and he said that wasn't exactly what he meant. In fact, he said a little incredulously, he didn't know until that morning that his uncle had never voted for a Democrat for president. It wasn't so much that the two had an open, ongoing political conversation as that Dave felt like they *could* have one. He equated his remark about "poetry people" to his uncle's statement that most of his neighbors support Trump.

"We mostly spend time with people who see the world the way we see it," Dave said, lamenting the present lack of healthy dialogue among Americans of divergent opinions. He invoked the long-term, odd-couple friendship between Supreme Court justices Ruth Bader Ginsburg and Antonin Scalia, who intentionally engaged over their ideological opposition. "I'm not sure that sort of thing is possible these days," he continued. "But I'd like to think that my uncle and I both accept that we don't have the answers. I liked that he asked, 'Who do you like on your side?' If we could do more of that, it would be better. I know that's Pollyannaish, but it's like that group in Texas—let's just talk about it."

Although it's true that Dave's travels as an advocate of poetry didn't often expose him or his audience to contrary political viewpoints, it did allow him new insight into the importance of the poet's voice during clamorous times. As Bertolt Brecht famously noted, "you can't write poems about trees when the woods are full of policemen."

I asked him what power poetry can hold in times like these, and he laughed.

"But it seems like we're always in 'these times,'" he said. "I think poetry says the things it's said to most moments: things are much more complicated than we can ever manage to express. Most poems should enlarge our sense of politics. It's the job of poetry to try to complicate. Poetry acknowledges that life is much more complicated than anything we can say about it, and especially anything politics can say about it."

As the lunch wound down, I asked Dave a version of the question I'd been asking everywhere I went—what was his biggest concern in the context of the coming election?

"All of them?" he joked, then drew serious.

"We're staring down the barrel of climate change. We're at the point of climate catastrophe, and we're doing this at the beginning of a new Gilded Age. I find it increasingly difficult to separate these problems. People ask, 'Are you worried about poetry?' Poetry will always be around as long as there's humanity. *That's* what I'm worried about. Will *we* be around?"

It's not easy here. The neighborhoods beyond downtown Martins Ferry climb like ladders up hillsides. After parting ways with Dave and Dan that Saturday, I embarked on a tour of the town and its surroundings and soon found myself negotiating roads so steep I worried during one harrowing turn that my car would tip and roll. Narrow, too. On some stretches, the only choice is to go forward hoping for no vehicle to approach from the opposite direction. And I realized: this is what it's like to leave one's driveway every morning and return, and to do it again the next day and the next. Who would live here? This is always the question.

And yet these difficult streets are lined with mostly well-kept houses constructed in defiance, with asymmetrical foundations to compensate for the terrain, cleverly tilted driveways, stockade fences creeping uphill on ascending stilts. All of it an acceptance of what life has handed them and a choice not to flee in pursuit of some easier way, but to adapt. Martins Ferry is a mystery of worry and hope. If there's a stubbornness here, if there is bitterness and anger, it ought at least to be understood. There is something to learn from the people who endure.

James Wright wrote another poem about his hometown, called "Beautiful Ohio," which happens to share its title with the state song. The two odes could not be more different. The anthem is fond, and false. Wright's poem is neither of those.

The narrator of his "Beautiful Ohio" sits on a railroad tie watching a sewer pipe expel its contents into the Ohio River. He seems to recognize some shared humanity in this—these are his people and he is one of them (sewage after all being the great equalizer). Of the spew before him, he concludes:

> *I know what we call it*
> *Most of the time.*
> *But I have my own song for it,*
> *And sometimes, even today,*
> *I call it beauty.*

It's easy to tell a place like Martins Ferry that all it needs is another steel factory to make everything better again. I've been hearing that same code for decades, but it rings less true and less relevant with each passing year. We need—and are actively inventing—new ways to thrive. The dark parts of the Rust Belt are real, and if there was an easy answer, we'd have recognized it ourselves a long time ago. The truth of life in this region is that struggle is a sort of birthright, and it has inspired energy and innovation in the generation that has followed the industrial decline. I see it all the time. I'm seeing it in a devastated Lordstown, trying to kindle a new electric vehicle economy from the ruins of old memory. I heard it in my visit with Bret Davis, who advances the tradition of his family farm with technology and proactive outward engagement, informed by the old ways but knowing they are not enough.

We're also smart enough to recognize the irony of the state anthem, "Beautiful Ohio," which derives originally from a sappy song about two lovers drifting down a moonlit stream in a red canoe. Except for the title, it's got nothing to do specifically with

Ohio, and I have no idea how it ever got to be our song. The anthem was updated in 1989 with new lyrics, and though it does generically capture some of the scenic beauty of the state—"golden grain," "lovely flowers," and the silhouettes of cities—it also turns a wooden ear to certain key difficulties. The first of the song's two verses is delivered by a wanderer from afar, seeking a place to belong and finding it in "beautiful Ohio." The second verse pays homage to a place where "mighty factories seem to hum a tune, so grand." The problem is, by 1989 two main troubles were actively distilling in Ohio: loss of population, and loss of factories. No wanderers were seeking Ohio, however beautiful it was (and is). Between 1970 and 1980, the state's population growth was nearly flat, inching upward by just 1.4 percent, a trend that has continued. And the mighty factories were not exactly humming. In fact, the first recorded usage of the term *Rust Belt* had occurred in that same decade, and the exodus of factory jobs was our biggest problem by the time those new lyrics appeared.

A word I've come to rely on is one that was applied to my hometown of Akron in a 1926 article in the *American Mercury* magazine, which described the place as "unbeautiful." It doesn't mean ugly; rather, it describes a place for which glamour is not the point. There is plenty of beauty here, especially in the ways people endure, but it is not easily captured in a state-sanctioned jingle or the superficiality of election-year snapshots.

Back down from the hillside, I parked my car in front of the library, near the brown Ohio Historical Marker whose gold letter-ing pays tribute to Martins Ferry's two literary figureheads: James Wright on one side, and William Dean Howells, the novelist, critic, and playwright celebrated as "the dean of American letters," on the other. I set off walking. My initial pursuit was uncertain and overly literal. I wanted to try to locate Wright's sewer pipe, figuring the water treatment plant at the river's edge might be a good place to start. But I didn't have much success, access to the river hindered by fences and thick underbrush. Instead, I cut back toward the town center. Dan Lucas had alerted me during our breakfast that the local hospital, the place I'd perceived three years earlier as an employment hub, had since closed, and as I approached its parking lot, the emptiness was striking, particularly as it opened a vista into the adjacent Walnut Grove Cemetery. The unemployment rate in Belmont County, which includes Martins Ferry, had fluctuated throughout 2019 from a high of 7 percent to a low of 4 percent, always above the national rate, which had hovered around 3.7 percent all year.

As I continued through the little downtown, I found it eerily quiet, devoid of foot traffic, despite the warm, pleasant autumn afternoon. I walked for nearly two hours and encountered exactly three other people on the street. But as I passed under the crudely fanciful WANETA TRIBE 75 IMPROVED ORDER OF REDMEN sign hanging from the side of the local bingo hall and turned the corner back toward the library, I spotted a storefront whose name I immediately recognized: Z's Jewelry, the shop damaged in the 2016 fire, whose owner had vowed not to give up.

I tried the door. It opened.

14

A BEGINNING

The rest of Leonte Cooper's life began with his final descent down the shadowy staircase of the old house his mother rented in the middle of Akron, lugging the second of two plastic laundry baskets into which he'd dumped just about everything he owned. The other basket was already in the trunk of his mom's aging gray Nissan, stuffed with clothes, shoes, books, and pictures, the inventory of someone who had never lived in more than one room. He pushed the screen door open with his shoulder, shooing the big black dog back into the house, and made his way out to the driveway and into the hazy afternoon sun, opened the car door and wedged the basket into the backseat. He returned to the kitchen one last time to say goodbye to his father, a man he didn't know very well, who had spent most of Leonte's childhood in and out of jail.

His father handed him a crumpled wad of bills.

"This should be enough to get you there," he said.

Leonte thanked him and headed out to the car. I followed.

"I am super stoked," he said to me across the top of the Nissan as I opened the passenger door. Twenty-two years old, he smiled eagerly, his eyes alit with the same optimism I'd seen the first time I met him, nearly a year before, and which had remained in all our interactions since, a spirit I still wondered about, considering everything.

We slid into our seats. I pulled on the seat belt webbing. It didn't move.

"Yeah, they don't work," Cooper said with an apologetic grin.

I nodded, hoping my face didn't betray my sudden concern about the quality of his driving skills and the unavoidable implication of a young black man being pulled over for a seat belt violation. The trip to Columbus would take us two hours down I-71 to our destination, the Ohio State University student housing complex where Leonte had a late-afternoon move-in appointment. With a headful of lively black dreadlocks and a thin beard, dressed in camouflage cargo shorts and a patterned black T-shirt, a pair of Beats hanging on his neck, he could be any of the millions of young Americans setting off for a college campus in the late summer of 2019. He had big hopes, big plans; he'd spent the summer reading Thomas Payne's *Common Sense* and studying for the LSAT, just for practice, and attending Toastmasters meetings, readying himself for Ohio State's mock trial team, which, he informed me as we made our way toward the highway, had been ranked fifth in the nation the previous year. He would be studying political science, with plans for law school to follow. He knew the exact GPA and LSAT scores he'd need to get into the best programs, already calculating his path.

"I want to do so much," he said. "I want to do Model UN. I already joined student government. . . . I can't wait! I've been out of school too long."

He didn't just want to earn a law degree; he wanted to combine it with an MBA. And he didn't want to get into just any law school; he was aiming for the Ivy League. He wanted to study abroad. He wanted to be accepted into Phi Beta Kappa. He wanted to become president of student government.

He would talk like this all the way to Columbus, so full of energy, so fully aware that this was not just the next phase of his life but the manifestation of a course correction to a life that could have gone far differently.

I first met Cooper by chance at the Akron campus of Stark State College, where he was working toward an associate degree. I was there for an informal author event at the campus bookstore. Cooper happened by, saw the book propped up on the table next to where I was standing, and asked about the title— *The Hard Way on Purpose*. I explained that it was a book about living in the Rust Belt and the title was my take on the way we tend to do things in our part of the world. He gave me that smile, and said yeah, he got that, and immediately engaged me with questions. He was kinetic, magnetic. When I finally got a chance to turn the conversation toward him, I asked what he was studying, and he told me he was majoring in political science, using the two-year community college to fulfill his general studies requirements before transferring to the much more expensive Ohio State.

"Then what?" I asked him.

"I want to do law school," he said. "I want to make a difference."

"Stay in Ohio," I told him. "We need you."

Months later, I saw his face again, also by chance, as I was driving through town, Cooper in a royal blue Stark State T-shirt, looking at me from the back of a city bus. Not the young man himself, but his image on an ad panel for the college. I suppose I was surprised to see him in that form, but not completely. I'd left our brief interaction with a sense that he was special somehow. But now, seeing him this way, as a public example of possibility, I wondered.

The further I had traveled in this strange unraveling year, the more vexed I had become about the question I was chasing, the question of whether America was broken, of whether Donald Trump and a binarily divided Congress and a degraded national dialogue were matters of the moment or our new way of being. The question kept growing like a barnacle clung to titanic battles of impeachment and television clamor, unbreachable division and personal powerlessness in the face of brazen lies and insults and the people who defend them. I am not a person who despairs easily and yet I had begun to wonder what was worth yearning for. What even is an American dream? Is it still a list of goals pinned above a young man's pillow?

Leonte Cooper was, more than anything, an echo of my own children, a year or so in age from each of them, setting off just as both of them were—Evan into the dangerous work of trying to save people, Lia soon to begin graduate school to learn how to help people heal—all of them full of ideas and plans and promise. As a father and as a citizen of a place whose conscience now seems desperately important—Ohio as a counterpoint to cynicism (*I want to believe this*)—I needed to understand him better. I needed him as proof.

We met again at a neighborhood café on a Sunday afternoon in the summertime, not long after he'd graduated from Stark State. He'd walked to our meeting from church, a few miles through central Akron. He didn't have a car. He was trying to save up for one, he told me, working as chairman of the youth advisory board for a local program battling homelessness.

I learned that day that Cooper had arrived at the community college following a failed first stab at adulthood. After graduating high school, skating by with decent grades but little effort, he'd enlisted in the army, not so much with a sense of purpose but owing more to a lack of it. An uncle had served and suggested it might be a course for Cooper to follow. So he signed up and was ordered to report to Fort Meade in Maryland. When he passed through the metal detector at the entrance, he was pulled aside. The guards found the two big bottles of alcohol he'd stashed in his bag. He was turned away, required to serve a ninety-day suspension before he'd even begun. It didn't go much better from there.

He hated boot camp, the screaming and yelling, the constant thumb of authority. He rebelled, causing trouble in formation, being a smart aleck, laughing outright when his drill sergeant barked, "You are not going to make it." Cooper, who told me he has gone by his surname ever since the military drilled it into him, was hanging out with other troublemakers, partying and getting reprimanded for one infraction after another. He was depressed and said he considered suicide.

Finally, he said, he'd had enough. Faced with the threat of dishonorable discharge, he went into a self-imposed exile, quit drinking, and devoted himself to Christianity. He did all this alone, he said, a desperate and resolute decision to save himself. He reemerged as a changed person, with a first mission to prove himself to his superiors.

"Once I became a Christian and began building a spiritual life, you start to reflect on yourself," he said. "During that time, I had to realize what I wanted to do. My sergeants were like, 'whoa.' It was like an overnight transformation."

I probed further. Was there a mentor, a program, some structure that guided him toward this change? No, he said flatly. He just decided he had to take control. No relapse? I asked. No, he said, with the same composition. I would ask about this again in the months that followed and, always, he would downplay what struck me as a dramatic transformation. He conveyed it as something that simply had to be done.

He returned to his unit intent on repairing his reputation,

cutting off his association with the friends he'd been getting into trouble with, surprising his superiors by winning a commendation for the cleanest room in his platoon. He gained trust and was granted privileges, eventually earning a promotion to the rank of Student Master Sergeant. He left the army with an honorable discharge. He applied for and received a Pell Grant, which would allow him to complete community college without debt. He returned to Akron and enrolled at Stark State, the first in his family to attend college.

"When I came to community college, I knew exactly what I wanted to do," he said.

But all this new promise and resolve came with a new set of struggles. With little saved from his military pay and only a part-time job, his father fresh out of jail and his mother still raising two children and struggling to make ends meet, he moved into Akron's Spring Hill Apartments, the same government-subsidized housing project where LeBron James had lived during high school, in one of the city's most crime-ridden neighborhoods. In the time he lived there, he said, two residents were shot, one injured during a robbery and the other killed in a drug deal. Cooper could smell the pot smoke in the hallways and knew that he could knock on the door next to his and buy anything he wanted. This was not so much a temptation as a reminder of something he didn't want to be anymore.

"I can't stand to be around it," he said. "I feel like my spiritual taste buds have changed."

With no car and unable to afford a bus pass, Cooper walked to and from campus every day, more than an hour each way, leaving at daybreak and returning home well after dark.

He earned an honors scholarship at the community college and became active in student organizations. He was named to the All-Ohio Academic Team and was accepted into Phi Theta Kappa, the international honors society for two-year colleges. He maintained a perfect 4.0 GPA throughout his time there. When he graduated in May 2019, he reached out to the uncle who had guided him toward the military.

"I think he had given up on me," Cooper said. "I think it was one of my biggest moments, when I was able to send him a message and say I graduated. That was big."

The Columbus skyline came into view, the GPS directing Cooper's borrowed Nissan toward Woody Hayes Drive. This was his first time seeing the campus. He'd made all his applications from afar and hadn't been able to afford a visit. With only the income from his summer job at the homeless nonprofit, he'd moved back in with his family for the few months leading to this departure, with a Pell Grant and a partial scholarship from the Ohio Legislative Black Caucus covering most of his school costs and just enough money in his pocket to get started. Now it was all here in front of him.

"I love it. I *love* it," he said, shaking his head as he passed between the glassy buildings of the sprawling, 1,665-acre campus. Navigating one-way streets, he circled the block twice, found a parking spot, and entered the lobby of the newly opened five-story housing complex on High Street, the main drag through the college district, which dominates the city's north side, the third-largest college campus in the country. There, he was greeted by a trio of cheery student assistants in polo shirts and lanyards. He signed his papers, received his key, and took the elevator up to the third floor. "*My* floor," he said as the elevator car rose. The bell dinged, the doors parted, and Cooper stepped into a hallway that opened to a brightly sunlit communal study area, with chairs and tables, a shiny new coffee maker, and a wide view of the campus.

He followed the apartment numbers down the hallway to his

new front door, inserted the key, turned it, and entered to the smell of fresh paint and new carpet.

"It's nice!" he exclaimed, taking it in. "Wow—this is crazy. I've got a stove!"

He hadn't yet met his roommate, a fifth-year biomedical engineering student from Syria who wouldn't check in till later. Cooper opened doors and peeked around corners, tentative at first, almost as if he didn't belong. I would be leaving him from here, joining Gina and heading to a hotel as we continued our travels through Ohio. Cooper had originally planned to drive back to Akron that night, but when he saw his bed, it seemed almost a revelation. He had sheets, he announced with the same tone of wonder that had declared the fact of a stove. He could stay.

We went back down the elevator, returned to his car, and carried up the baskets. He set them by his closet, a jumble of his old life to be organized into a new order.

"This feels perfect," he said.

I left him there, believing that his beginning was a kind of ending.

Throughout all these months, my mind had returned frequently to something I'd heard Warren Buffet say a few years before, when I'd gone to hear him speak at an event in Cleveland. He was asked about the division of the country, about the effect the newly elected Donald Trump was having on the nature of the presidency, on the expectation and tenor of leadership, about the strange times we were living in. He smiled in that narrow way you see from people who have seen and done things that we have not, the thing we call wisdom.

America, he said simply, will always prevail. He urged against reacting to whatever the moment suggests, insisting that in the long view, we have always been okay, that times have been worse than now and we have endured them, and there is no evidence to prove anything other than that: America will prevail because that's what America has always done. He said this in the context of his children and their future, children, he made clear, who were not allowed to benefit from his fortune, who'd been required to make their own path, as though they could be proof of his promise.

I had found Cooper in the midst of his own American path, after his fall, after the test of his first hard journey, in a new ascendancy, at a point of departure and a point of arrival. He believed in grace. He believed in himself. Others believed in him. As I followed him on Facebook and in occasional correspondence through his first semester, I observed a growing engagement with the world of ideas, the emergence of a voice. He posted about school vouchers and Black History Month. He commented on the new Amazon facility in his hometown and on Medicare-for-all. He had never voted in a presidential election, and in early 2020, now at age twenty-three, he was listening and reading, giving a great deal of thought and attention to the various candidates, wholly open and decidedly undecided. With the primary season underway, an Akron councilwoman had invited him to volunteer for Bernie Sanders's statewide campaign, and he had asked her—naively, he acknowledged—if that meant he would be required to vote for him. His decision would come, he had told me, but not until he determined who was right for him. He didn't yet know how or when that would happen.

I went to visit him on campus on a snowy Saturday in the Spring 2020 semester. Still without a car, he'd hitched a ride from his roommate to the Panera Bread restaurant where we'd arranged to meet. He arrived in a bluster of snow, dressed in a red Ohio State hoodie, track pants, and a red knit cap with earflaps. He pulled it off to reveal the dreadlocks now dyed gold.

"A lot has *changed*," he said after I greeted him and asked how he was doing. He drew out that last word in a way I recognized from our previous conversations, the way he weighted his stories and exclamations, the hint of a preacher's lilt, the roundness of someone in a sequence of discovery.

We ordered sandwiches and settled at a counter at the edge of a dining room bustling with students. I asked him what he meant by change and he told me the biggest had been a move from his student housing complex to a shared apartment far from campus. He had arrived determined to complete his undergraduate studies without debt, but with a rent payment of $1,000 a month, he had already fallen behind. So he'd departed from the place that had felt like a whole new life in favor of an old building nearly an hour-long bus ride from campus. Much like his community college experience, he left home every morning at daybreak and stayed on campus until after dark, attending classes—ethics, language, reasoning, history—studying in between, and keeping busy with various student organizations, exercising at the rec center, socializing with newfound friends.

Already holding a position in student government and serving as a student representative on faculty senate, he was preparing to run for a campus general assembly seat, "so you can actually make policy," he said. After his schooling, he wanted to start his career in the private sector, but the ultimate goal was a life in public service.

Already, however, he was developing concern about what that would mean. Before he'd arrived on campus, he had expressed his dismay about the rising tension within public discourse.

"If you don't believe what I believe," he'd told me the previous summer, "the conclusion is not that we disagree. The conclusion is that we can't be friends. What does that say about the culture of our country?"

Now, in classrooms and in political organizations, in social conversations and at campus events, he was finding a new voice of his own and with it a new kind of tension, the question of how to express it and what would happen when it met with opposing, sometimes inscrutable forces. What he had found, in essence, is the question I had been chasing, the question of the individual, the question of the voter, the question of the candidate, the question of Ohio, the question of America:

Who will listen to me? And what do they want in return?

Cooper admitted he was struggling with this. He said:

I don't even feel like I should talk during class sometimes. Like maybe I shouldn't put this out there. Because it's really polarized out there right now. And people that don't study politics don't debate anymore about politics. They get mad if you have a different opinion than them. I have friends that are very far left and friends that are very far right. And we talk about issues all the time. But when you're talking to the average person that just hears what's been put out there, just hears people say, "Well, the Democrats just want open borders; the Republicans are just racist"—that's what they believe. So when you confront them with the issue, they're like, you automatically want open borders or you're automatically a racist. And that's not fair. And it makes it hard to talk about politics like that.

He does keep quiet in class sometimes, he said. He doesn't want to be misunderstood, judged, disliked. He feels as though it's fruitless to try to convince people of something in an environment when the idea of listening has become so corrupted. He wants others to understand that he is open to having his mind changed, and he wants to believe that he could have healthy discourse with someone who felt the same way. But how does one even get to that point of understanding?

He told me about a recent controversy on campus. The undergraduate student government had failed to recognize Black History Month and when students complained, a representative of the group responded that it was "not in their systems or processes" to acknowledge every cultural commemoration. In response, students in support of the recognition organized a protest, resulting in a demonstration in which African American students flooded the chambers for a student government meeting, which, Cooper noted, was held in a campus building constructed on what was once an Underground Railroad site. More than fifty students spoke in protest at a forum that lasted five and a half hours, finally resulting in unanimous passage of a resolution to recognize Black History Month.

The result was not what impressed Cooper so much as the effort behind it.

"It takes a lot of organizing, a lot of effort, a lot of sacrifice," he said.

This was a lesson in power, in how it is controlled by those who already have it and how much work it takes to challenge it. He sounded almost weary when he projected that single protest outward into the context of a deeply divided nation.

I do have hope for the country, but I'm gonna be honest. I'm a little bit uncertain with what's going on now, especially now that I'm here on this campus talking to people. At Stark State, there weren't a lot of people that loved politics, that knew much about it. But here, there's people that have aspirations to go to Congress someday. When I see that, hearing what they think makes me a little bit nervous, because some of them really do want to use government to force their ideas on other people. And a lot of them are really excited about doing that. And that bothers me. And I feel like if I go to another school that's even more civically engaged, I'll see it even more. And that's the future of who is going to be in office.

I asked him if he'd lost any of the optimism I'd seen when we'd first arrived on campus six months before. This is what I'd really come to hear: how hope sounded now in the voice of a person who had been saved by it.

"I do still have high hopes," he said, nodding in a way that caused those gold dreadlocks to shimmer in the restaurant's fluorescent light. "I guess maybe it's the idea of the future—I'm just really, really optimistic about it. My roommate just the other day said sometimes he'll see me studying all night, and he's like, 'When I was in college, if I had to stay up all night studying for a test, it wasn't getting done.'

"I think it's just figuring out what I really love, and it's politics. That's what I love. And really, really, *really* studying history to see where I am now. I feel like I have a better idea of the whole picture for myself, and some kind of, like, spiritual connection to really, really make a balance. It just makes me feel like there is a purpose behind life, and if I don't get to that purpose, then there's gonna be an empty void that's gonna be there forever. So I do want to get there, eventually."

Eventually. Maybe that was it. The wisdom of patience, the hope of promise, even on a winter afternoon in Ohio, when the thin gray light has to be enough to believe in the sun.

15

CIRCLE

On Christmas Eve, 1818, more than five hundred men arranged themselves in a wide circle surrounding the twenty-five square miles of Ohio's burgeoning Hinckley Township, steeled by whiskey and heavily armed for a "war of extermination." Just fifteen years into statehood, the area still known as the Western Reserve of Connecticut was heavily wooded and snarling with bears, wolves, deer, and wildcats, as well as smaller creatures— squirrels, snakes, turkeys, raccoons, foxes. The indigenous people who had lived in the territory for thousands of years had recently been pushed out by American settlers. Now, intent on taming the land they'd claimed, these men awaited their signal. When it came, they began moving as one, slowly toward the center, constricting, constricting, whooping and waving, firing away, driving all the animals inward till they were concentrated in a small area, at which time the throng massacred every living thing save themselves. Despite such an ill-advised configuration, only two hunters were wounded. The wildlife did not fare so well.

According to a local history, the group killed twenty-one bears, seventeen wolves, three hundred deer, and mounds of turkeys, foxes, and raccoons. The settlers lit bonfires and feasted through the night, then carried home all the meat they could, leaving the rest to rot. In the spring, buzzards migrating back from the South came upon the site and commenced on the turkey-vulture version of an orgy. This windfall apparently became implanted in their genetic memory. Each March 15, that same site fills with sky-watching visitors as the black-feathered, red-faced carrion seekers make their famous return to Hinckley, great numbers of them darkening the late-winter sky, cheered by a throng of partiers akin to the Gobblers Knob pilgrims who gather in Punxsutawney every year to watch for the shadow of a groundhog.

On Buzzard Day 2020, Gina and I drove out through the rural suburbs and pulled into the parking lot of the Cleveland Metroparks's "Top O' Ledges Reservation." Normally, thousands of people roam the parkland and gather in Hinckley's town center, necks craned skyward, looking for the first buzzard. But this year was different. We were just days into the disorientation and anxiety of a pandemic, the coronavirus that had suddenly closed our schools and emptied store shelves of bread and toilet paper, pushing us into something called "social distance" and knocking an already ill-at-ease American populace completely off kilter. Restaurant workers, barbers, tattoo artists, and movie ushers were abruptly ordered off work, the stock market was screaming in freefall, gun dealers were overwhelmed with buyers, airlines over-whelmed with cancelations. The park system had called off its Buzzard Day program and the Hinckley Chamber of Commerce had postponed the township's sixty-third annual festival.

As the federal government fumbled to respond to the fast-developing crisis, Ohio emerged as a beacon of leadership, a bellwether. Governor Mike DeWine held daily briefings with clear, fact-based updates, a steady demeanor, and decisive actions, joined each day by the state's white-lab-coated Department of

Health director, Dr. Amy Acton, whose turns at the lectern were characterized by empathy and precise metaphors—measures of precaution described as layers of Swiss cheese, fast-changing data likened to "viewing a star at a distance"—to put science and statistics into everyday perspective, issuing logic and common sense. DeWine was lauded nationally for being ahead of the curve in declaring a state of emergency, following the lead of science, limiting public gatherings, ordering bars and restaurants to close, establishing a stay-at-home order, and further actions. He was the first governor in the country to close schools and bucked the trend of some other Republican governors as he quietly resisted President Trump's pressure for an early end to stay-at-home restrictions. As the early events escalated, the *Washington Post* described DeWine's and Acton's joint response as "a national guide to the crisis." Ohio's primary election was scheduled for two days after Buzzard Day, but by the end of Monday, the governor would call for its postponement, stemming the public gathering. Even though his own primary campaign was stalled by the order, Joe Biden singled out DeWine for "stepping up during this time of crisis to fill the [leadership] void and protect our most vulnerable."

Only a half dozen cars were in the reservation's parking lot when we arrived at midday. I pulled into a space, feeling an odd instinct to keep a few empty spots between the next car and mine. Gina and I stepped out into the cool March air, zipping our jackets tight against it, and trudged across a lawn that was not green but the memory of green from a season before, passing then into the woods. The day was pleasant, sunshine sifting through the latticework of leafless treetops, a few wispy clouds above, leaves crunching underfoot, birds chirping, a distant caviling of crows. I tried to watch the sky while simultaneously following the trail but tripped on an exposed tree root, then a rock, stumbling forward, causing Gina to laugh at me in the way she laughs at Jerry Lewis, which is not one of my favorite things about her.

I wanted to see a buzzard right away. I don't know why. I don't know if it was impatience or unease, a newly important desire for the expected to happen.

"Just wait," she said. "Let's find a sunny spot and stop."

A woman approached from the opposite direction. She smiled, nodded hello, but also eased to a greater distance and pulled her coat collar up to shield her nose and mouth. We were all suddenly fearful, including of each other, a fever of its own before any actual sign of fever. The world off kilter, the funhouse mirror I'd sensed a year before, was warping into a new distortion.

I'm here at the end of the story of a year, knowing that the story continues beyond my telling, that the world changes and just keeps changing, believing that it endures. And yet, like anyone else, I am time after time awed and unsettled by its change. I'm writing this worried and uncertain. Lia, laid off from her restaurant job—would she be still leaving for graduate school in May? Evan, departing every afternoon for yet another new danger on his police beat, picking up firehouse shifts on his days off. Gina's middle-aged sister, already without health insurance after her husband's recent job loss, was suddenly cut off from her job waiting tables. Our life savings had lost so much value in a week that the numbers read like nonsense. Gina and I were scrambling to figure out how to engage with students we suddenly would not be seeing each day, simultaneously thankful for employment. No one we knew was sick yet, but surely that would change. The worst was the feeling of not knowing how to feel.

The immediate effect of the pandemic, before the coming reality of deaths, was contained in new jargon—"social distance," "shelter in place"—a government-decreed isolation into the silos of social media and cultural alienation and selective consumption of news and information. *We're all in this together,* people kept saying. But really, we were all in it apart.

We passed trees whose smooth gray trunks were scarred by love— JEFF + JAIME FOREVER, TOOTCH + JENNY, KEMS - DEMS 1955— and the inevitable hieroglyph: a three-foot penis spray-painted in green. We left the trail and crossed over fallen trees, sidestepping down a rocky incline to position ourselves cautiously at the dizzying lip of a steep rock ledge, a vantage that allowed us the wide, swelling view of a valley and hillside beyond.

We stood there side by side, looking up. Surrounded by old trees, slightly recoiled by the drop of the cliff, perched on the cold rock, watching for a bird or birds that may or may not come, a vulture bent on survival, taking what it finds—nothing in that moment was more true than the indifference of nature. It will do what it will do despite our delusion of society or command. The pull of the moon, a tremor below, the rise of the sea, the spread of a germ, the disquiet of a blizzard in Ohio.

The heart wants what it wants,
which is everything.

Dave Lucas, Ohio's poet laureate, wrote those lines in the middle of a poem called "Meditation at Five Islands." The declaration has always felt to me like the farthest extent of human capacity, but also its stark limitation.

Many years ago, an Ohio Wyandot Indian named Turk declared that this land "belongs in common to us all.... The Great Spirit above is the true and only owner of this soil; and He has given us all an equal right to it."

What strange days these were. Governor DeWine and Dr. Acton

had been drawing us to the television every afternoon, always two o'clock, explaining what they could explain in terms as human as possible, sometimes allowing the effect on their own lives. Mike DeWine announced Ohio's first death, a seventy-six-year-old man he knew personally. Amy Acton shared the story of the abuse and homelessness she'd suffered during her childhood in the Mahoning Valley as a point of insight into the public fear. "Life feels like it's shutting down," she said, "but I feel like life is waking us up."

What do we call this paradox, the comfort when someone we trust tells us the truth about bad things? Is that leadership? Is that government? Or is it just the best that one human can do for another who comes asking?

We stood there for a long time, together in a narrow sunbeam, not speaking, trying to take in all of the sky. And then there it came, alone, arcing wide and steady on an updraft, unmistakable from the pictures I'd studied, the black crucifixion of the underside, the wide wings tipped in white. It turned a slow circle, looking for something it still believes is here.

BIBLIOGRAPHY OF SORTS

These works were mostly literally and sometimes also figuratively influential to this book:

Abernathy, Penelope Muse. "The Expanding News Desert: 2018 Report." University of North Carolina Hussman School of Journalism and Media.

Anderson, Sherwood. *Winesburg, Ohio*. New York: Signet Classics, 2005.

Armon, Rick. *50 Must-Try Craft Beers of Ohio*. Athens: Ohio University Press, 2017.

———. *Ohio Breweries*. Mechanicsburg, PA: Stackpole Books, 2011.

Borowiec, Andrew. *Along the Ohio*. Baltimore, MD: Johns Hopkins University Press, 2000.

———. *Wheeling, West Virginia*. Almada, Portugal: Camera Infinita Books, 2018.

Catte, Elizabeth. *What You Are Getting Wrong About Appalachia*. Cleveland: Belt Publishing, 2018.

CBRE Research. "Trading Places: Retail Properties Converted to Industrial Use." CBRE, January 30, 2019.

Chamberlain, Libby, ed. *Pantsuit Nation*. New York: Flatiron Books, 2017.

Coffey, Daniel J., John C. Green, David B. Cohen, and Stephen C. Brooks. *Buckeye Battleground: Ohio, Campaigns, and Elections in the Twenty-First Century*. Akron, OH: University of Akron Press, 2011.

Crout, George C., and W. E. Rosenfelt. *Ohio: Its People and Culture*. Minneapolis: T. S. Denison & Co., 1977.

Curnutte, Mark. *Across the Color Line: Reporting 25 Years in Black Cincinnati*. Cincinnati, OH: University of Cincinnati Press, 2019.

Cutter, Matthew. *Closer You Are: The Story of Robert Pollard and Guided By Voices*. New York: Da Capo Press, 2018.

Frey, William H. "Black-White Segregation Edges Downward Since 2000, Census Shows." Brookings Institution, December 17, 2018.

Friedlander, Lee. *Industrial Valleys: Ohio & Pennsylvania*. New York: Callaway Editions, 1982.

Glaser, Elton, and William Greenway, eds. *I Have My Own Song for It: Modern Poems of Ohio*. Akron, OH: University of Akron Press, 2002.

Goldbach, Eliese Colette. *Rust: A Memoir of Steel and Grit*. New York: Flatiron Books, 2020.

Goldstein, Amy. *Janesville: An American Story*. New York: Simon & Schuster, 2017.

Gopnik, Adam. *A Thousand Small Sanities: The Moral Adventure of Liberalism*. New York: Basic Books, 2019.

Hiatt, Brian. *Bruce Springsteen: The Stories Behind the Songs*. New York: Harry N. Abrams, 2019.

Jennings, La Vinia Delois. *Margaret Garner: The Premiere Performances of Toni Morrison's Libretto*. Charlottesville: University of Virginia Press, 2016.

Joo, Johnny. *Ohio's Forgotten History*. Self-publication, 2019.

Knepper, George W. *Ohio and Its People*. Kent, OH: Kent State University Press, 1989.

———. *An Ohio Portrait*. Columbus: Ohio State Historical Society, 1976.

Macy, Beth. *Dopesick: Dealers, Doctors, and the Drug Company that Addicted America*. Boston, MA: Little, Brown, 2018.

Maharidge, Dale, and Michael Williamson. *Journey to Nowhere: The Saga of the New Underclass*. New York: Hyperion, 1996.

Marino, Jacqueline, and Will Miller, eds. *Car Bombs to Cookie Tables: The Youngstown Anthology*. Cleveland, OH: Belt Publishing, 2015.

McClelland, Edward. *How to Speak Midwestern*. Cleveland, OH: Belt Publishing, 2016.

McQuade, Zan, ed. *The Cincinnati Anthology*. Cleveland, OH: Belt Publishing, 2014.

Morrison, Toni. *Beloved*. New York: Alfred A. Knopf, 1987.

Piiparinen, Richey, and Anne Trubek, eds. *Rust Belt Chic: The Cleveland Anthology*. Cleveland, OH: Belt Publishing, 2012.

Segedy, Jason, ed. *The Akron Anthology*. Cleveland, OH: Belt Publishing, 2016.

Smarsh, Sarah. *Heartland: A Memoir of Working Hard and Being Broke in the Richest Country on Earth*. New York: Scribner, 2018.

Springsteen, Bruce. *Born to Run*. New York: Simon & Schuster, 2016.

Traficant: The Congressman of Crimetown. Directed by Eric Murphy. Los Angeles: Steel Valley Films, 2015. DVD.

Trubek, Anne, ed. *Voices from the Rust Belt*. New York: Picador, 2018.

Vance, J. D. *Hillbilly Elegy: A Memoir of a Family and Culture in Crisis*. New York: Harper, 2016.

Waddington, David. *Policing Public Disorder*. Portland, OR: Willan Publishing, 2007.

Watts, Lisa, ed. *Good Roots: Writers Reflect on Growing Up in Ohio*. Athens: Ohio University Press, 2006.

Wright, James. *Above the River: The Complete Poems*. New York: Farrar, Straus and Giroux, 1992.

ACKNOWLEDGMENTS

If you're even reading this page, you're either (1) someone who helped, (2) one of my cousins or something, or (3) looking to see how the sausage was made.

So. If you appear in the preceding pages: thank you. You didn't have to talk, or show me around, or meet me for coffee, or open up your home or your workplace or your life story, or help me understand what I was trying to understand even when I seemed a little dense, but you did, but you did, but you did. And I thank you.

Three people made this book happen. First came Daniel Greenberg, agent extraordinaire, who understood what this should be from the start, certainly before I did, and as always supported me at the worst times and as always made the good times roll. Thanks as well to all the keenly talented and helpful people at Levine Greenberg Rostan Literary Agency.

Next came Brant Rumble, who is the shit. That's probably a bad thing to call one's editor, but really, he is. The. Shit. (Reader, if you are reading this, that means he didn't delete it. That's the kind of awesome editor Brant Rumble is.) I am blessed to have had such a simpatico soul with me for so long and through so many strange turns along the way. I couldn't imagine a better person to work with and also call a friend. Deep gratitude to everyone else at Hachette Books as well, especially Susan Weinberg, Mary Ann

Naples, Michelle Aielli, Michael Barrs, Sarah Falter, Anna Hall, Amanda Kain, and Mollie Weisenfeld.

Finally, from before the beginning and through after the end, my wife, Gina, was supportive, patient, and insightful—the best traveling companion, auxiliary notetaker, sometime photographer, Ohio geological expert, drinking buddy, associate DJ, navigator (both literal and figurative), room-service advocate, and conscience a person could ever dream of.

If you are reading this because you are my cousin, you know enough about me already. And yes, we all know it was Billy who sat in the cupcakes. Hahaha.

The following people kicked in generous, often crucial support, providing information, making connections, offering direction, synching schedules, helping me understand what I was trying to ask for, vouching for my character, nagging on my behalf, etc.: Matthew Akers, Ken Bindas, Andrew Borowiec, Catey Breck, Alison Caplan, Alexandra Nicholis Coon, Mark Curnutte, John Faherty, Doug Gillard, John C. Green and everyone else at the Bliss Institute of Applied Politics, Kymberli Hagelberg, Debbie Hayes, Norma Hill, Amy Hunter, William Jones, Kyle Kutuchief, Eric Murphy, Fedearia Nicholson, Doug Oplinger, Sarah Pollard, Sean Posey, James Renner, Cristopher Shell, Arin Miller Tait, Dennis Willard, and Matthew Wyszynski. Less directly, but no less vitally, thanks to all the journalists, especially at local newspapers, whose first draft of history was a constant and irreplaceable source of information about many events described herein.

Thanks to News Director Andrew Meyer and Director of Programming Ele Ellis and the rest of the staff at NPR station WKSU in Kent, Ohio, for producing a series of conversations that among other things helped me better understand what I was finding along the way.

These smart, generous friends read this before it was a book and offered valuable feedback to help make it a better one: Chris Drabick, Chris Eck, Bob Ethington, Gina Giffels, Chuck Klosterman, Dave Lucas, and Eric Nuzum.

Chris Drabick's debut novel, *The Way We Get By,* is in bookstores now. It's terrific. You should read it. The title is from a Spoon song. That's awesome. Eric Nuzum's latest book, *Make Noise,* will make you smarter in ways you never dreamed. Chuck Klosterman is writing one right now that will blow your little mind.

See, this is the kind of trenchant inside information you get if you read far enough into an acknowledgments page.

Thanks to my students, colleagues, and friends at the University of Akron and in the Northeast Ohio Master of Fine Arts (NEOMFA) program in creative writing for their commiseration and inspiration.

Finally, I offer most grateful acknowledgment to the University of Akron Faculty Research Fellowship for generous support during this project and to the Chautauqua Institution for the first opportunity to present this work in public.

Vote.